STAR WARS

LEGACY

VOLUME II

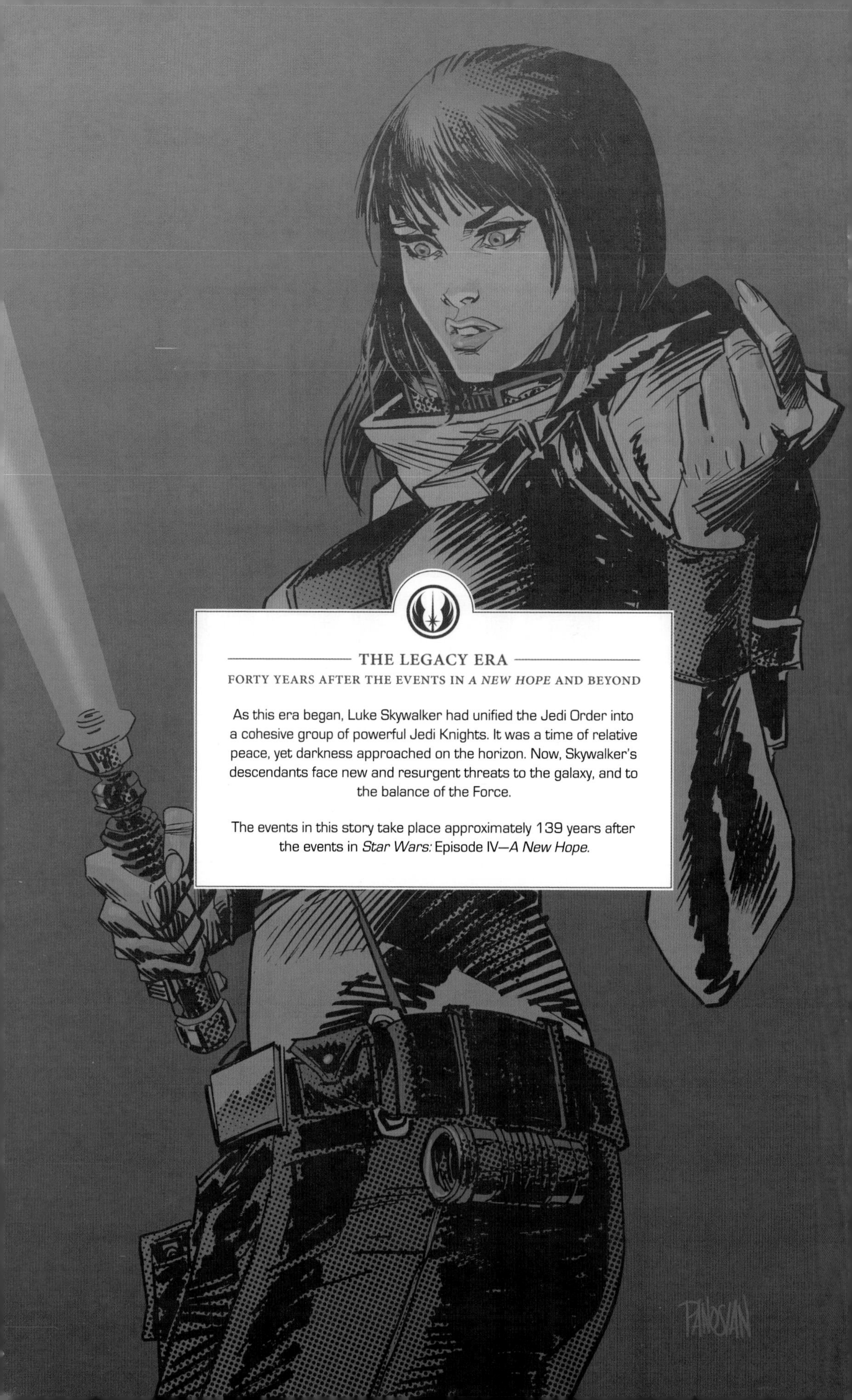
PANOSIAN

## THE LEGACY ERA

FORTY YEARS AFTER THE EVENTS IN *A NEW HOPE* AND BEYOND

As this era began, Luke Skywalker had unified the Jedi Order into a cohesive group of powerful Jedi Knights. It was a time of relative peace, yet darkness approached on the horizon. Now, Skywalker's descendants face new and resurgent threats to the galaxy, and to the balance of the Force.

The events in this story take place approximately 139 years after the events in *Star Wars:* Episode IV—*A New Hope*.

BOOK 3
# WANTED: ANIA SOLO

STAR WARS®
LEGACY
VOLUME II

SCRIPT
CORINNA BECHKO   GABRIEL HARDMAN

ART
GABRIEL HARDMAN

COLORS
JORDAN BOYD

LETTERING
MICHAEL HEISLER

FRONT COVER ART
AGUSTIN ALESSIO

DARK HORSE BOOKS   LUCAS BOOKS

PRESIDENT AND PUBLISHER
MIKE RICHARDSON

COLLECTION DESIGNER
RICK DeLUCCO

EDITOR
RANDY STRADLEY

ASSISTANT EDITOR
FREDDYE LINS

NEIL HANKERSON EXECUTIVE VICE PRESIDENT    TOM WEDDLE CHIEF FINANCIAL OFFICER
RANDY STRADLEY VICE PRESIDENT OF PUBLISHING    MICHAEL MARTENS VICE PRESIDENT OF
BOOK TRADE SALES    ANITA NELSON VICE PRESIDENT OF BUSINESS AFFAIRS    SCOTT ALLIE
EDITOR IN CHIEF    MATT PARKINSON VICE PRESIDENT OF MARKETING    DAVID SCROGGY VICE
PRESIDENT OF PRODUCT DEVELOPMENT    DALE LaFOUNTAIN VICE PRESIDENT OF INFORMATION
TECHNOLOGY    DARLENE VOGEL SENIOR DIRECTOR OF PRINT, DESIGN, AND PRODUCTION
KEN LIZZI GENERAL COUNSEL    DAVEY ESTRADA EDITORIAL DIRECTOR    CHRIS WARNER SENIOR
BOOKS EDITOR    DIANA SCHUTZ EXECUTIVE EDITOR    CARY GRAZZINI DIRECTOR OF PRINT AND
DEVELOPMENT    LIA RIBACCHI ART DIRECTOR    CARA NIECE DIRECTOR OF SCHEDULING    TIM WIESCH
DIRECTOR OF INTERNATIONAL LICENSING    MARK BERNARDI DIRECTOR OF DIGITAL PUBLISHING

SPECIAL THANKS TO JENNIFER HEDDLE, LELAND CHEE, TROY ALDERS, CAROL ROEDER,
JANN MOORHEAD, AND DAVID ANDERMAN AT LUCAS LICENSING.

ART ON PAGES 2 AND 6 BY DAN PANOSIAN

This volume collects issues #11–#15 of the Dark Horse comic-book series Star Wars: Legacy Volume II.

Published by Dark Horse Books
A division of Dark Horse Comics, Inc.
10956 SE Main Street, Milwaukie, OR 97222

DarkHorse.com  StarWars.com

International Licensing: 503-905-2377

To find a comics shop in your area, call the Comic Shop Locator Service toll-free at 1-888-266-4226.

Library of Congress Cataloging-in-Publication Data

Bechko, Corinna, 1973-
Star Wars Legacy II. Volume II, Book II, Outcasts of the broken ring / script, Corinna Bechko, Gabriel Hardman ; art, Brian
Albert Thies ; colors, Rachelle Rosenberg ; lettering, Michael Heisler ; front cover art, Agustin Alessio.
    pages cm
Summary: "Ania Solo and Imperial Knight Jao Assam break with the Galactic Triumvirate to track down the Sith Darth
Wredd. The trail leads Ania and Jao to a dead planet–and another Sith Lord and his army of pirates"– Provided by publisher.
ISBN 978-1-61655-310-4 (v. 2) – ISBN 978-1-61655-381-4 (v. 3)
1. Star Wars fiction–Comic books, strips, etc. 2. Graphic novels. I. Hardman, Gabriel. II. Title. III. Title: Outcasts of the broken
ring.
PN6728.S73B444 2014
741.5'973–dc23
                        2013050883

First edition: August 2014
ISBN 978-1-61655-381-4

10 9 8 7 6 5 4 3 2 1
Printed in China

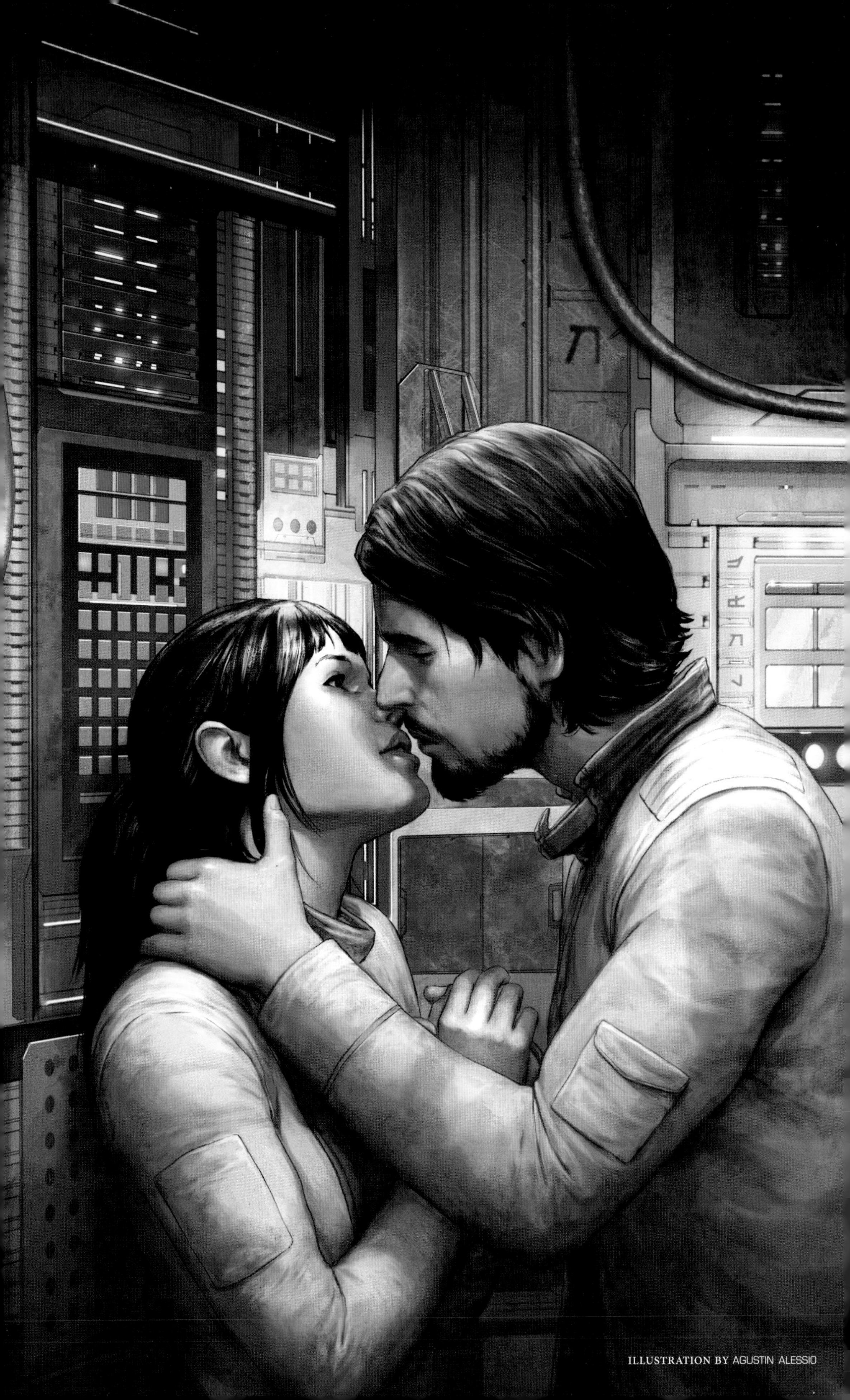

ILLUSTRATION BY AGUSTIN ALESSIO

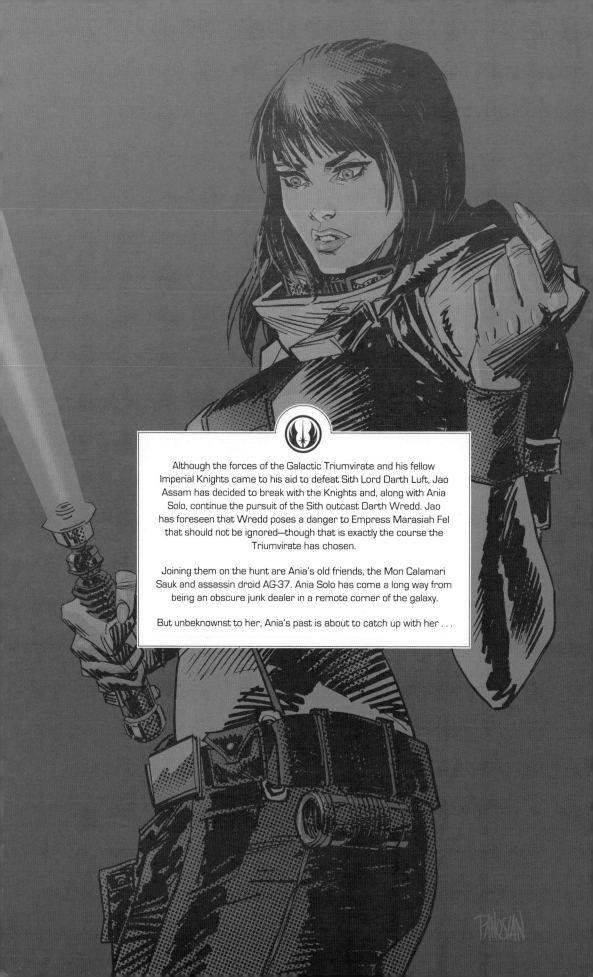

Although the forces of the Galactic Triumvirate and his fellow Imperial Knights came to his aid to defeat Sith Lord Darth Luft, Jao Assam has decided to break with the Knights and, along with Ania Solo, continue the pursuit of the Sith outcast Darth Wredd. Jao has foreseen that Wredd poses a danger to Empress Marasiah Fel that should not be ignored—though that is exactly the course the Triumvirate has chosen.

Joining them on the hunt are Ania's old friends, the Mon Calamari Sauk and assassin droid AG-37. Ania Solo has come a long way from being an obscure junk dealer in a remote corner of the galaxy.

But unbeknownst to her, Ania's past is about to catch up with her . . .

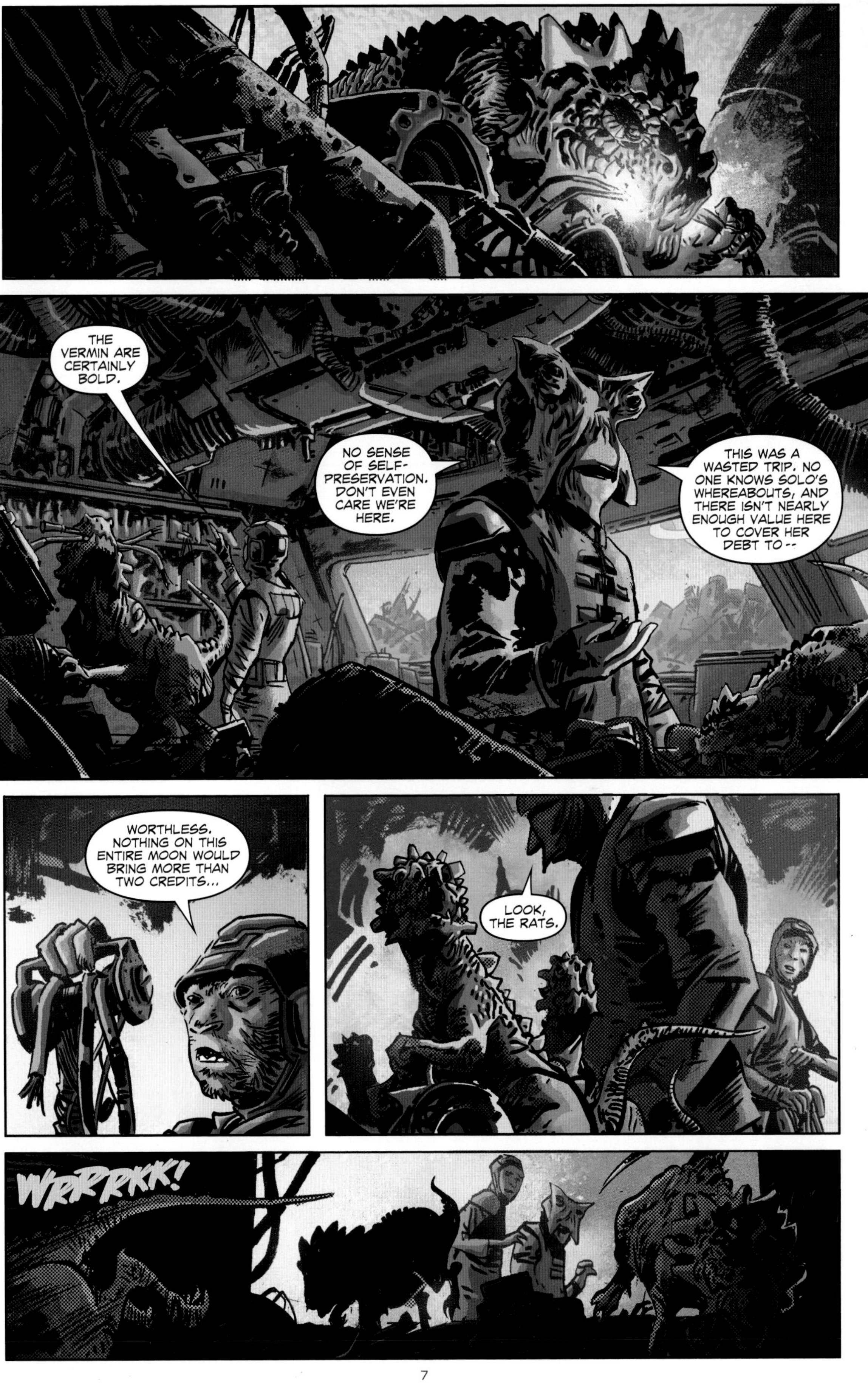
THE VERMIN ARE CERTAINLY BOLD.
NO SENSE OF SELF-PRESERVATION. DON'T EVEN CARE WE'RE HERE.
THIS WAS A WASTED TRIP. NO ONE KNOWS SOLO'S WHEREABOUTS, AND THERE ISN'T NEARLY ENOUGH VALUE HERE TO COVER HER DEBT TO --
WORTHLESS. NOTHING ON THIS ENTIRE MOON WOULD BRING MORE THAN TWO CREDITS...
LOOK, THE RATS.
WRRRKK!

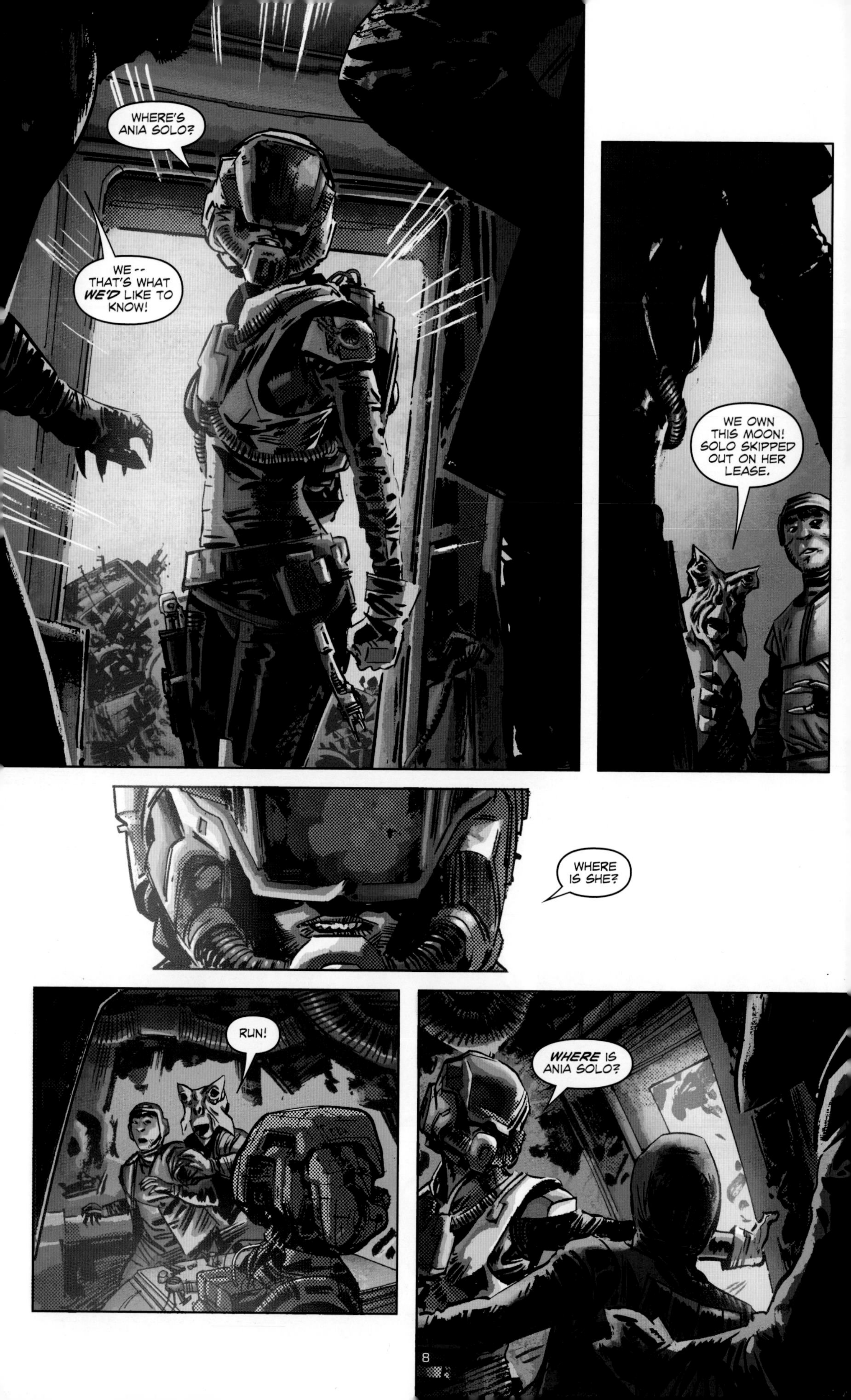
WHERE'S ANIA SOLO?
WE -- THAT'S WHAT WE'D LIKE TO KNOW!
WE OWN THIS MOON! SOLO SKIPPED OUT ON HER LEASE.
WHERE IS SHE?
RUN!
WHERE IS ANIA SOLO?
8

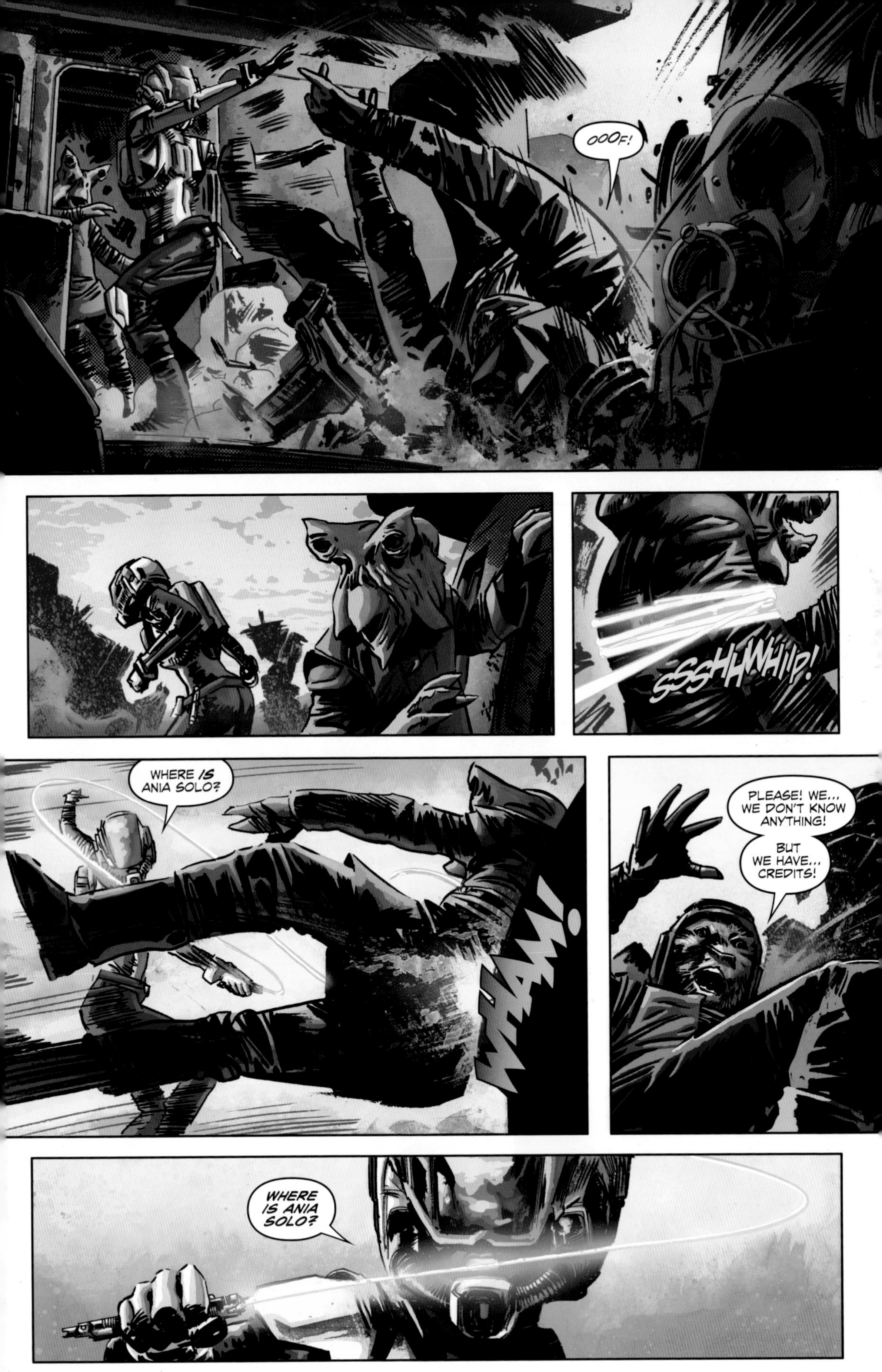
OOOF!
SSSHHWHIIP!
WHERE IS ANIA SOLO?
WHAM!
PLEASE! WE... WE DON'T KNOW ANYTHING!
BUT WE HAVE... CREDITS!
WHERE IS ANIA SOLO?

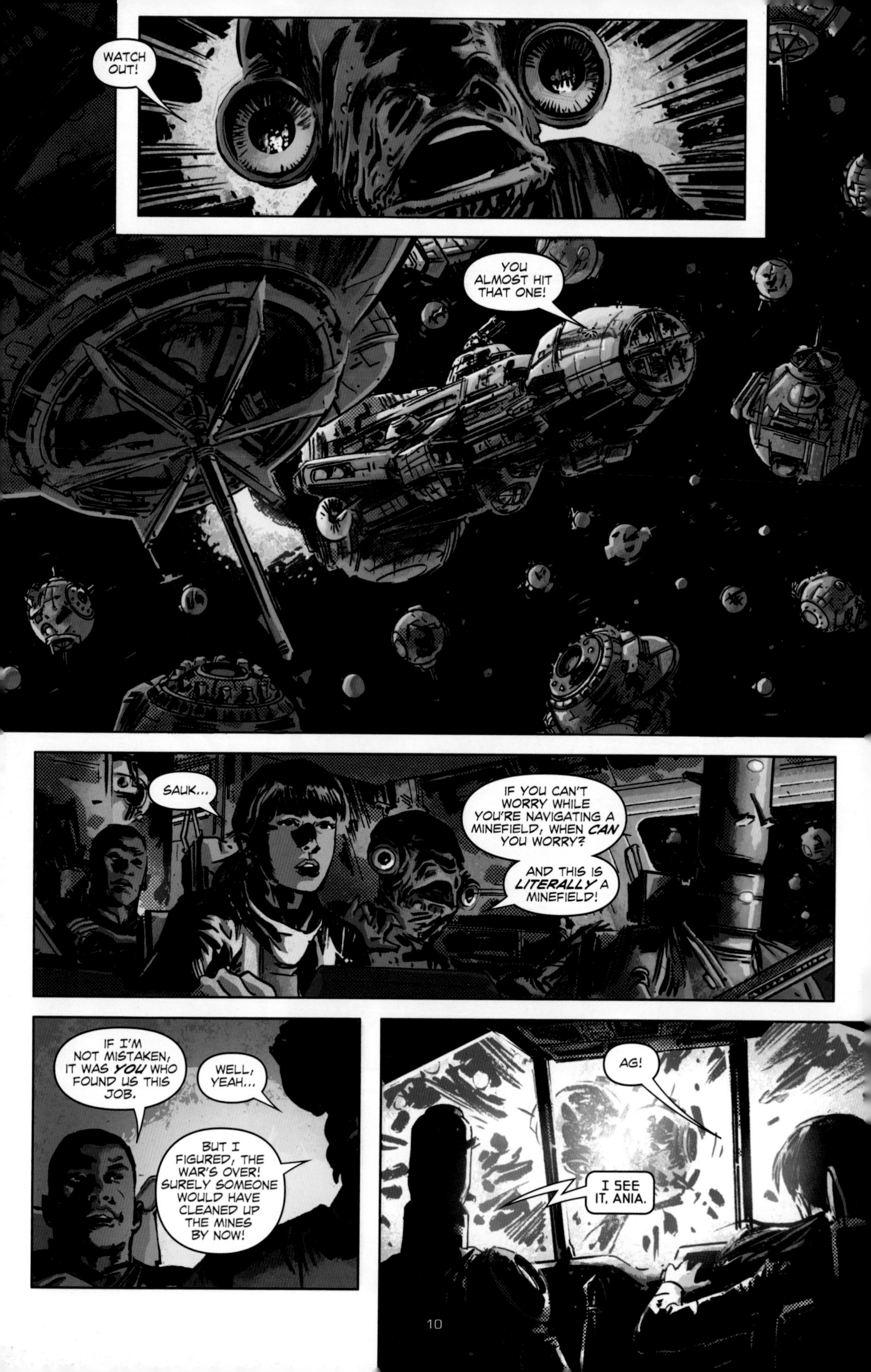
WATCH OUT!
YOU ALMOST HIT THAT ONE!
SAUK...
IF YOU CAN'T WORRY WHILE YOU'RE NAVIGATING A MINEFIELD, WHEN *CAN* YOU WORRY?
AND THIS IS *LITERALLY* A MINEFIELD!
IF I'M NOT MISTAKEN, IT WAS *YOU* WHO FOUND US THIS JOB.
WELL, YEAH...
BUT I FIGURED, THE WAR'S OVER! SURELY SOMEONE WOULD HAVE CLEANED UP THE MINES BY NOW!
AG!
I SEE IT, ANIA.

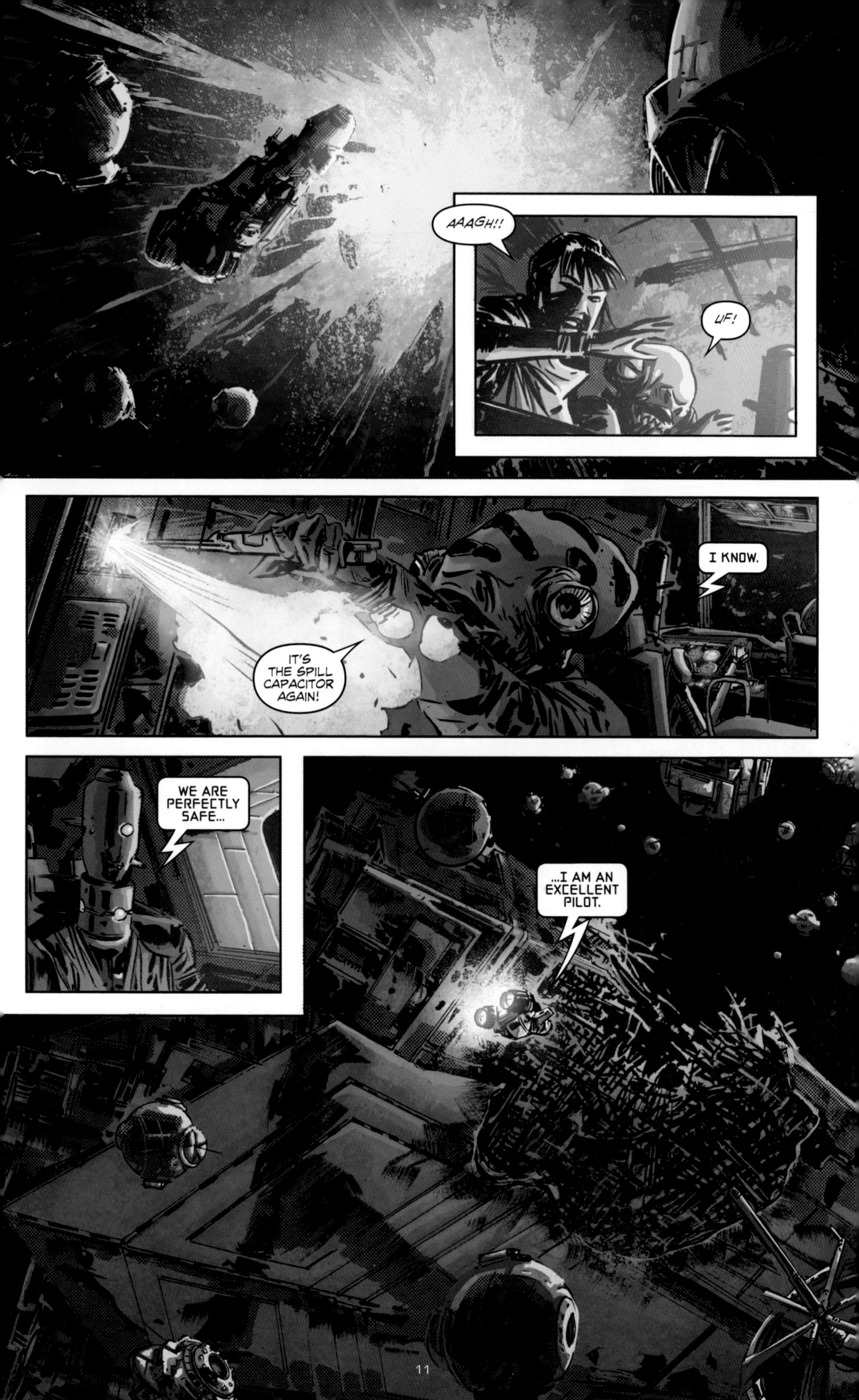
AAAGH!!
UF!
IT'S THE SPILL CAPACITOR AGAIN!
I KNOW.
WE ARE PERFECTLY SAFE...
...I AM AN EXCELLENT PILOT.

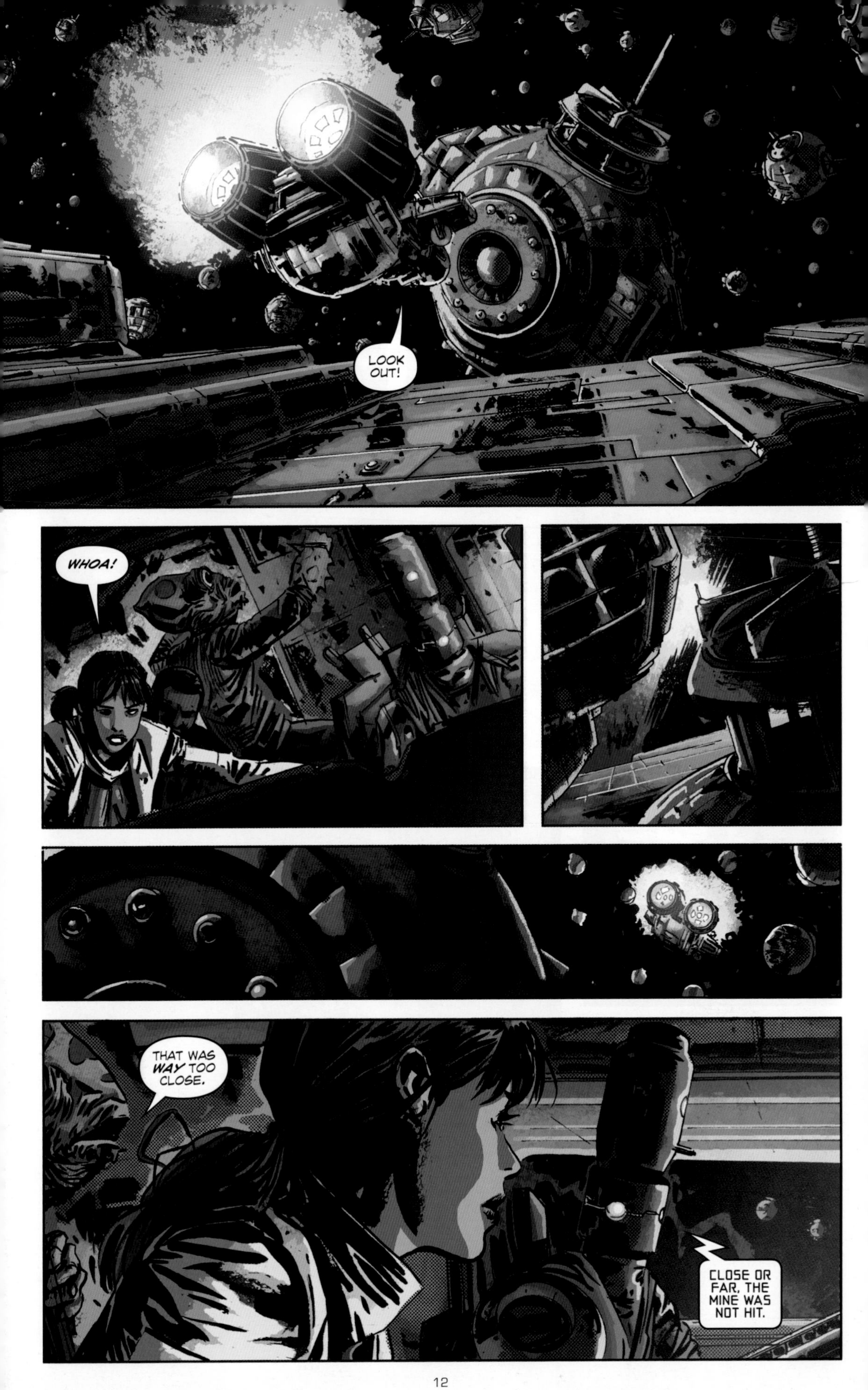
LOOK OUT!
WHOA!
THAT WAS WAY TOO CLOSE.
CLOSE OR FAR, THE MINE WAS NOT HIT.

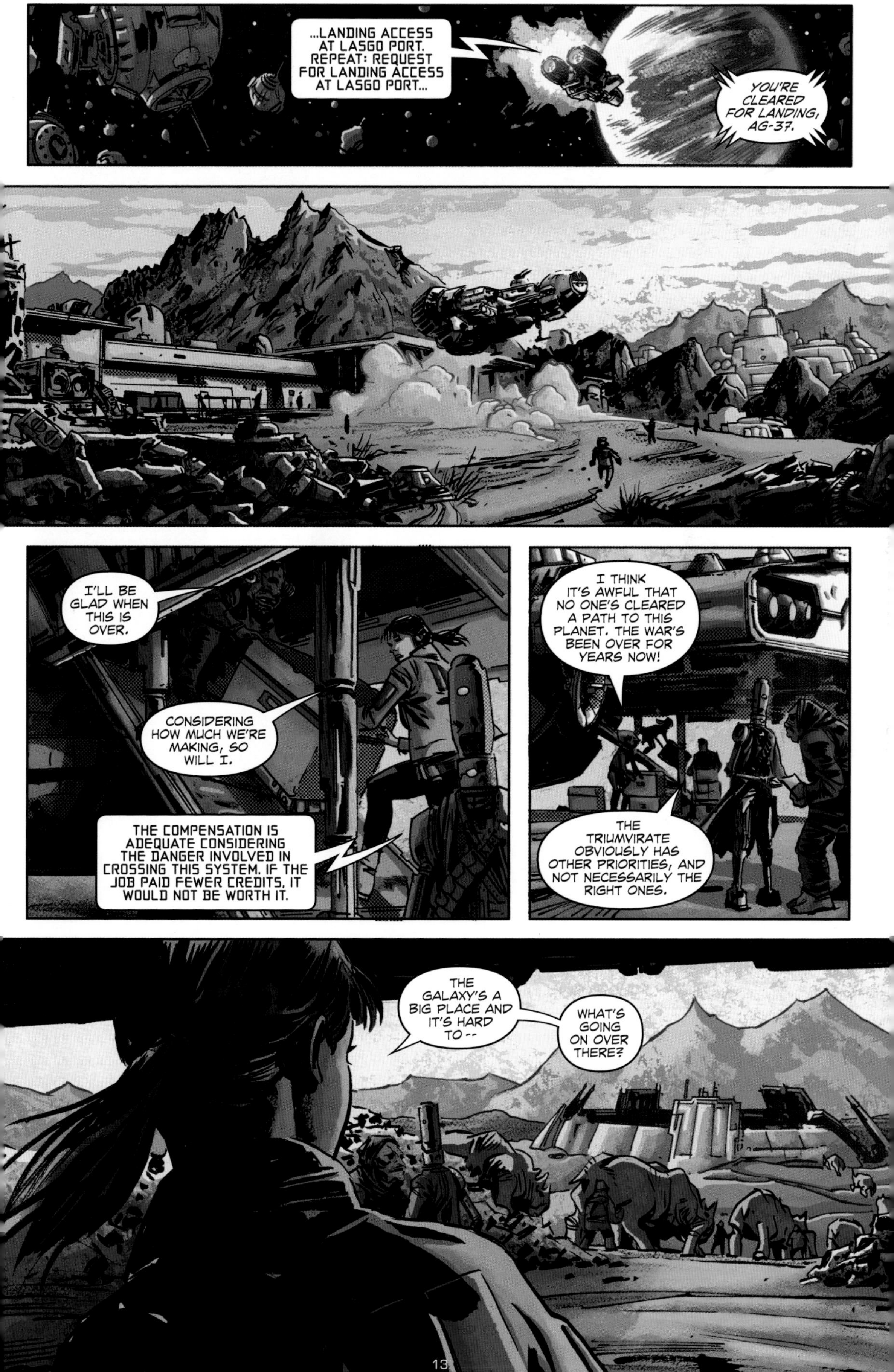

...LANDING ACCESS AT LASGO PORT. REPEAT: REQUEST FOR LANDING ACCESS AT LASGO PORT...
YOU'RE CLEARED FOR LANDING, AG-37.
I'LL BE GLAD WHEN THIS IS OVER.
CONSIDERING HOW MUCH WE'RE MAKING, SO WILL I.
THE COMPENSATION IS ADEQUATE CONSIDERING THE DANGER INVOLVED IN CROSSING THIS SYSTEM. IF THE JOB PAID FEWER CREDITS, IT WOULD NOT BE WORTH IT.
I THINK IT'S AWFUL THAT NO ONE'S CLEARED A PATH TO THIS PLANET. THE WAR'S BEEN OVER FOR YEARS NOW!
THE TRIUMVIRATE OBVIOUSLY HAS OTHER PRIORITIES, AND NOT NECESSARILY THE RIGHT ONES.
THE GALAXY'S A BIG PLACE AND IT'S HARD TO --
WHAT'S GOING ON OVER THERE?

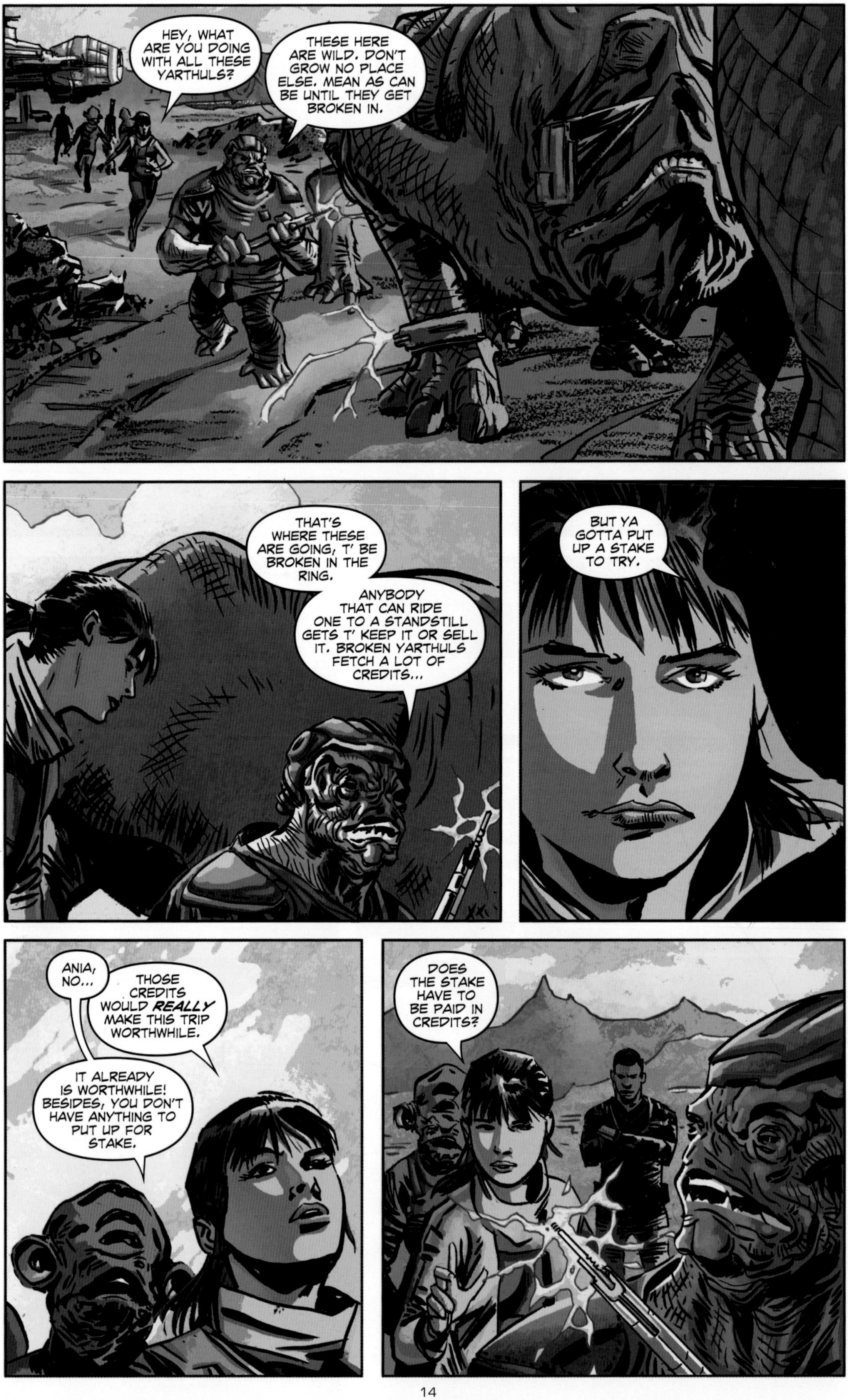
HEY, WHAT ARE YOU DOING WITH ALL THESE YARTHULS?
THESE HERE ARE WILD. DON'T GROW NO PLACE ELSE. MEAN AS CAN BE UNTIL THEY GET BROKEN IN.
THAT'S WHERE THESE ARE GOING, T' BE BROKEN IN THE RING.
ANYBODY THAT CAN RIDE ONE TO A STANDSTILL GETS T' KEEP IT OR SELL IT. BROKEN YARTHULS FETCH A LOT OF CREDITS...
BUT YA GOTTA PUT UP A STAKE TO TRY.
ANIA, NO...
THOSE CREDITS WOULD REALLY MAKE THIS TRIP WORTHWHILE.
IT ALREADY IS WORTHWHILE! BESIDES, YOU DON'T HAVE ANYTHING TO PUT UP FOR STAKE.
DOES THE STAKE HAVE TO BE PAID IN CREDITS?

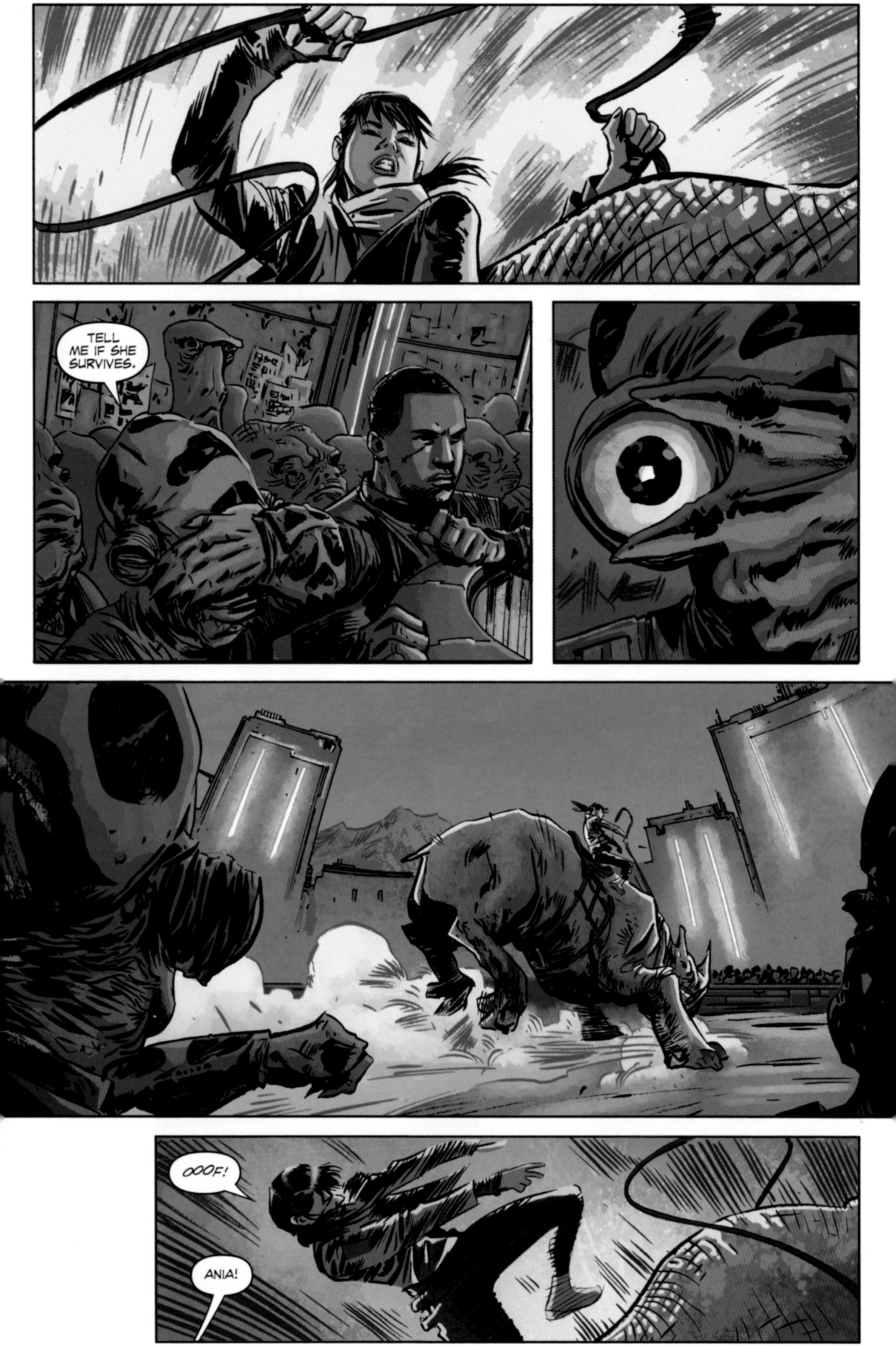
TELL ME IF SHE SURVIVES.
OOOF!
ANIA!

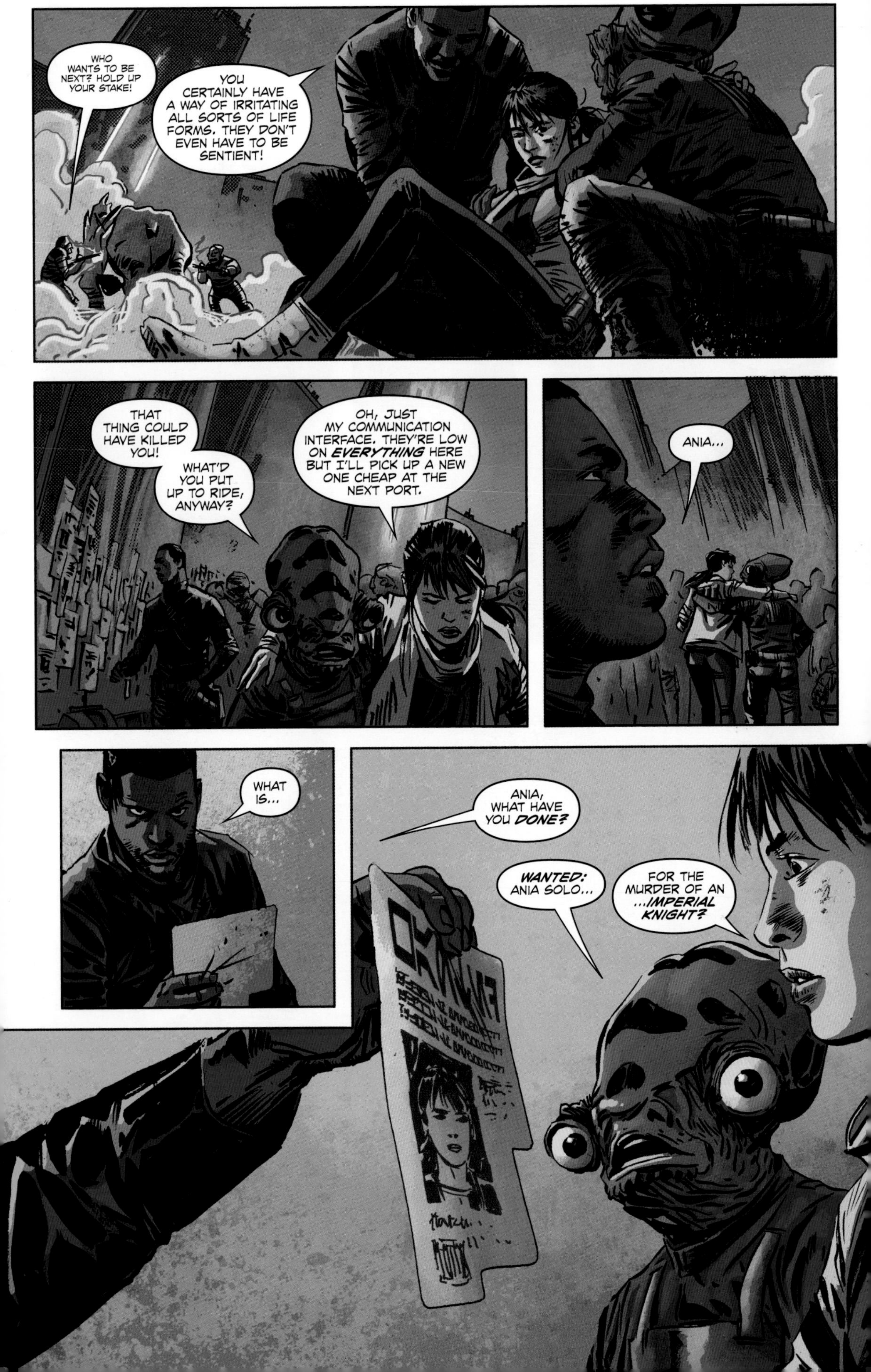
WHO WANTS TO BE NEXT? HOLD UP YOUR STAKE!
YOU CERTAINLY HAVE A WAY OF IRRITATING ALL SORTS OF LIFE FORMS. THEY DON'T EVEN HAVE TO BE SENTIENT!
THAT THING COULD HAVE KILLED YOU!
WHAT'D YOU PUT UP TO RIDE, ANYWAY?
OH, JUST MY COMMUNICATION INTERFACE. THEY'RE LOW ON EVERYTHING HERE BUT I'LL PICK UP A NEW ONE CHEAP AT THE NEXT PORT.
ANIA...
WHAT IS...
ANIA, WHAT HAVE YOU DONE?
WANTED: ANIA SOLO...
FOR THE MURDER OF AN ...IMPERIAL KNIGHT?

BUT I'D NEVER EVEN SEEN AN IMPERIAL KNIGHT BEFORE I MET YOU!

THEN WHY WERE YOU HIDING OUT IN THE CARRERAS SYSTEM?

THAT'S ABOUT AS FAR OFF THE GRID AS YOU CAN GET!

NOW WAIT A MINUTE! I THINK I DESERVE AN ANSWER!

YOU REALLY WANT TO KNOW?

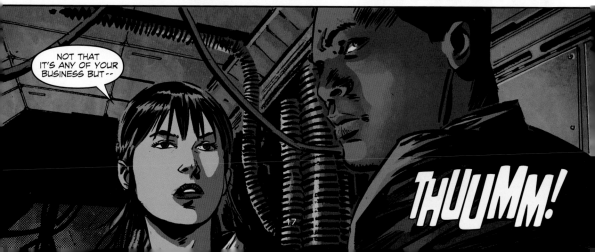

NOT THAT IT'S ANY OF YOUR BUSINESS BUT--

THUUMM!

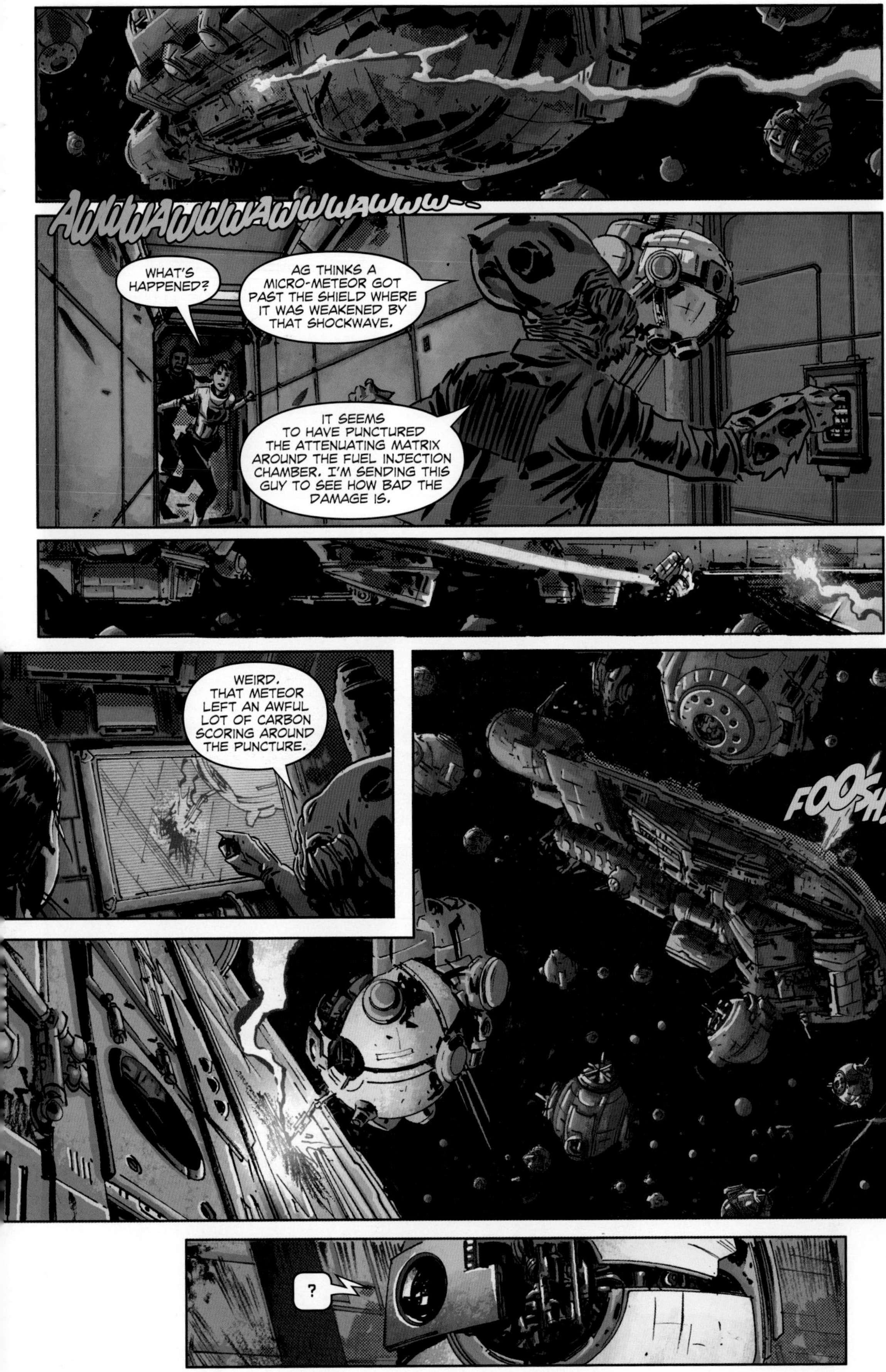
AWWWAWWWAWWWAWWW-
WHAT'S HAPPENED?
AG THINKS A MICRO-METEOR GOT PAST THE SHIELD WHERE IT WAS WEAKENED BY THAT SHOCKWAVE.
IT SEEMS TO HAVE PUNCTURED THE ATTENUATING MATRIX AROUND THE FUEL INJECTION CHAMBER. I'M SENDING THIS GUY TO SEE HOW BAD THE DAMAGE IS.
WEIRD. THAT METEOR LEFT AN AWFUL LOT OF CARBON SCORING AROUND THE PUNCTURE.
FOOSH!
?

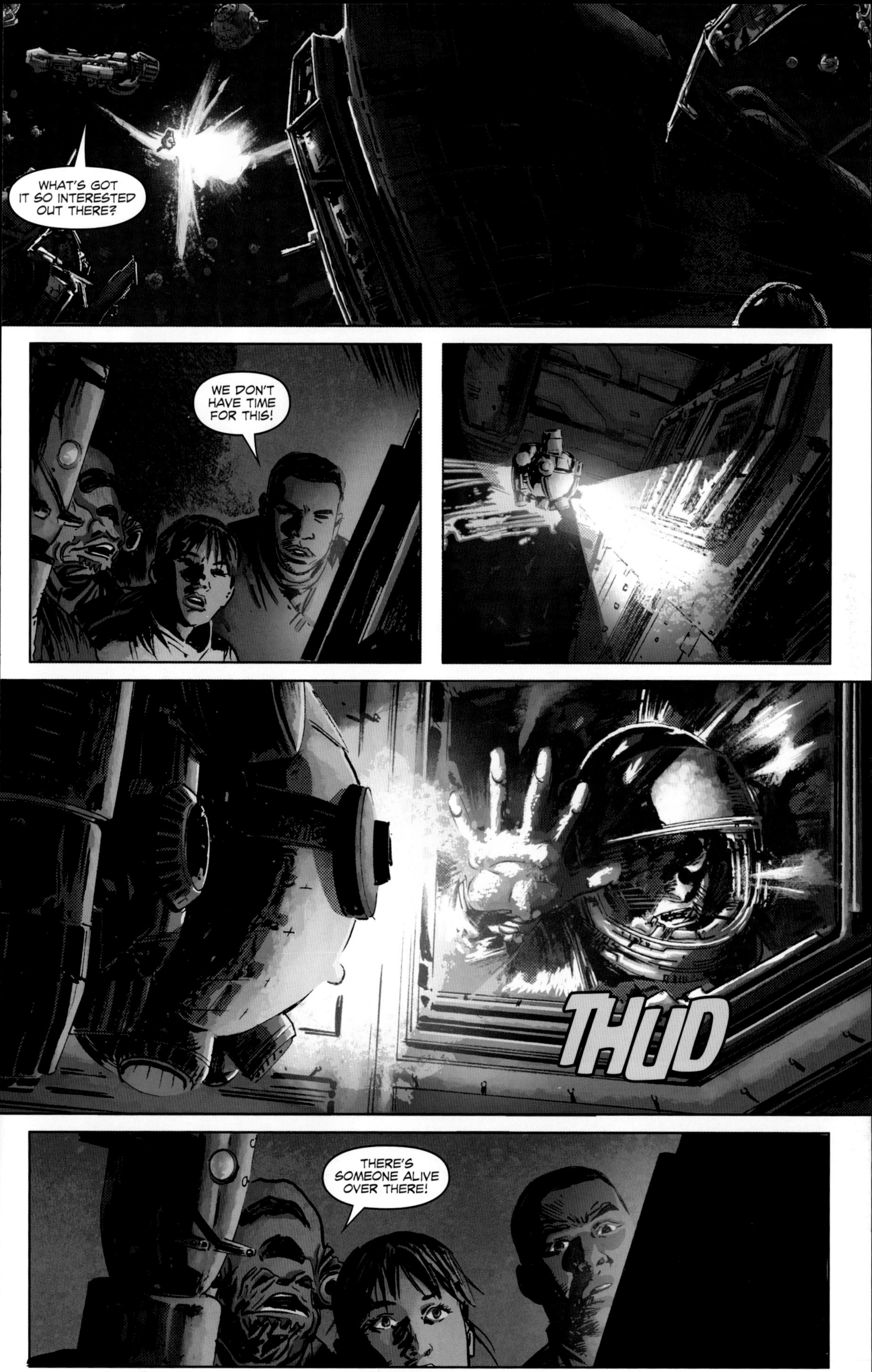
WHAT'S GOT IT SO INTERESTED OUT THERE?
WE DON'T HAVE TIME FOR THIS!
THUD
THERE'S SOMEONE ALIVE OVER THERE!

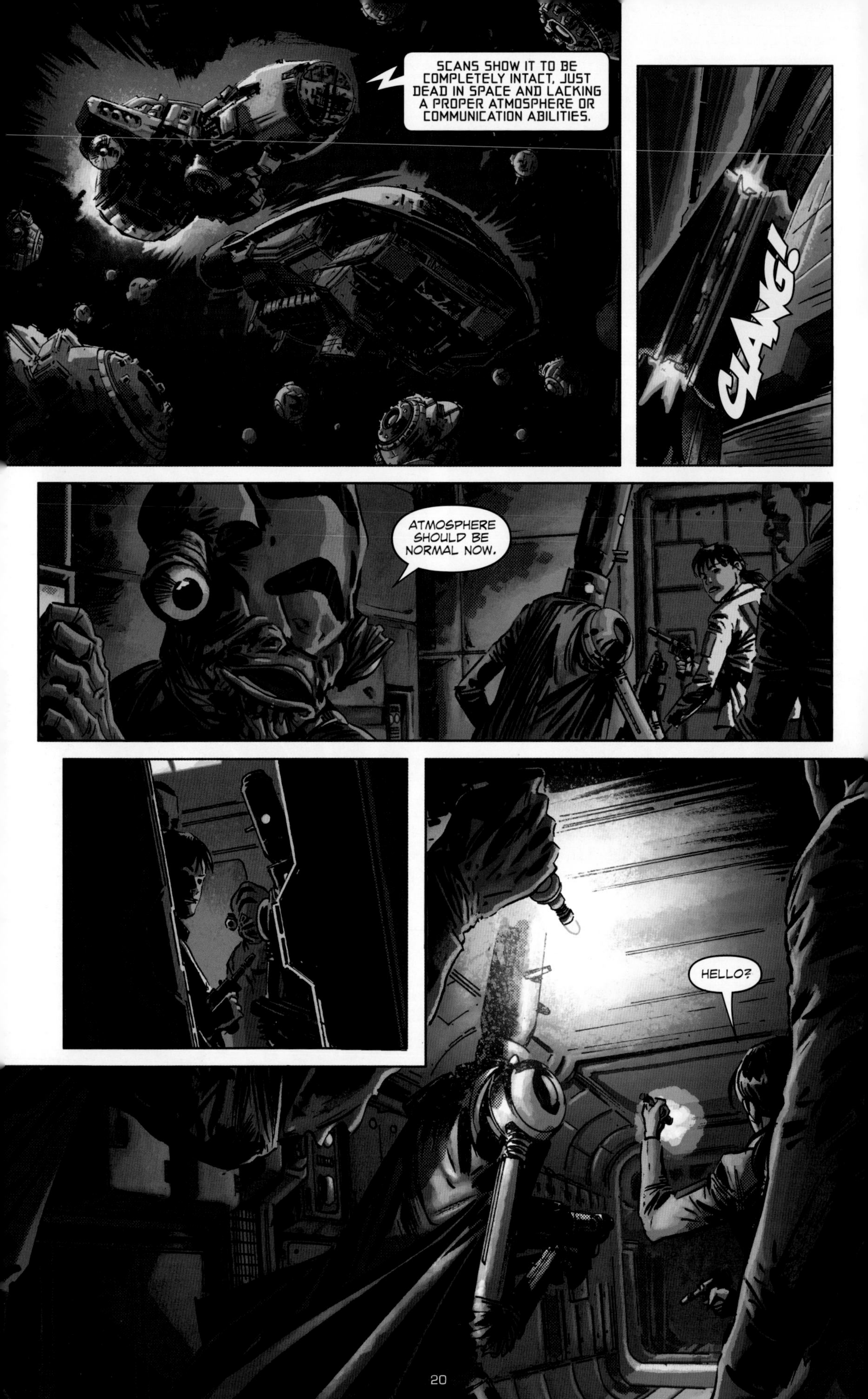
SCANS SHOW IT TO BE COMPLETELY INTACT, JUST DEAD IN SPACE AND LACKING A PROPER ATMOSPHERE OR COMMUNICATION ABILITIES.
CLANG!
ATMOSPHERE SHOULD BE NORMAL NOW.
HELLO?

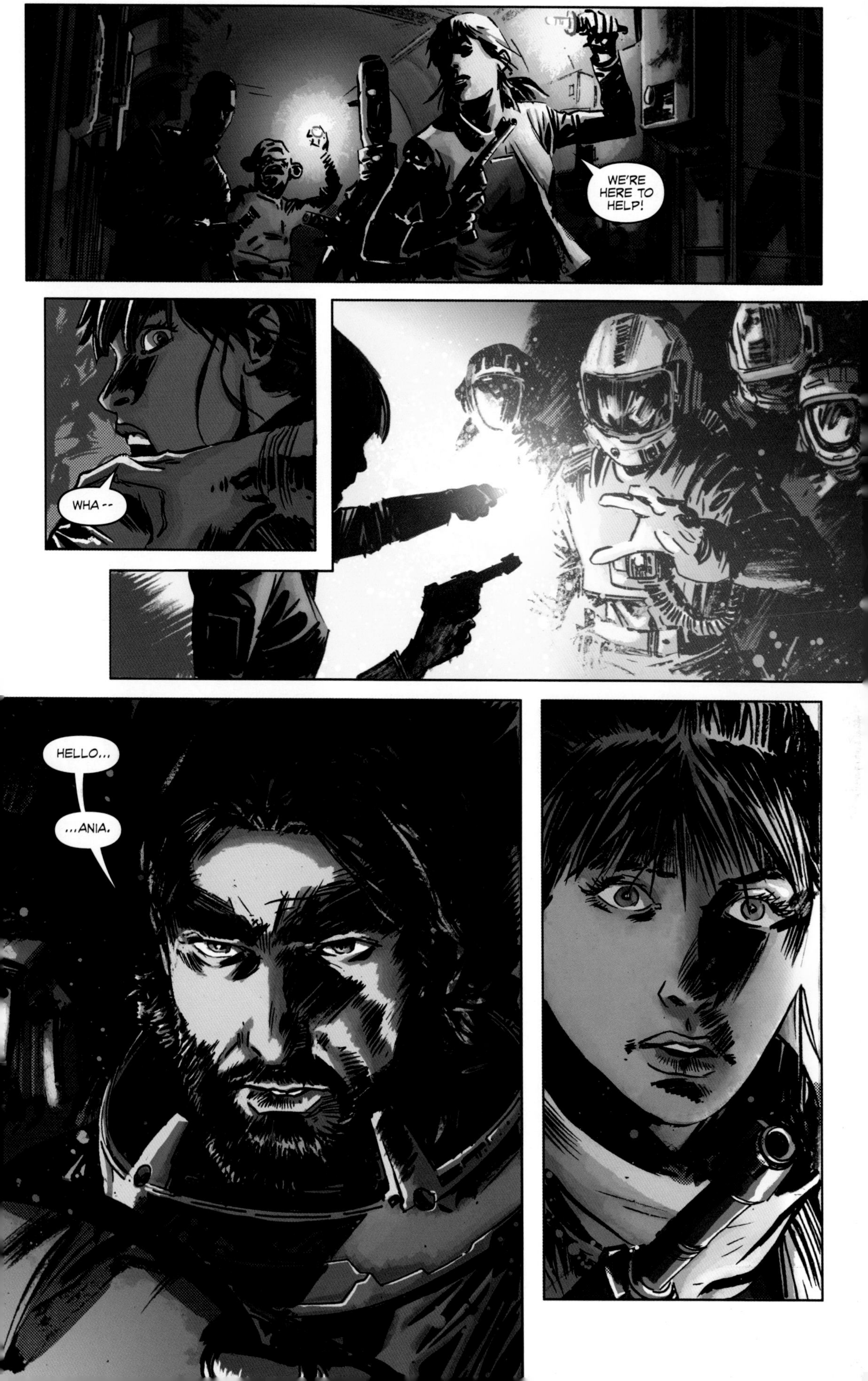
WE'RE HERE TO HELP!
WHA --
HELLO...
...ANIA.

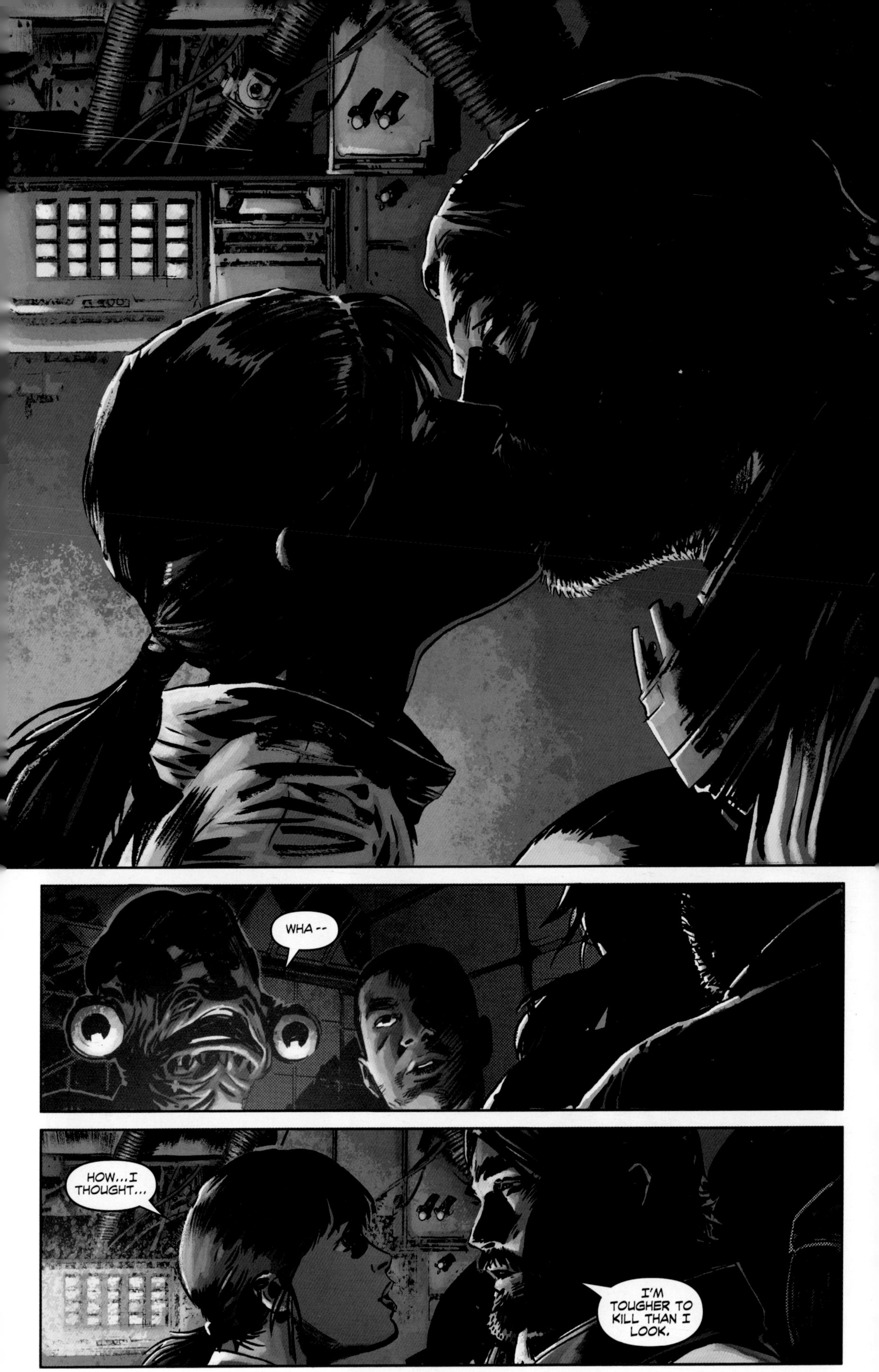
WHA --
HOW...I THOUGHT...
I'M TOUGHER TO KILL THAN I LOOK.

THIS IS **RAMID**, A FRIEND FROM WAY, WAY, WAY BACK.

I THINK YOU LEFT OUT A *"WAY."*

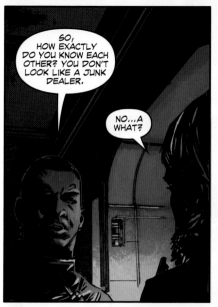

SO, HOW EXACTLY DO YOU KNOW EACH OTHER? YOU DON'T LOOK LIKE A JUNK DEALER.

NO...A WHAT?

TELL US WHAT'S WRONG WITH YOUR SHIP AND WE'LL FIX IT. SAUK IS A GENIUS ENGINEER! OR FAILING THAT WE COULD ALWAYS GIVE YOU A LIFT SOMEWHERE...

THE NET ISOLATOR GOT FRIED WHEN WE GOT TOO CLOSE TO ONE OF THESE DAMN MINES. THAT BLEW THE CONNECTION TO THE BOOSTER...THE PROBLEMS CASCADED FROM THERE. NO SHIELDS, NO TRAVEL.

ESPECIALLY NOT THROUGH A MINEFIELD.

THAT SOUNDS LIKE YOU JUST NEED A COUPLE OF NEW PARTS FOR THE INTEGRATION CIRCUIT. WHAT DO YOU THINK, SAUK?

I'M SURE WE COULD RIG SOMETHING FOR THAT. LET'S GO BACK TO AG'S SHIP AND SEE WHAT WE CAN COME UP WITH.

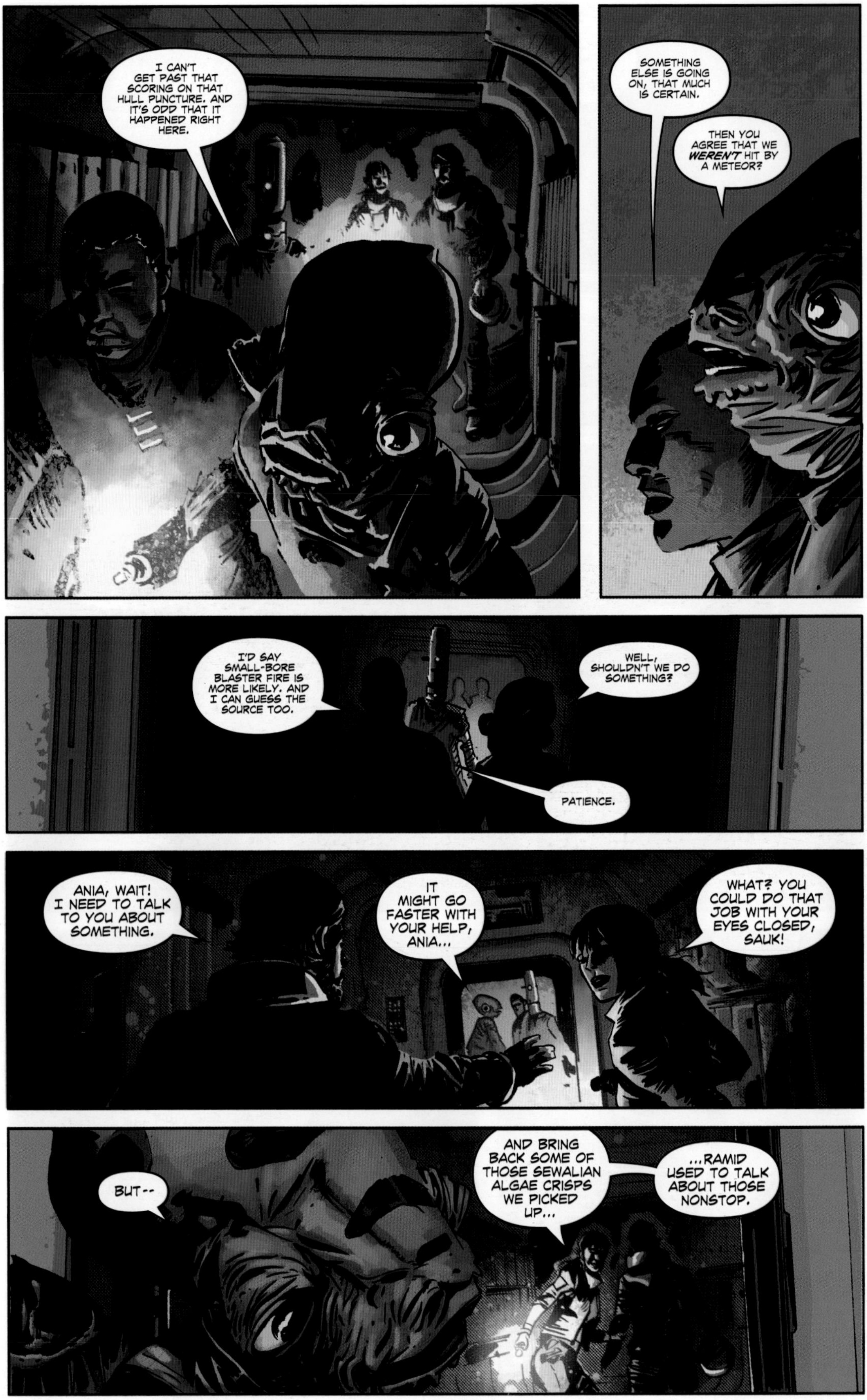
I CAN'T GET PAST THAT SCORING ON THAT HULL PUNCTURE. AND IT'S ODD THAT IT HAPPENED RIGHT HERE.
SOMETHING ELSE IS GOING ON, THAT MUCH IS CERTAIN.
THEN YOU AGREE THAT WE *WEREN'T* HIT BY A METEOR?
I'D SAY SMALL-BORE BLASTER FIRE IS MORE LIKELY. AND I CAN GUESS THE SOURCE TOO.
WELL, SHOULDN'T WE DO SOMETHING?
PATIENCE.
ANIA, WAIT! I NEED TO TALK TO YOU ABOUT SOMETHING.
IT MIGHT GO FASTER WITH YOUR HELP, ANIA...
WHAT? YOU COULD DO THAT JOB WITH YOUR EYES CLOSED, SAUK!
BUT--
AND BRING BACK SOME OF THOSE SEWALIAN ALGAE CRISPS WE PICKED UP...
...RAMID USED TO TALK ABOUT THOSE NONSTOP.

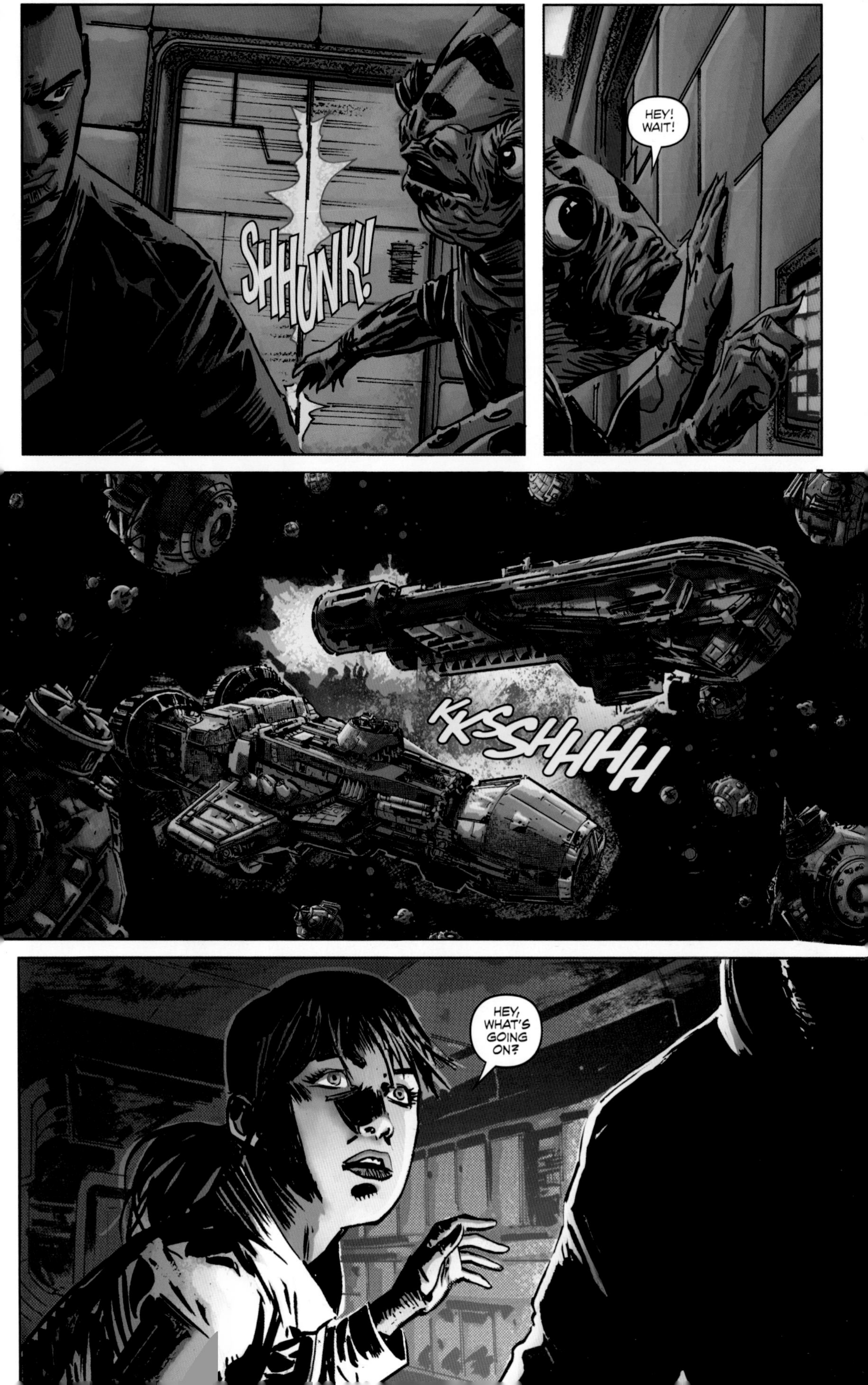
SHHUNK!
HEY! WAIT!
KKSSHHHH
HEY, WHAT'S GOING ON?

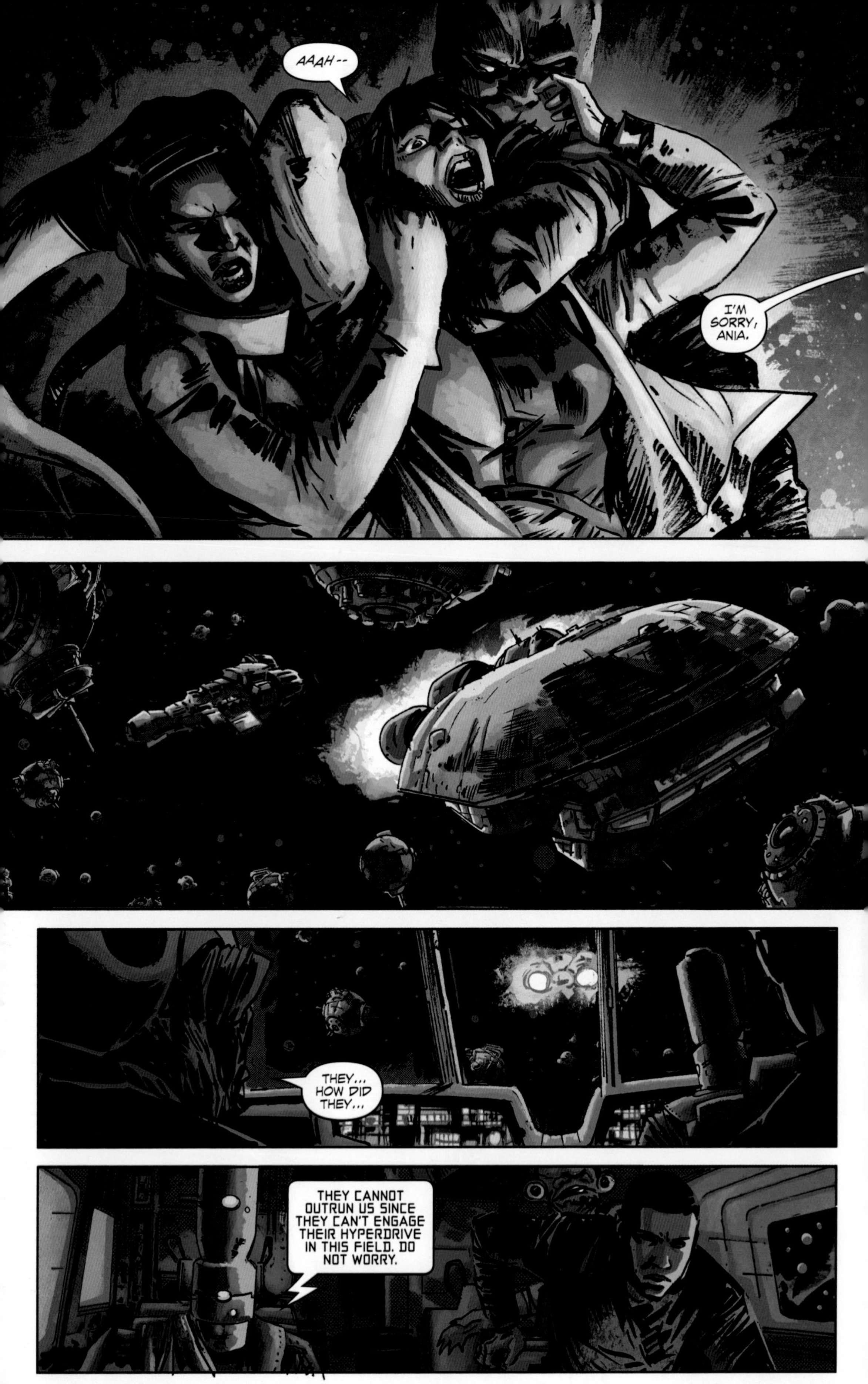
AAAH--
I'M SORRY, ANIA.
THEY... HOW DID THEY...
THEY CANNOT OUTRUN US SINCE THEY CAN'T ENGAGE THEIR HYPERDRIVE IN THIS FIELD. DO NOT WORRY.

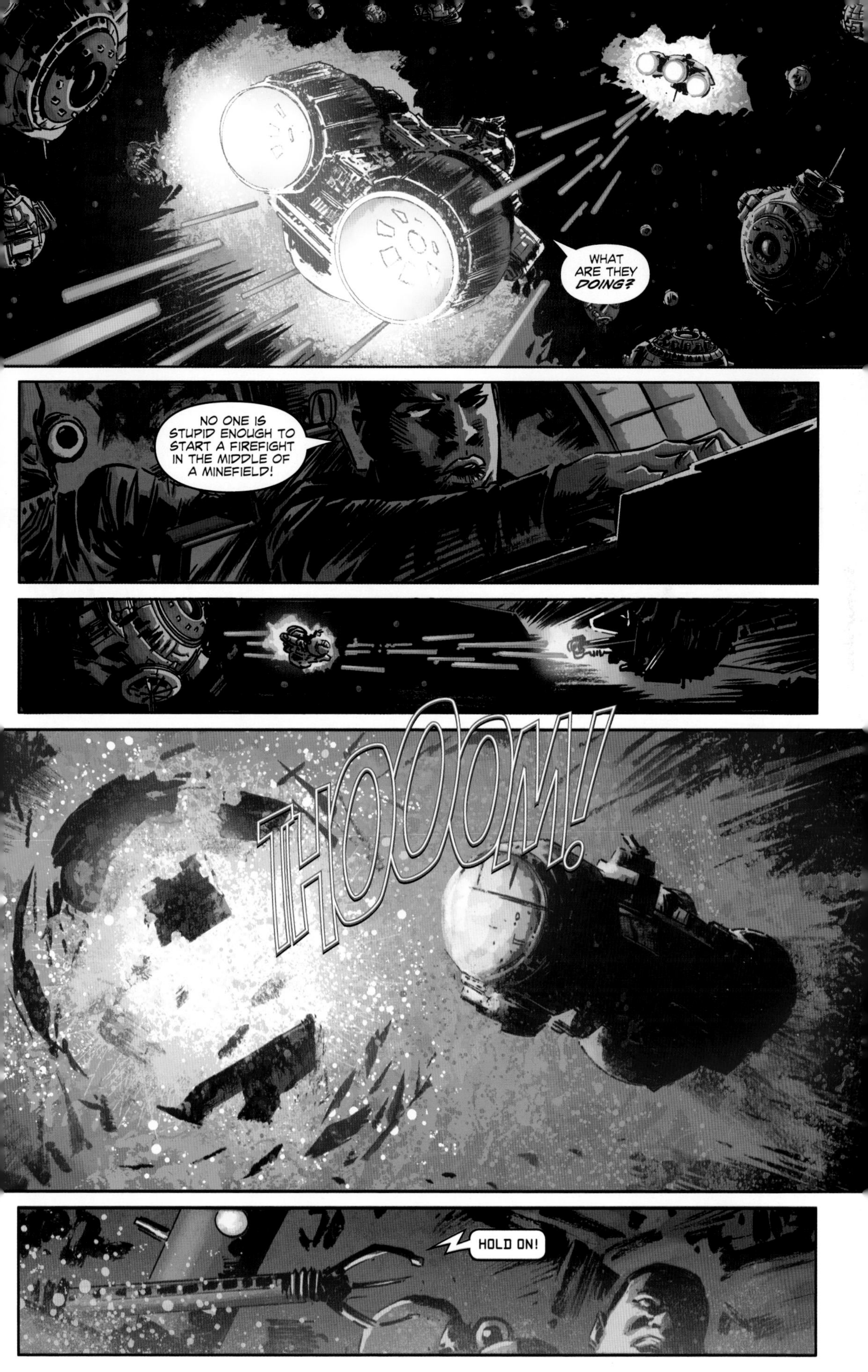
WHAT ARE THEY *DOING?*
NO ONE IS STUPID ENOUGH TO START A FIREFIGHT IN THE MIDDLE OF A MINEFIELD!
THOOOOM!
HOLD ON!

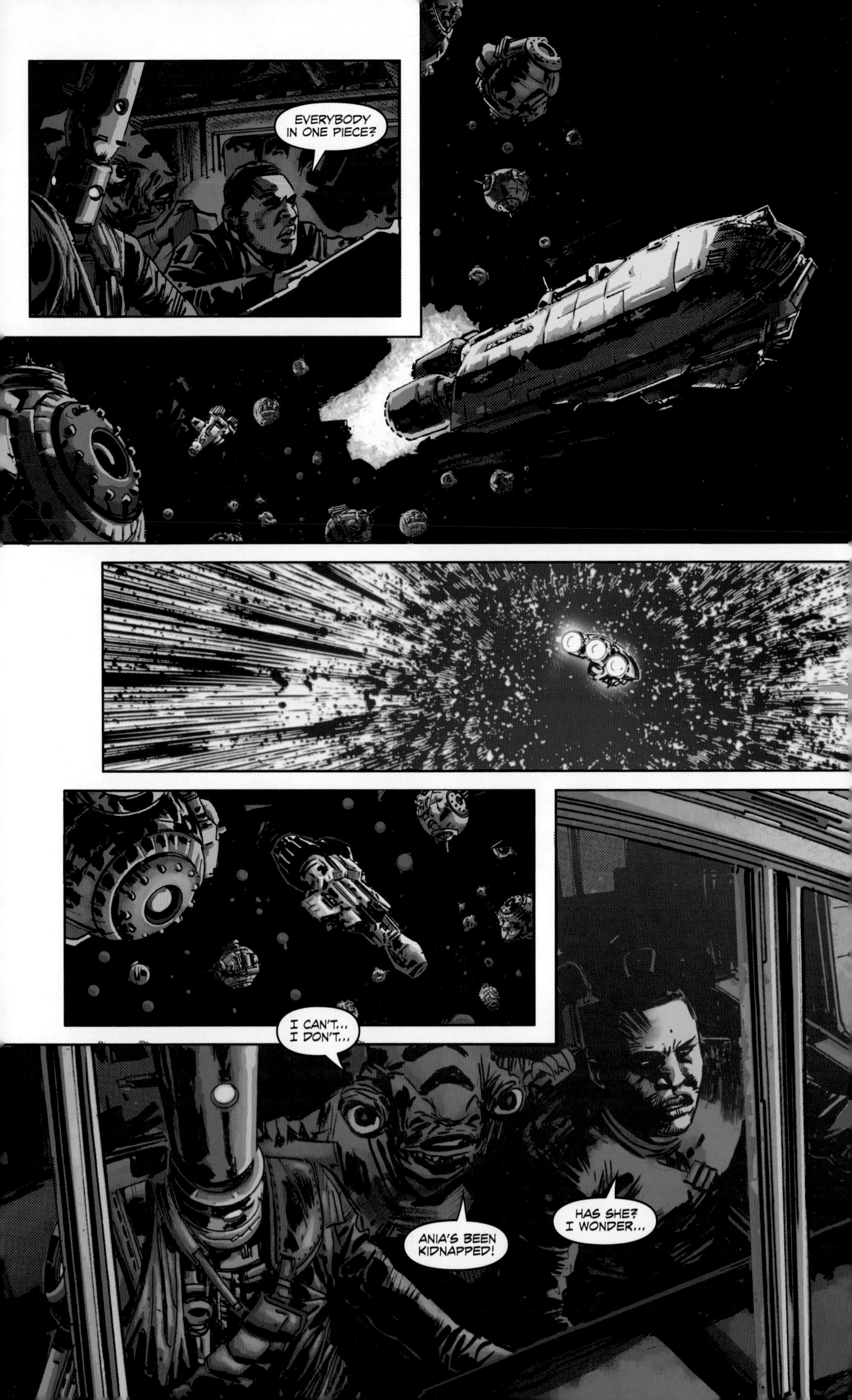
EVERYBODY IN ONE PIECE?
I CAN'T... I DON'T...
ANIA'S BEEN KIDNAPPED!
HAS SHE? I WONDER...

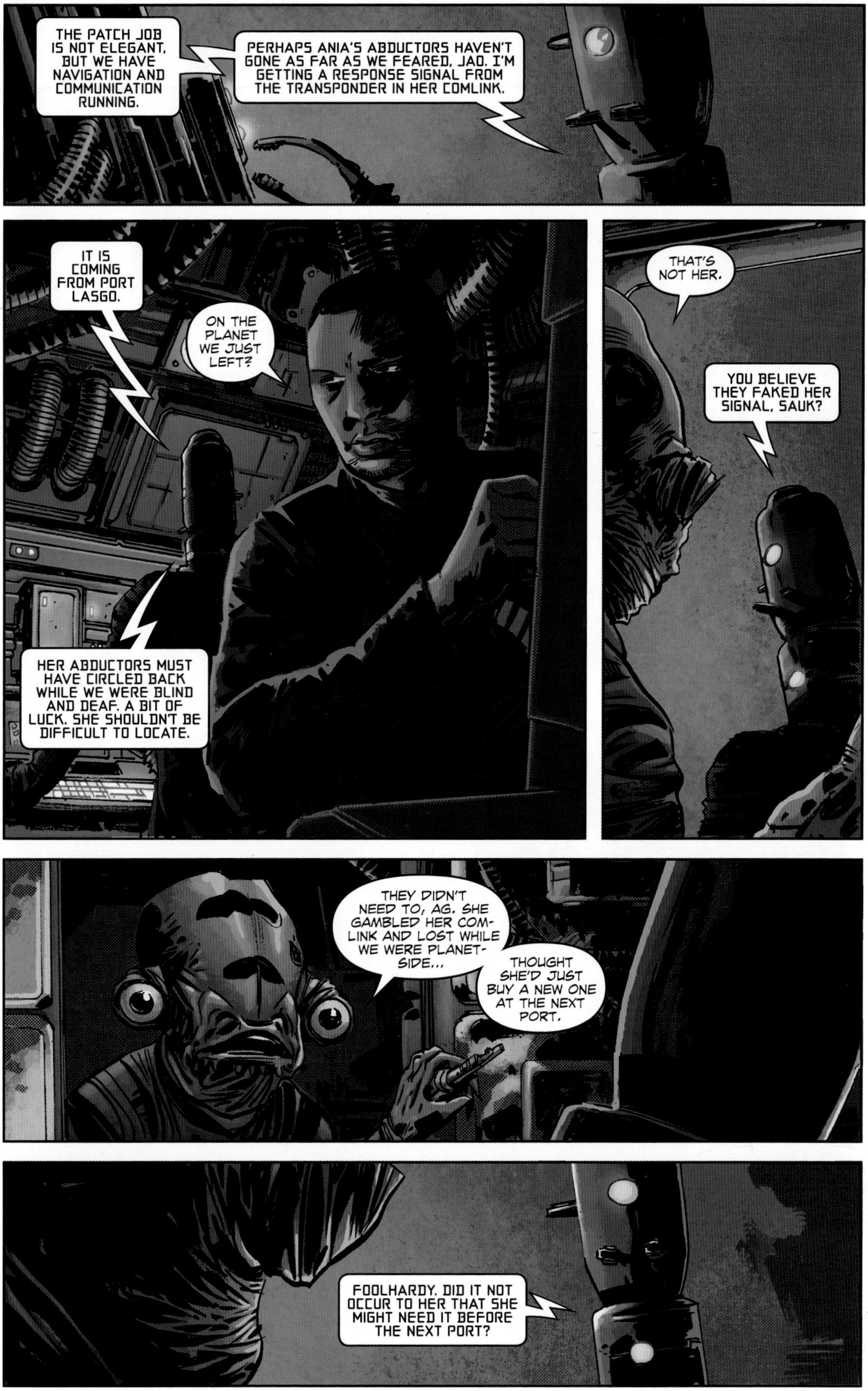
THE PATCH JOB IS NOT ELEGANT, BUT WE HAVE NAVIGATION AND COMMUNICATION RUNNING.
PERHAPS ANIA'S ABDUCTORS HAVEN'T GONE AS FAR AS WE FEARED, JAO. I'M GETTING A RESPONSE SIGNAL FROM THE TRANSPONDER IN HER COMLINK.
IT IS COMING FROM PORT LASGO.
ON THE PLANET WE JUST LEFT?
HER ABDUCTORS MUST HAVE CIRCLED BACK WHILE WE WERE BLIND AND DEAF. A BIT OF LUCK. SHE SHOULDN'T BE DIFFICULT TO LOCATE.
THAT'S NOT HER.
YOU BELIEVE THEY FAKED HER SIGNAL, SAUK?
THEY DIDN'T NEED TO, AG. SHE GAMBLED HER COM-LINK AND LOST WHILE WE WERE PLANET-SIDE...
THOUGHT SHE'D JUST BUY A NEW ONE AT THE NEXT PORT.
FOOLHARDY. DID IT NOT OCCUR TO HER THAT SHE MIGHT NEED IT BEFORE THE NEXT PORT?

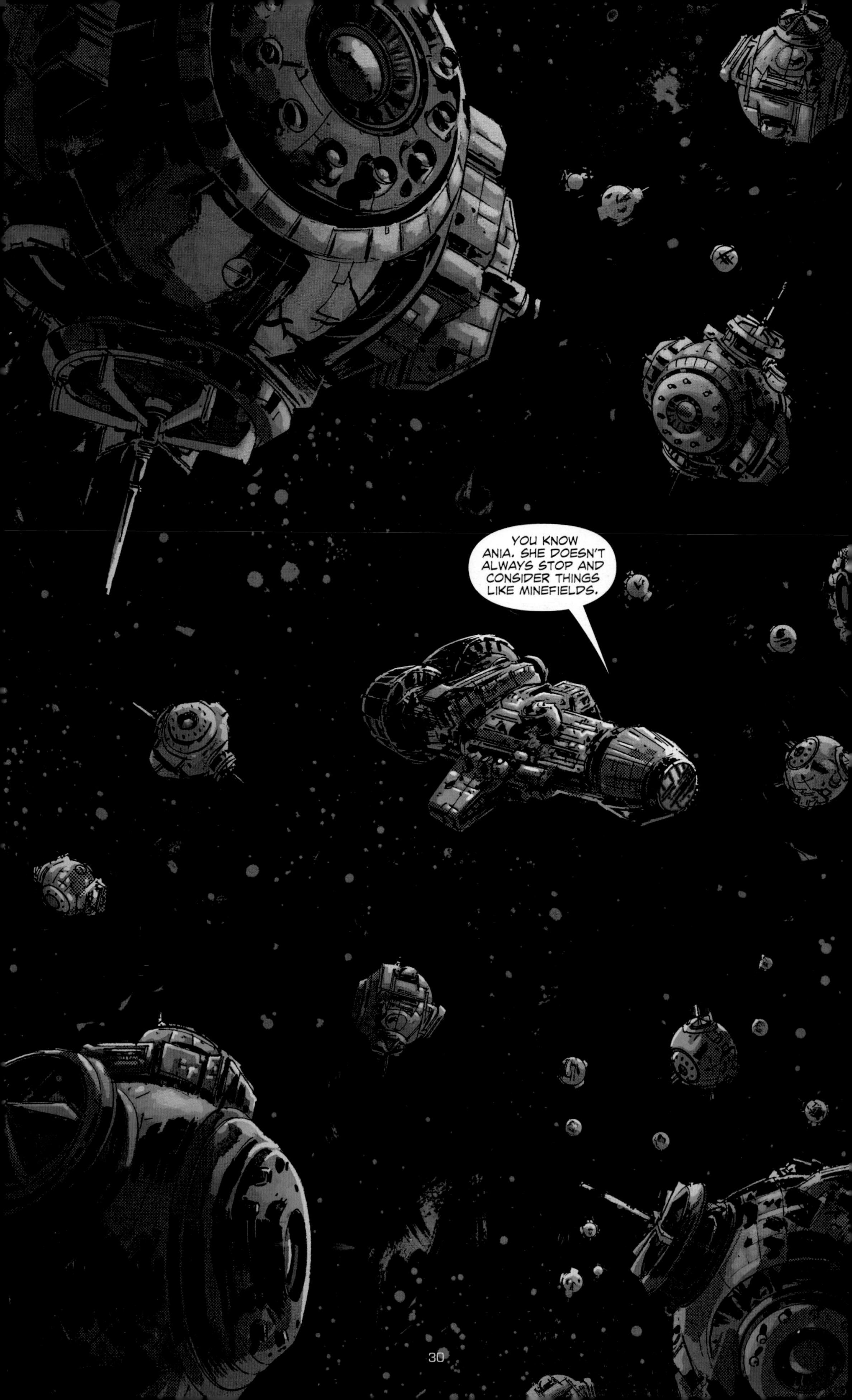
YOU KNOW ANIA. SHE DOESN'T ALWAYS STOP AND CONSIDER THINGS LIKE MINEFIELDS.

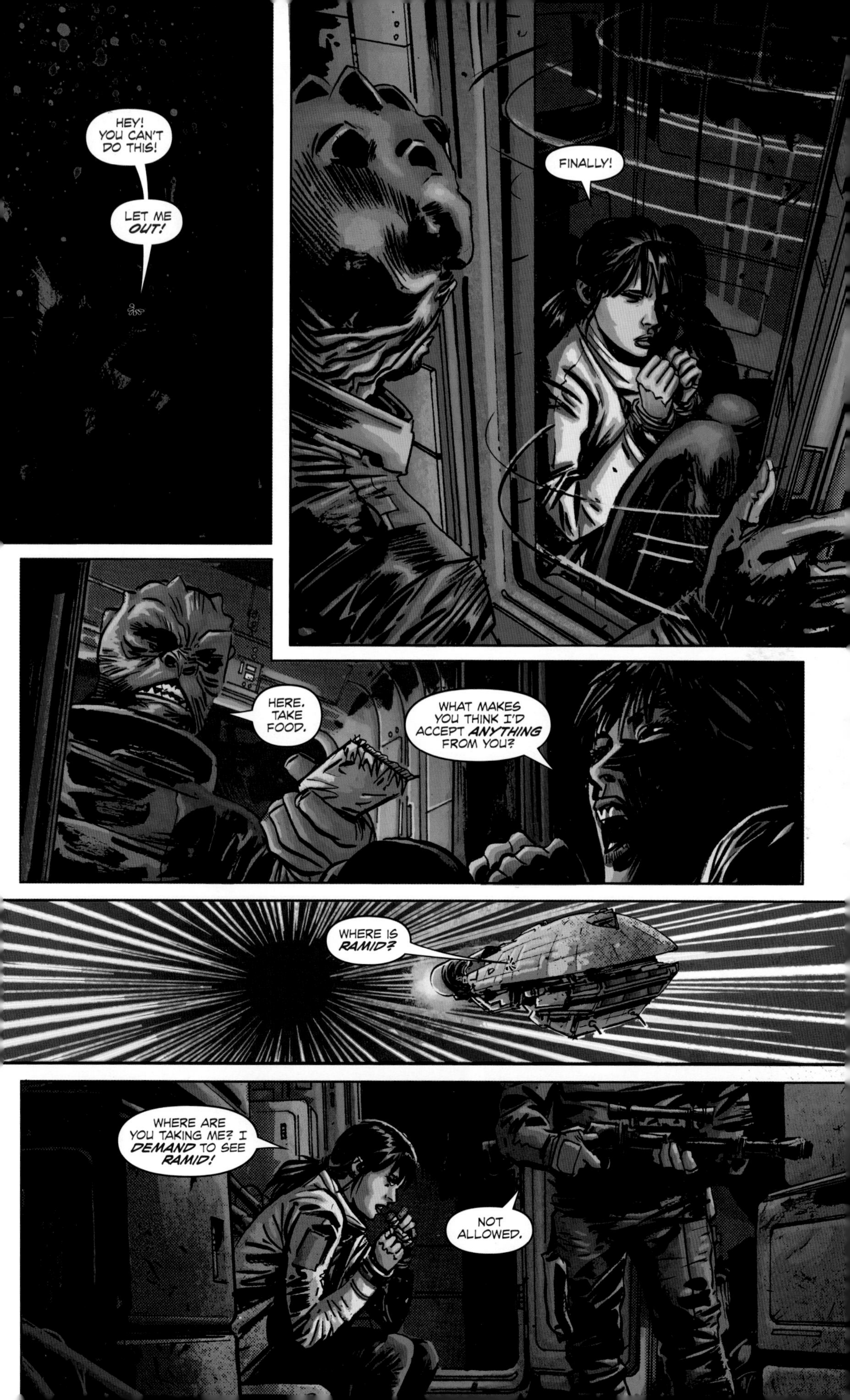
HEY! YOU CAN'T DO THIS!
LET ME *OUT!*
FINALLY!
HERE. TAKE FOOD.
WHAT MAKES YOU THINK I'D ACCEPT *ANYTHING* FROM YOU?
WHERE IS *RAMID?*
WHERE ARE YOU TAKING ME? I *DEMAND* TO SEE *RAMID!*
NOT ALLOWED.

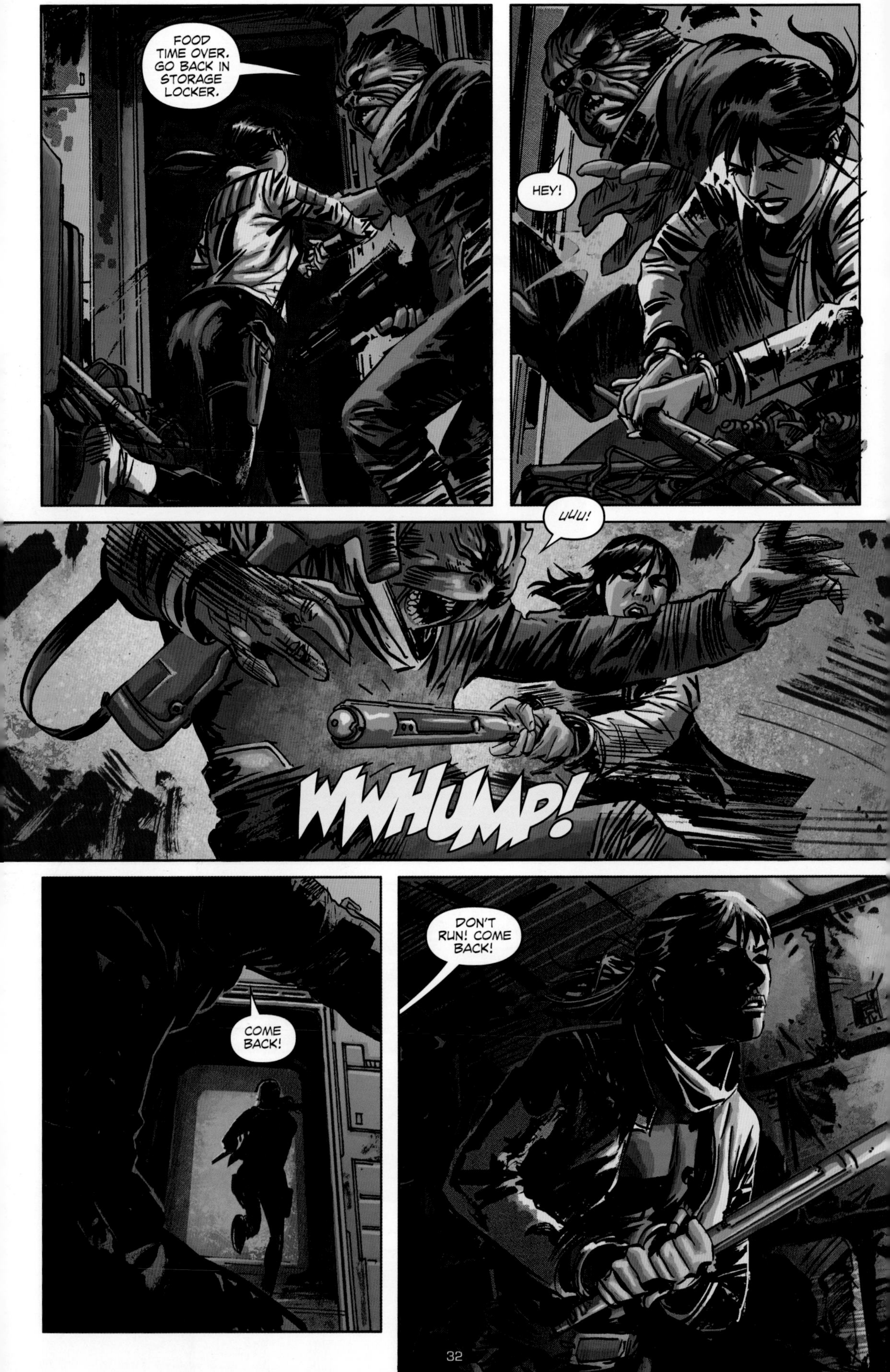
FOOD TIME OVER. GO BACK IN STORAGE LOCKER.
HEY!
UUU!
WWHUMP!
COME BACK!
DON'T RUN! COME BACK!

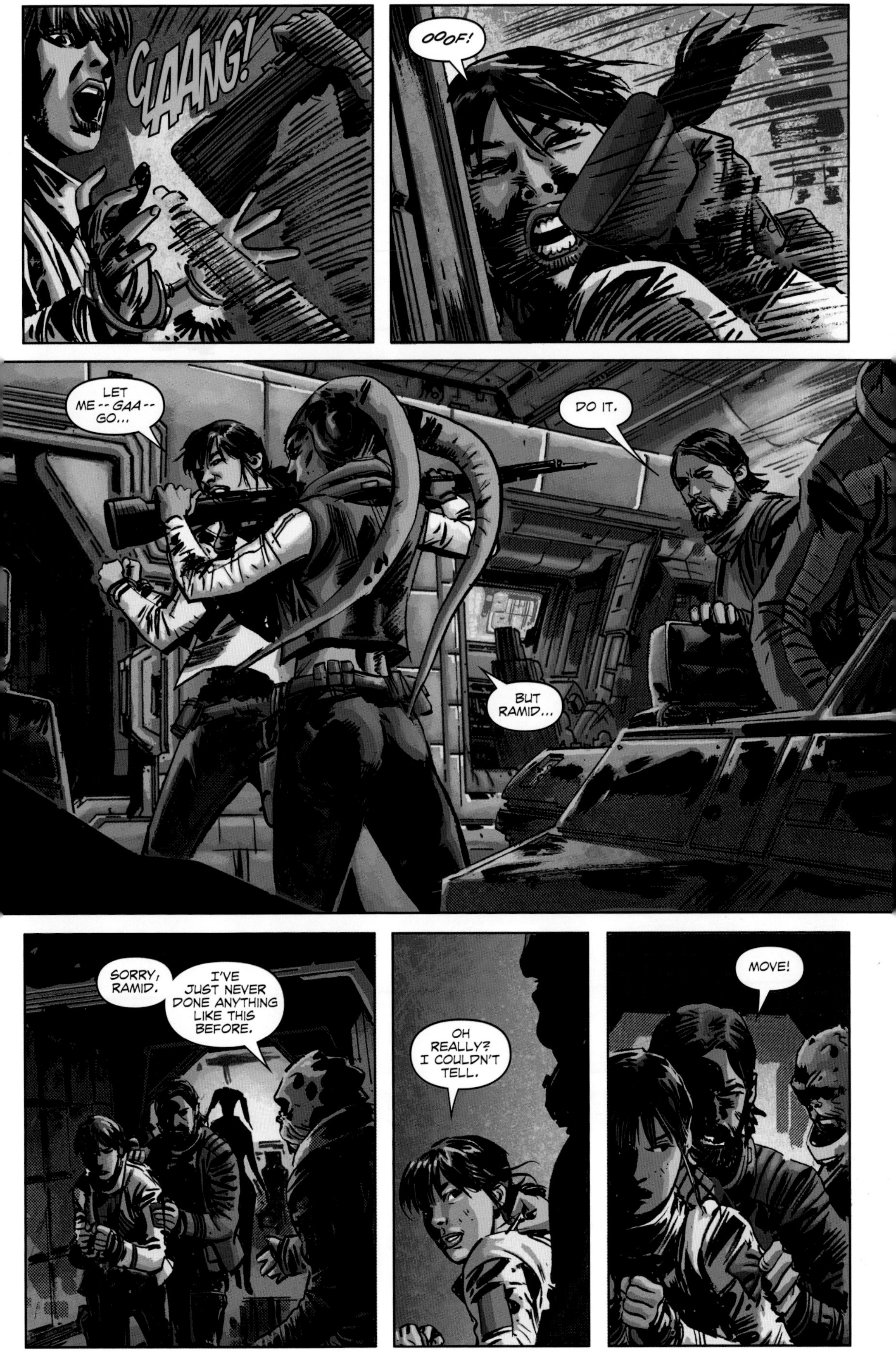
CLAANG!
OOOF!
LET ME -- GAA -- GO...
DO IT.
BUT RAMID...
SORRY, RAMID.
I'VE JUST NEVER DONE ANYTHING LIKE THIS BEFORE.
OH REALLY? I COULDN'T TELL.
MOVE!

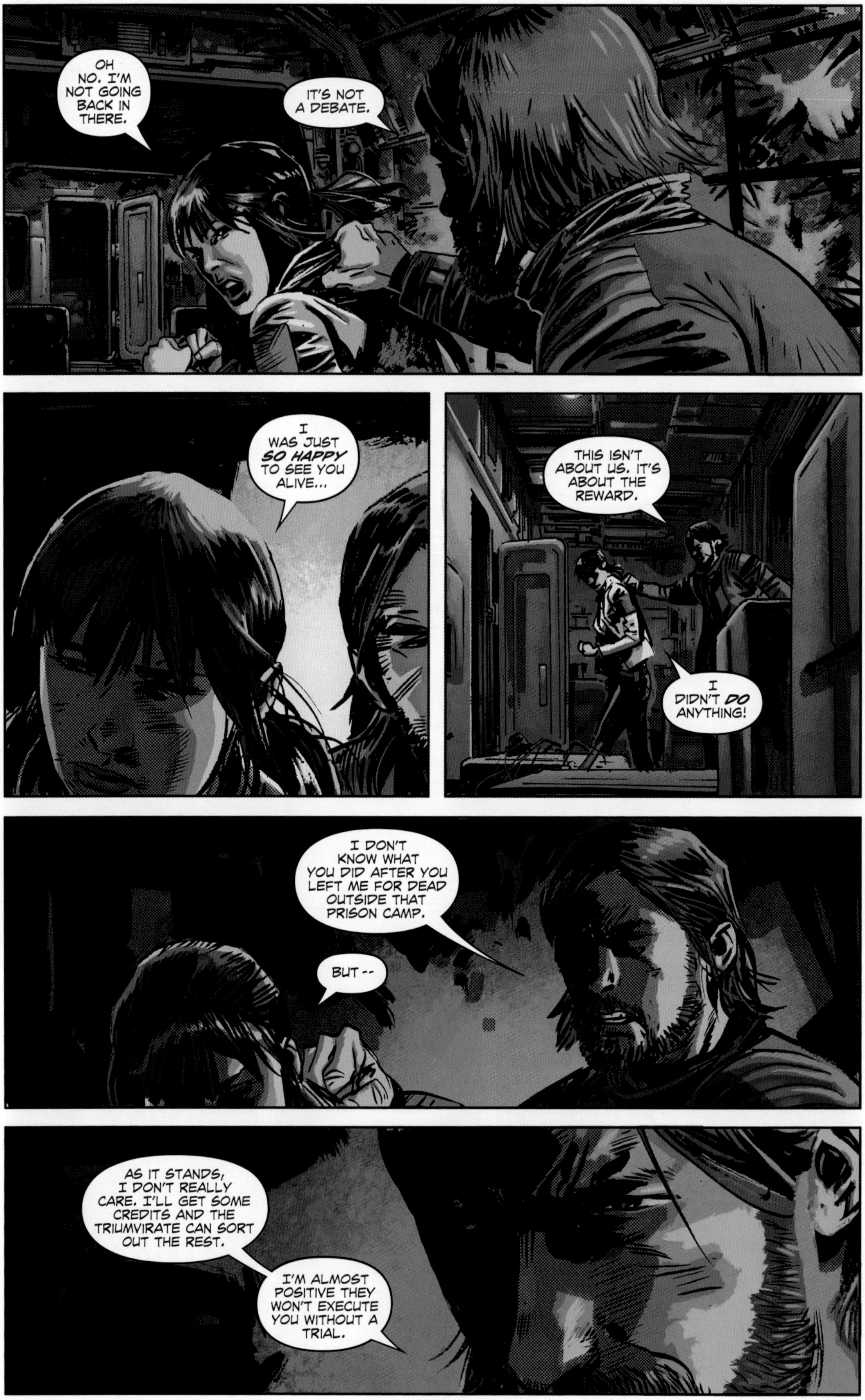
OH NO. I'M NOT GOING BACK IN THERE.
IT'S NOT A DEBATE.
I WAS JUST *SO HAPPY* TO SEE YOU ALIVE...
THIS ISN'T ABOUT US. IT'S ABOUT THE REWARD.
I DIDN'T *DO* ANYTHING!
I DON'T KNOW WHAT YOU DID AFTER YOU LEFT ME FOR DEAD OUTSIDE THAT PRISON CAMP.
BUT --
AS IT STANDS, I DON'T REALLY CARE. I'LL GET SOME CREDITS AND THE TRIUMVIRATE CAN SORT OUT THE REST.
I'M ALMOST POSITIVE THEY WON'T EXECUTE YOU WITHOUT A TRIAL.

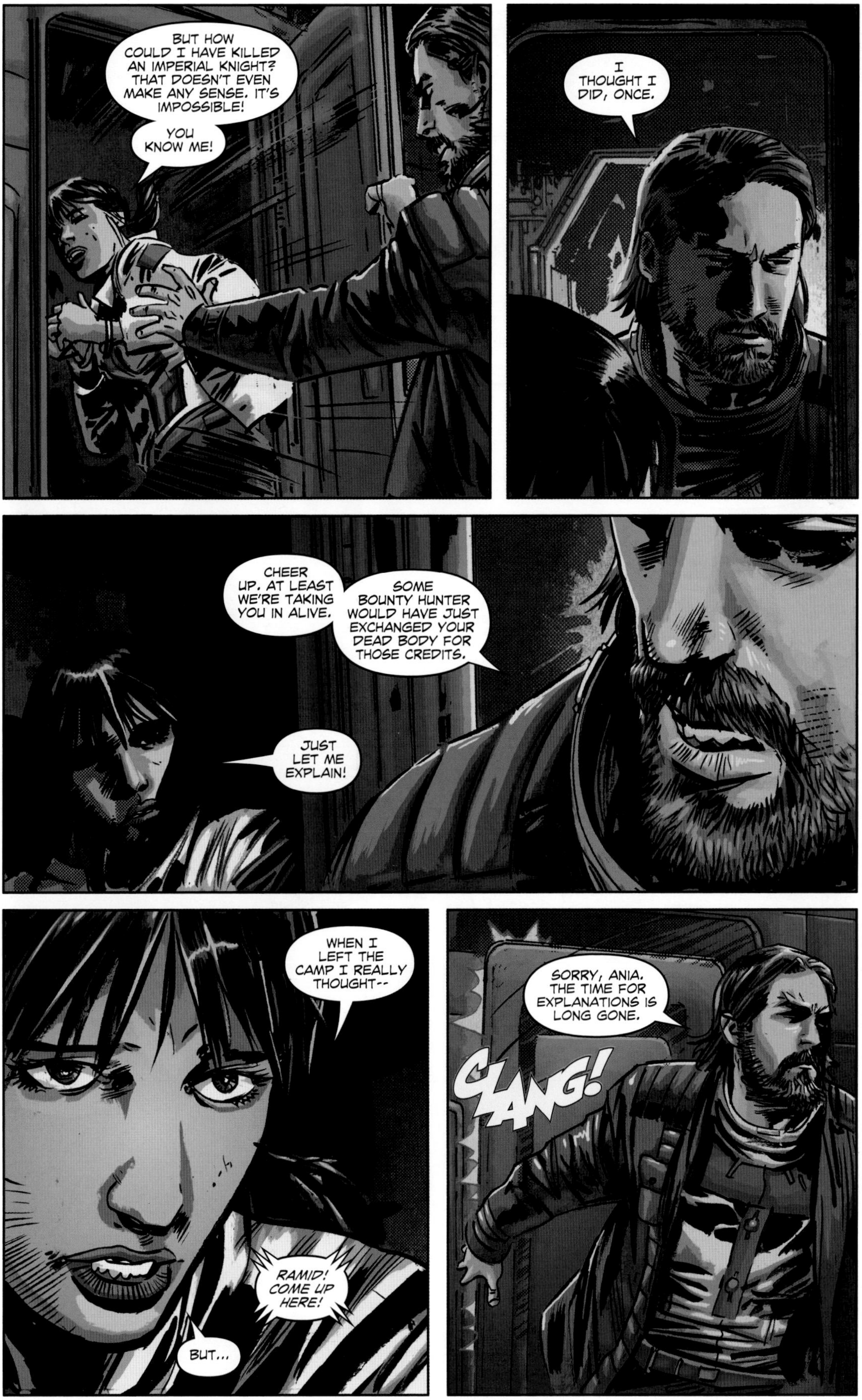
BUT HOW COULD I HAVE KILLED AN IMPERIAL KNIGHT? THAT DOESN'T EVEN MAKE ANY SENSE. IT'S IMPOSSIBLE!
YOU KNOW ME!
I THOUGHT I DID, ONCE.
CHEER UP. AT LEAST WE'RE TAKING YOU IN ALIVE.
SOME BOUNTY HUNTER WOULD HAVE JUST EXCHANGED YOUR DEAD BODY FOR THOSE CREDITS.
JUST LET ME EXPLAIN!
WHEN I LEFT THE CAMP I REALLY THOUGHT--
RAMID! COME UP HERE!
BUT...
SORRY, ANIA. THE TIME FOR EXPLANATIONS IS LONG GONE.
CLANG!

WE WENT OVER THE PLAN DOZENS OF TIMES! WHAT'S GONE WRONG?

IT WAS THAT COLD HYPERSPACE JUMP WE DID RIGHT OUT OF THE MINEFIELD. ATE UP A LOT MORE FUEL THAN WE WERE EXPECTING.

WE'RE NOT EXACTLY PROFESSIONAL KIDNAPPERS, RAMID. THERE WERE BOUND TO BE SOME HITCHES.

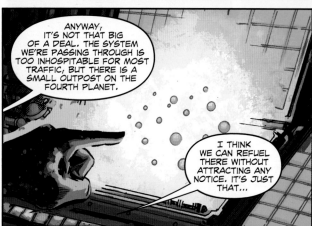

ANYWAY, IT'S NOT THAT BIG OF A DEAL. THE SYSTEM WE'RE PASSING THROUGH IS TOO INHOSPITABLE FOR MOST TRAFFIC, BUT THERE IS A SMALL OUTPOST ON THE FOURTH PLANET.

I THINK WE CAN REFUEL THERE WITHOUT ATTRACTING ANY NOTICE. IT'S JUST THAT...

WELL?

THERE'S ONLY ONE OUTPOST THERE BECAUSE IT'S *ALL* THIS PLANET CAN SUPPORT. NOT A NICE PLACE.

WE'LL HAVE TO BE CAREFUL -- GET OUR TRAJECTORY RIGHT. THOSE CLOUDS CONTAIN ACIDIC VAPOR. SOMETIMES IT RAINS MOLTEN SILICA OR SHARDS OF GLASS ON THE SURFACE.

IT RAINS *GLASS?*

WE WON'T WANT TO HANG AROUND.

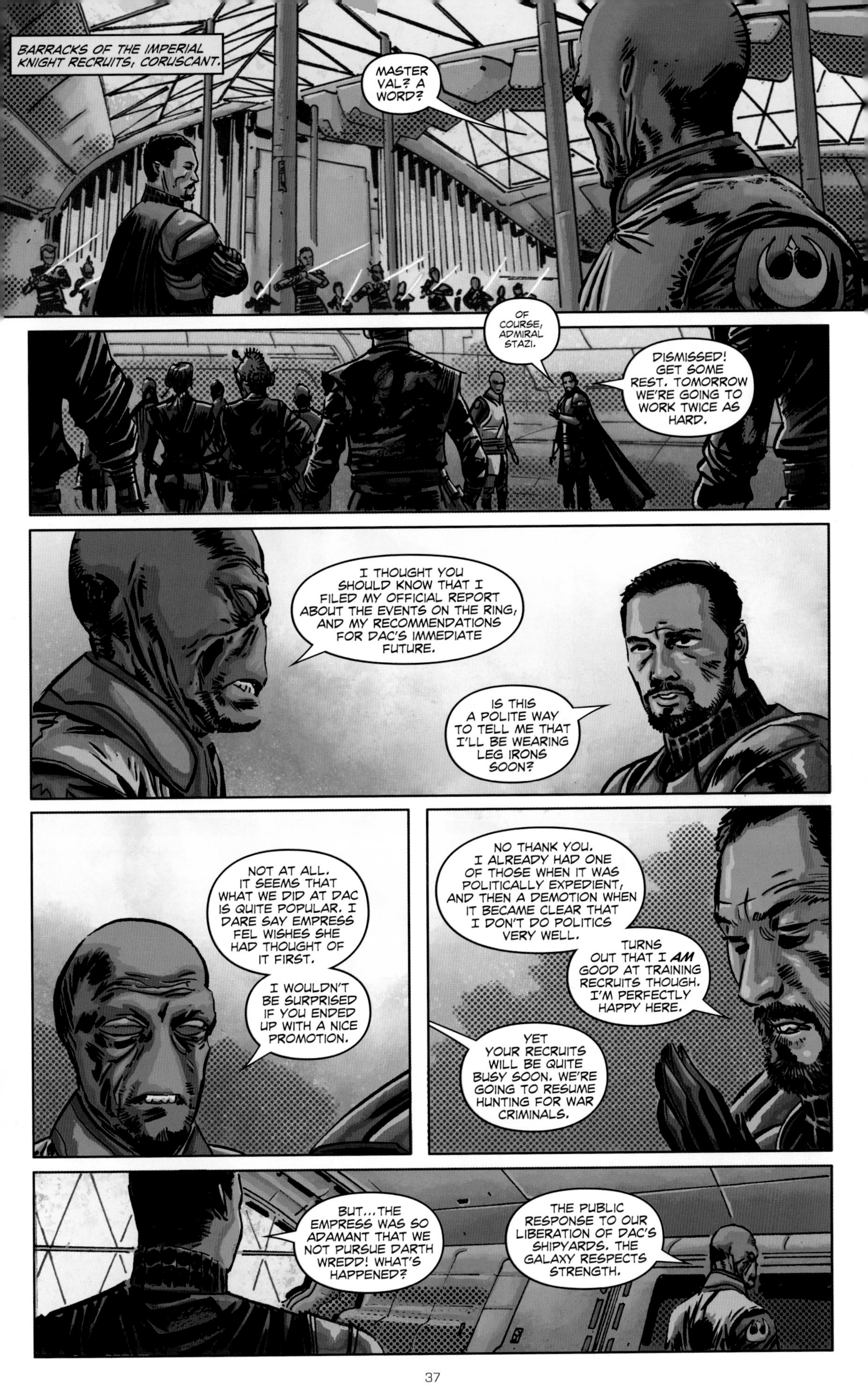
BARRACKS OF THE IMPERIAL KNIGHT RECRUITS, CORUSCANT.
MASTER VAL? A WORD?
OF COURSE, ADMIRAL STAZI.
DISMISSED! GET SOME REST. TOMORROW WE'RE GOING TO WORK TWICE AS HARD.
I THOUGHT YOU SHOULD KNOW THAT I FILED MY OFFICIAL REPORT ABOUT THE EVENTS ON THE RING, AND MY RECOMMENDATIONS FOR DAC'S IMMEDIATE FUTURE.
IS THIS A POLITE WAY TO TELL ME THAT I'LL BE WEARING LEG IRONS SOON?
NOT AT ALL. IT SEEMS THAT WHAT WE DID AT DAC IS QUITE POPULAR. I DARE SAY EMPRESS FEL WISHES SHE HAD THOUGHT OF IT FIRST.
I WOULDN'T BE SURPRISED IF YOU ENDED UP WITH A NICE PROMOTION.
NO THANK YOU. I ALREADY HAD ONE OF THOSE WHEN IT WAS POLITICALLY EXPEDIENT, AND THEN A DEMOTION WHEN IT BECAME CLEAR THAT I DON'T DO POLITICS VERY WELL.
TURNS OUT THAT I *AM* GOOD AT TRAINING RECRUITS THOUGH. I'M PERFECTLY HAPPY HERE.
YET YOUR RECRUITS WILL BE QUITE BUSY SOON. WE'RE GOING TO RESUME HUNTING FOR WAR CRIMINALS.
BUT...THE EMPRESS WAS SO ADAMANT THAT WE NOT PURSUE DARTH WREDD! WHAT'S HAPPENED?
THE PUBLIC RESPONSE TO OUR LIBERATION OF DAC'S SHIPYARDS. THE GALAXY RESPECTS STRENGTH.

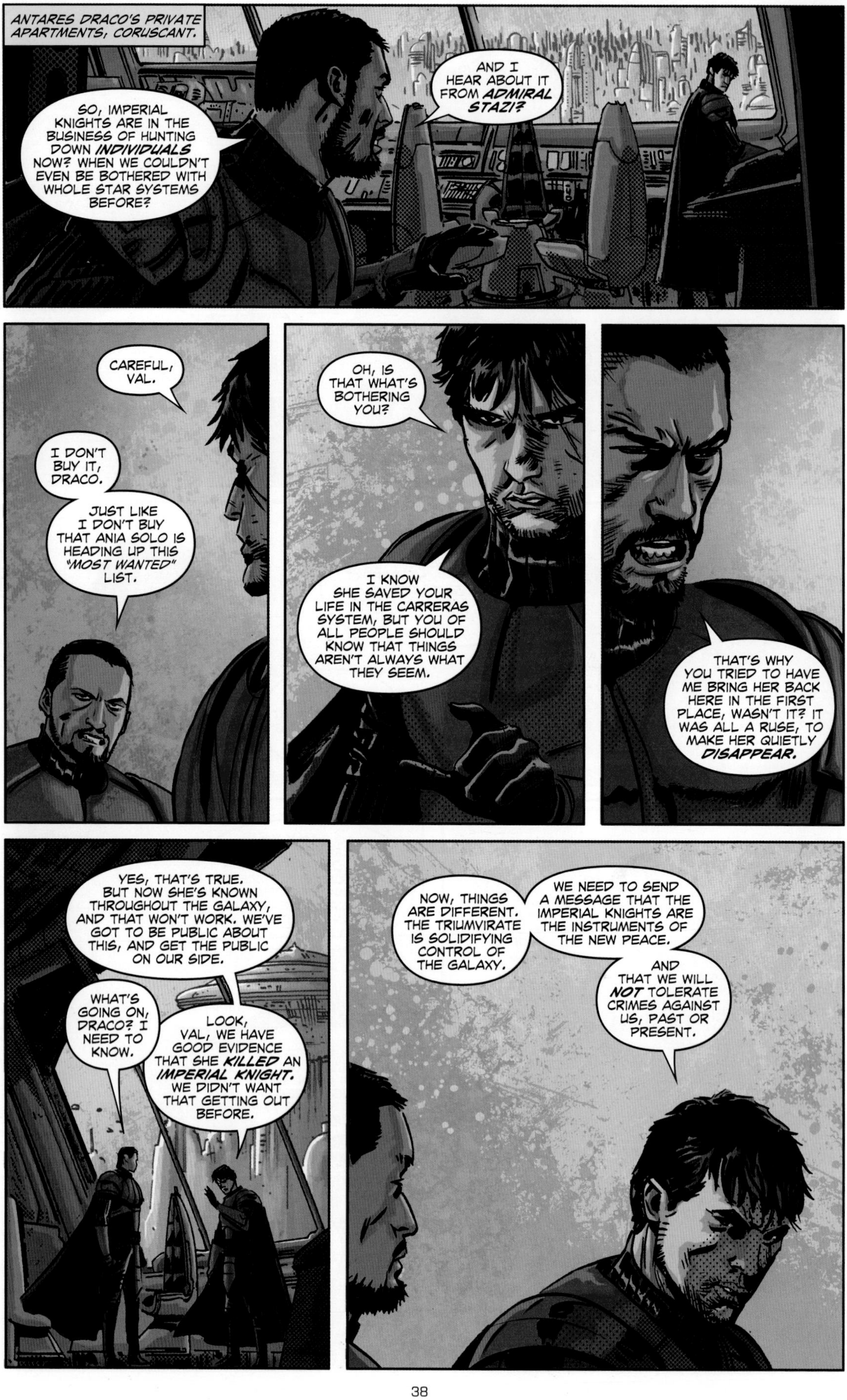
ANTARES DRACO'S PRIVATE APARTMENTS, CORUSCANT.
SO, IMPERIAL KNIGHTS ARE IN THE BUSINESS OF HUNTING DOWN INDIVIDUALS NOW? WHEN WE COULDN'T EVEN BE BOTHERED WITH WHOLE STAR SYSTEMS BEFORE?
AND I HEAR ABOUT IT FROM ADMIRAL STAZI?
CAREFUL, VAL.
I DON'T BUY IT, DRACO.
JUST LIKE I DON'T BUY THAT ANIA SOLO IS HEADING UP THIS "MOST WANTED" LIST.
OH, IS THAT WHAT'S BOTHERING YOU?
I KNOW SHE SAVED YOUR LIFE IN THE CARRERAS SYSTEM, BUT YOU OF ALL PEOPLE SHOULD KNOW THAT THINGS AREN'T ALWAYS WHAT THEY SEEM.
THAT'S WHY YOU TRIED TO HAVE ME BRING HER BACK HERE IN THE FIRST PLACE, WASN'T IT? IT WAS ALL A RUSE, TO MAKE HER QUIETLY DISAPPEAR.
YES, THAT'S TRUE. BUT NOW SHE'S KNOWN THROUGHOUT THE GALAXY, AND THAT WON'T WORK. WE'VE GOT TO BE PUBLIC ABOUT THIS, AND GET THE PUBLIC ON OUR SIDE.
WHAT'S GOING ON, DRACO? I NEED TO KNOW.
LOOK, VAL, WE HAVE GOOD EVIDENCE THAT SHE KILLED AN IMPERIAL KNIGHT. WE DIDN'T WANT THAT GETTING OUT BEFORE.
NOW, THINGS ARE DIFFERENT. THE TRIUMVIRATE IS SOLIDIFYING CONTROL OF THE GALAXY.
WE NEED TO SEND A MESSAGE THAT THE IMPERIAL KNIGHTS ARE THE INSTRUMENTS OF THE NEW PEACE.
AND THAT WE WILL NOT TOLERATE CRIMES AGAINST US, PAST OR PRESENT.

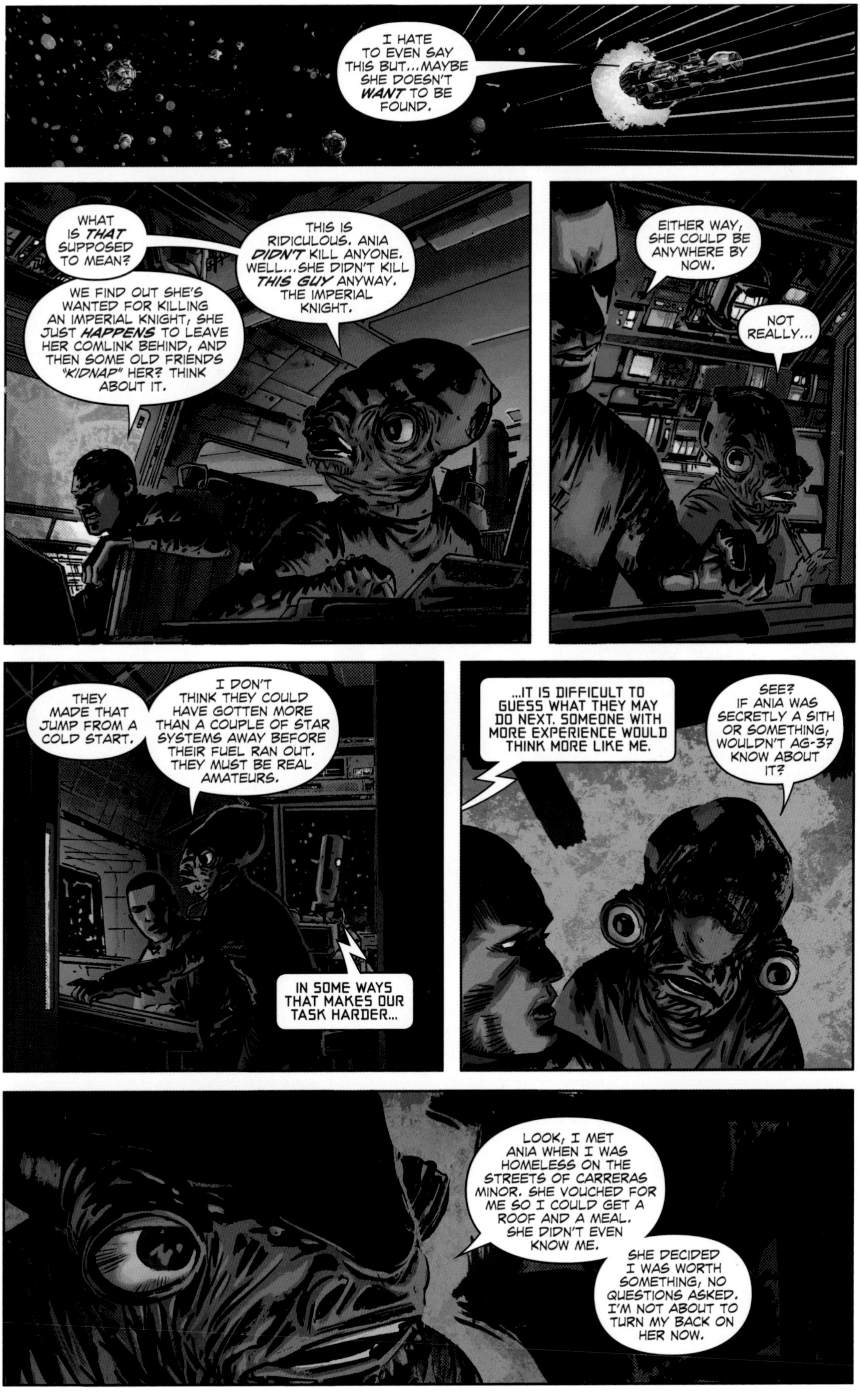
I HATE TO EVEN SAY THIS BUT...MAYBE SHE DOESN'T *WANT* TO BE FOUND.
WHAT IS *THAT* SUPPOSED TO MEAN?
WE FIND OUT SHE'S WANTED FOR KILLING AN IMPERIAL KNIGHT, SHE JUST *HAPPENS* TO LEAVE HER COMLINK BEHIND, AND THEN SOME OLD FRIENDS "*KIDNAP*" HER? THINK ABOUT IT.
THIS IS RIDICULOUS. ANIA *DIDN'T* KILL ANYONE. WELL...SHE DIDN'T KILL *THIS GUY* ANYWAY. THE IMPERIAL KNIGHT.
EITHER WAY, SHE COULD BE ANYWHERE BY NOW.
NOT REALLY...
THEY MADE THAT JUMP FROM A COLD START.
I DON'T THINK THEY COULD HAVE GOTTEN MORE THAN A COUPLE OF STAR SYSTEMS AWAY BEFORE THEIR FUEL RAN OUT. THEY MUST BE REAL AMATEURS.
IN SOME WAYS THAT MAKES OUR TASK HARDER...
...IT IS DIFFICULT TO GUESS WHAT THEY MAY DO NEXT. SOMEONE WITH MORE EXPERIENCE WOULD THINK MORE LIKE ME.
SEE? IF ANIA WAS SECRETLY A SITH OR SOMETHING, WOULDN'T AG-37 KNOW ABOUT IT?
LOOK, I MET ANIA WHEN I WAS HOMELESS ON THE STREETS OF CARRERAS MINOR. SHE VOUCHED FOR ME SO I COULD GET A ROOF AND A MEAL. SHE DIDN'T EVEN KNOW ME.
SHE DECIDED I WAS WORTH SOMETHING, NO QUESTIONS ASKED. I'M NOT ABOUT TO TURN MY BACK ON HER NOW.

AG, HOW LONG HAVE *YOU* KNOWN ANIA?

I FIRST ENCOUNTERED HER NEAR THE END OF THE MOST RECENT CIVIL WAR, IN THE SELVATAS SYSTEM.

WASN'T THERE A LARGE PRISON CAMP THERE?

WAS SHE AN INMATE?

THERE WERE A LOT OF POLITICAL PRISONERS BY THE END OF THE WAR.

LOTS OF LEGITIMATE PRISONERS TOO...

I NEVER INQUIRED ABOUT HER PARTICULAR CIRCUMSTANCES. IT DID NOT SEEM RELEVANT.

NOT RELE --

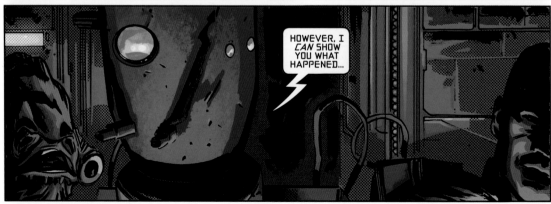

HOWEVER, I *CAN* SHOW YOU WHAT HAPPENED...

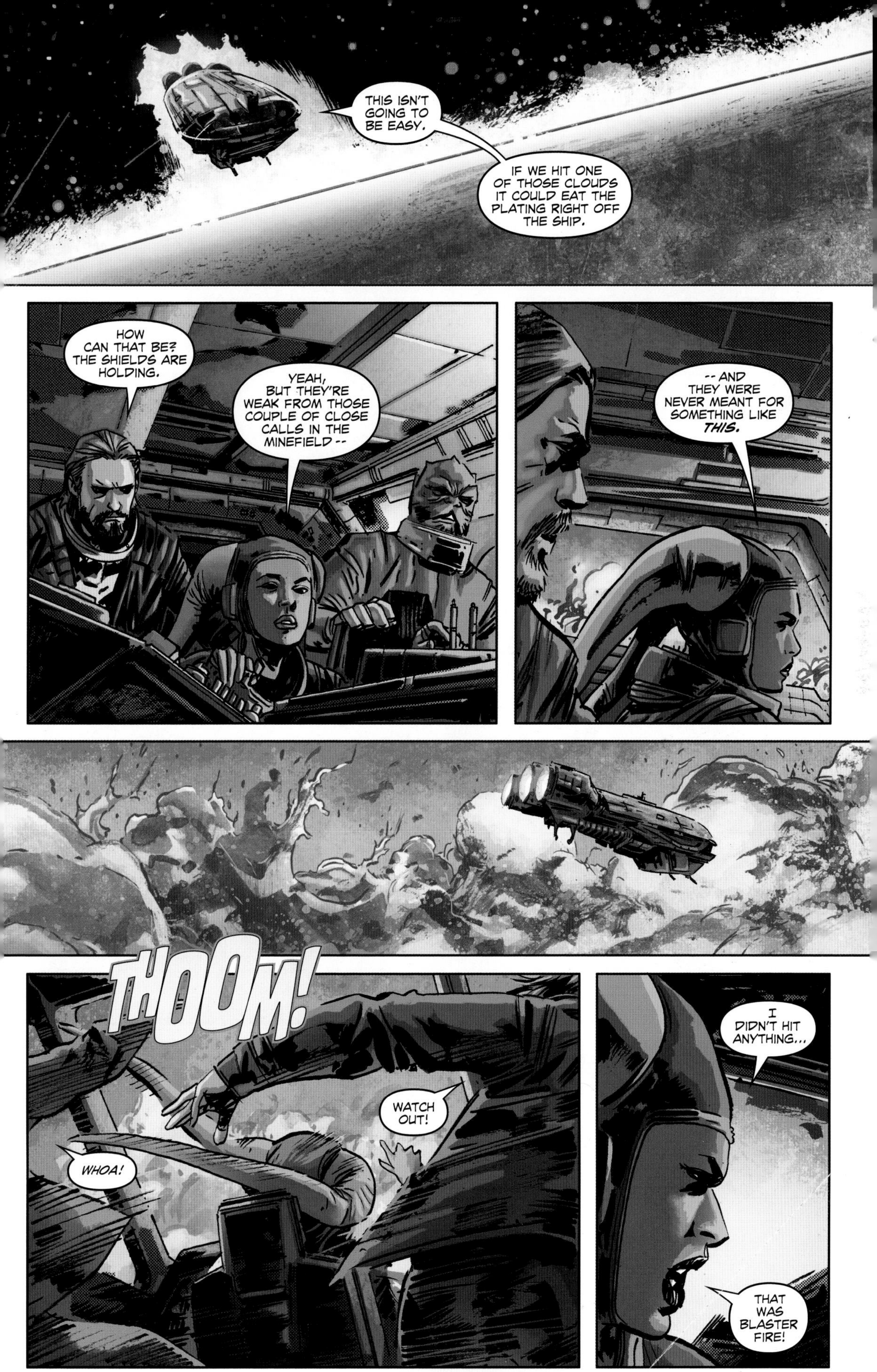

THIS ISN'T GOING TO BE EASY.
IF WE HIT ONE OF THOSE CLOUDS IT COULD EAT THE PLATING RIGHT OFF THE SHIP.
HOW CAN THAT BE? THE SHIELDS ARE HOLDING.
YEAH, BUT THEY'RE WEAK FROM THOSE COUPLE OF CLOSE CALLS IN THE MINEFIELD --
-- AND THEY WERE NEVER MEANT FOR SOMETHING LIKE *THIS.*
THOOM!
WATCH OUT!
*WHOA!*
I DIDN'T HIT ANYTHING...
THAT WAS BLASTER FIRE!

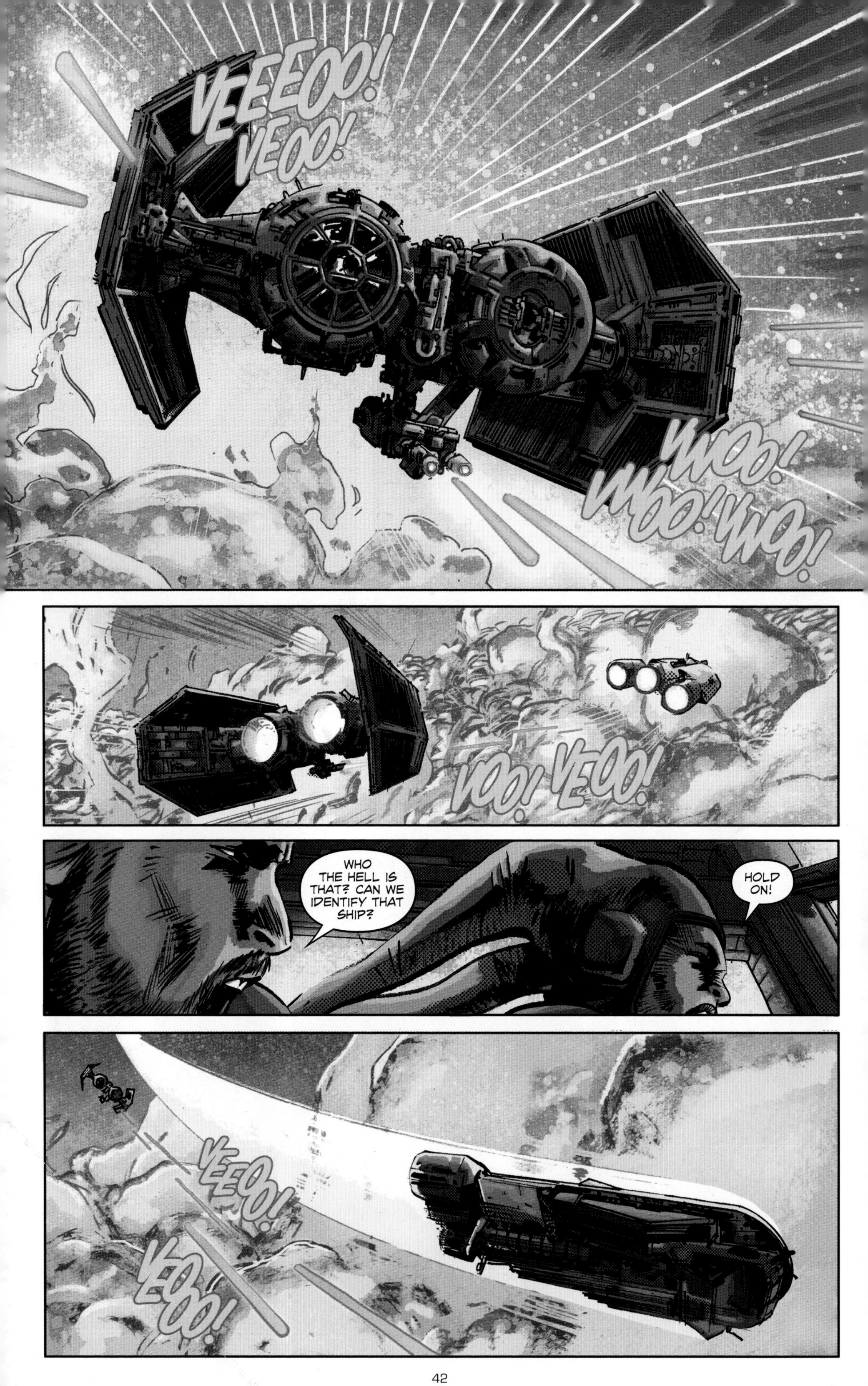
VEEEOO! VEOO!
VWOO! VWOO! VWOO!
VOO! VEOO!
WHO THE HELL IS THAT? CAN WE IDENTIFY THAT SHIP?
HOLD ON!
VEEOO!
VEOO!

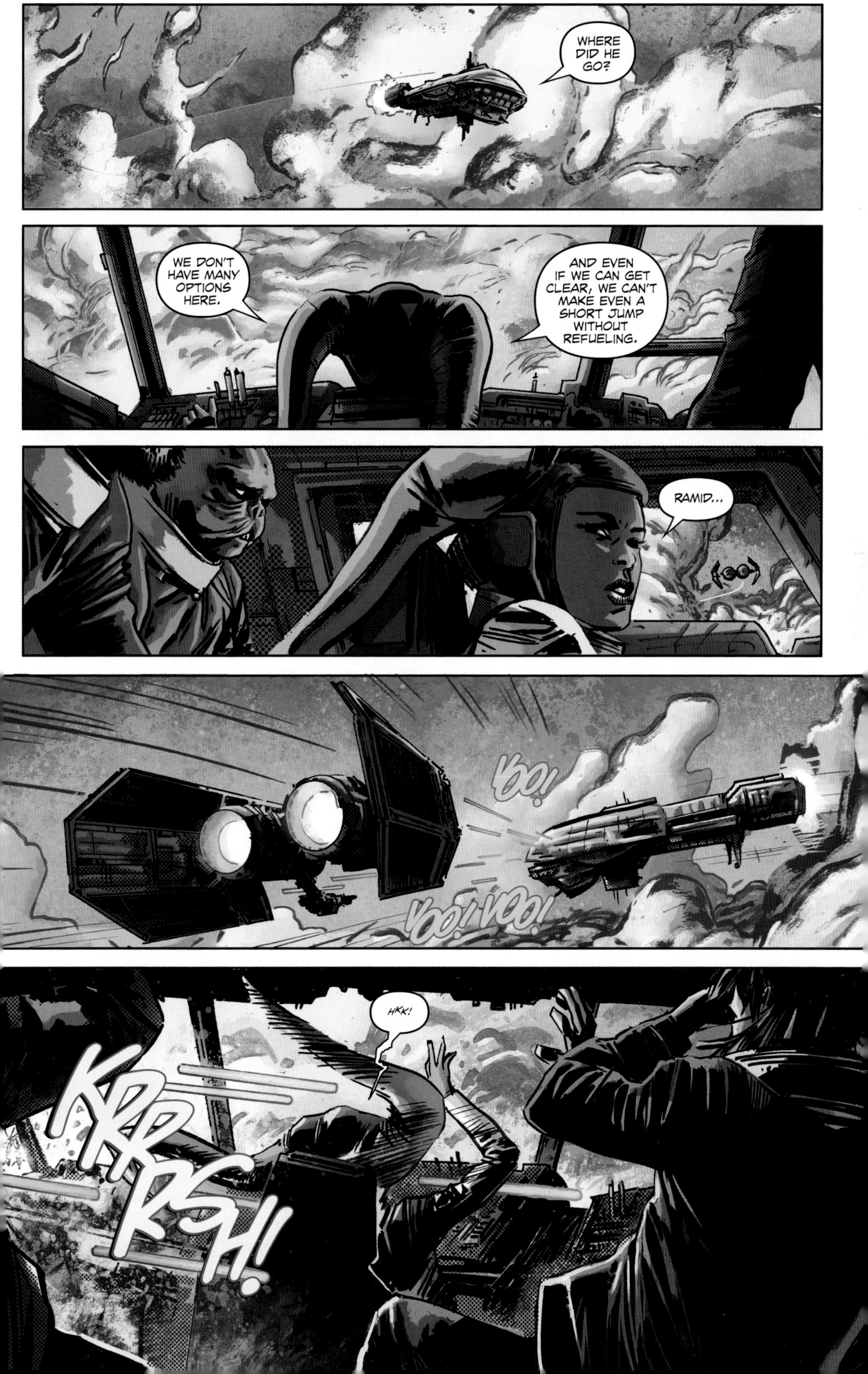
WHERE DID HE GO?
WE DON'T HAVE MANY OPTIONS HERE.
AND EVEN IF WE CAN GET CLEAR, WE CAN'T MAKE EVEN A SHORT JUMP WITHOUT REFUELING.
RAMID...
VOO!
VOO! VOO!
HKK!
KRRRSH!

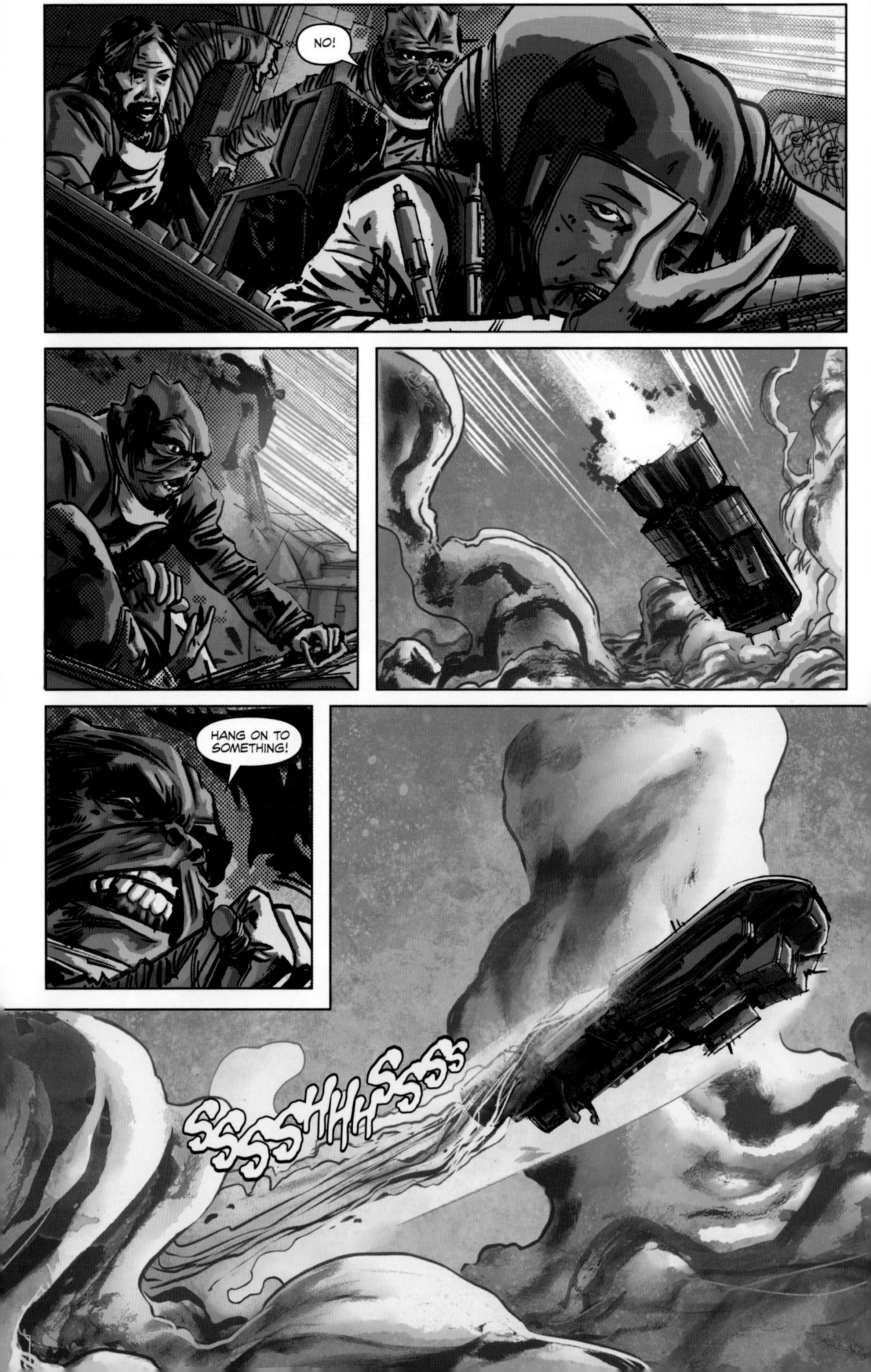
NO!
HANG ON TO SOMETHING!
SSSSHHHSSSS

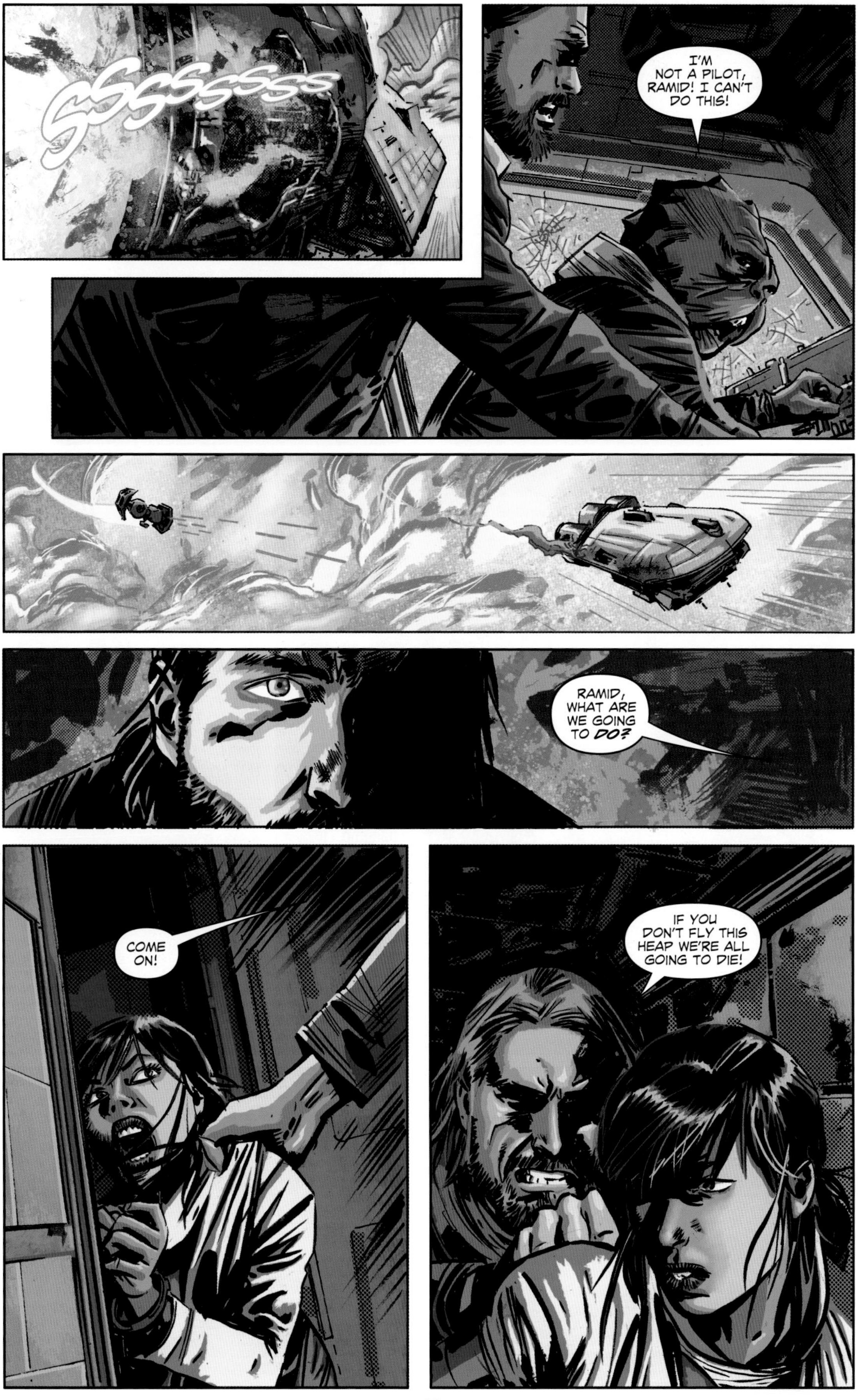
SSSSSSSS
I'M NOT A PILOT, RAMID! I CAN'T DO THIS!
RAMID, WHAT ARE WE GOING TO *DO?*
COME ON!
IF YOU DON'T FLY THIS HEAP WE'RE ALL GOING TO DIE!

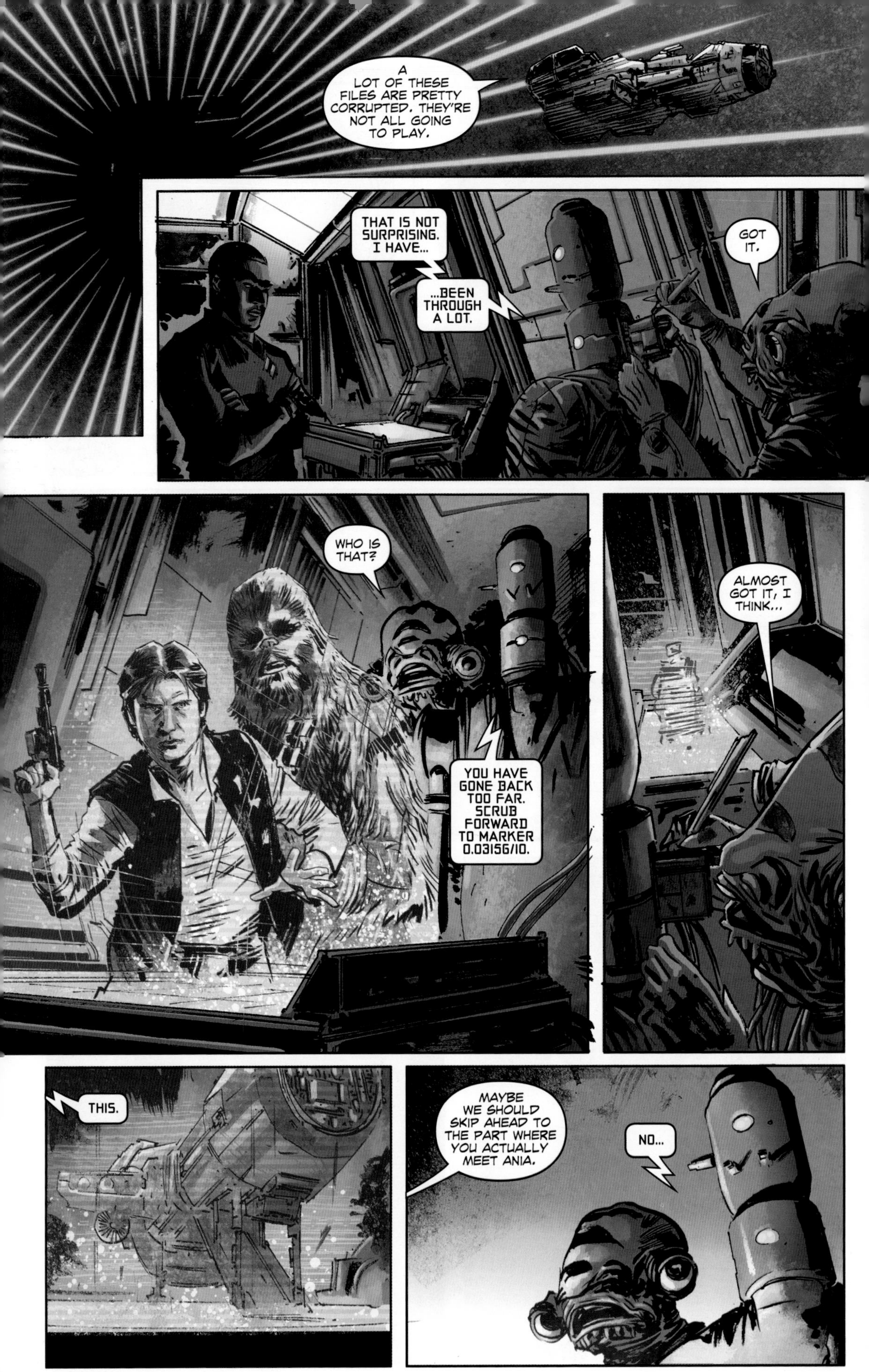
A LOT OF THESE FILES ARE PRETTY CORRUPTED. THEY'RE NOT ALL GOING TO PLAY.
THAT IS NOT SURPRISING. I HAVE...
...BEEN THROUGH A LOT.
GOT IT.
WHO IS THAT?
YOU HAVE GONE BACK TOO FAR. SCRUB FORWARD TO MARKER 0.03156/10.
ALMOST GOT IT, I THINK...
THIS.
MAYBE WE SHOULD SKIP AHEAD TO THE PART WHERE YOU ACTUALLY MEET ANIA.
NO...

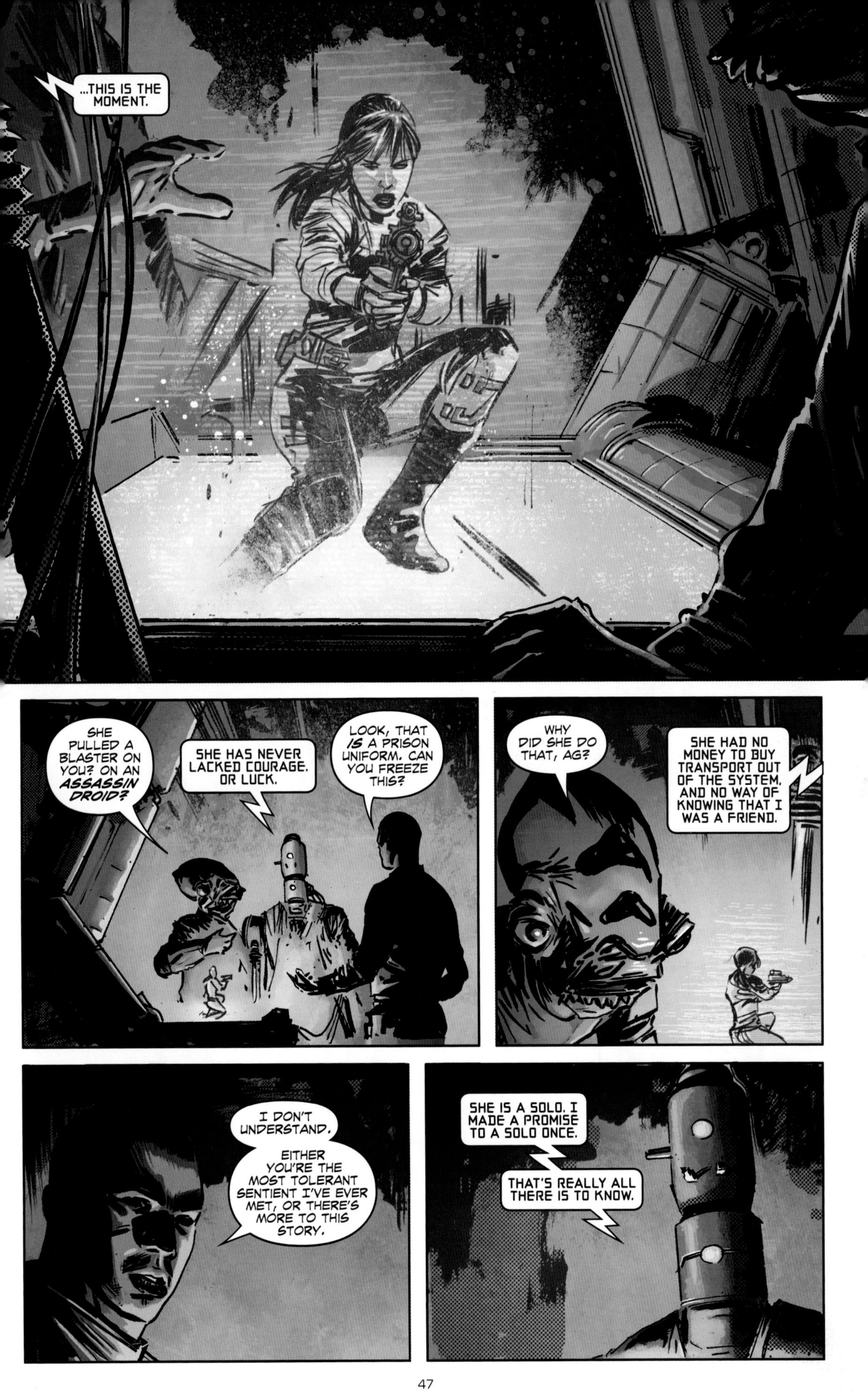
...THIS IS THE MOMENT.
SHE PULLED A BLASTER ON YOU? ON AN *ASSASSIN DROID?*
SHE HAS NEVER LACKED COURAGE. OR LUCK.
LOOK, THAT *IS* A PRISON UNIFORM. CAN YOU FREEZE THIS?
WHY DID SHE DO THAT, AG?
SHE HAD NO MONEY TO BUY TRANSPORT OUT OF THE SYSTEM, AND NO WAY OF KNOWING THAT I WAS A FRIEND.
I DON'T UNDERSTAND.
EITHER YOU'RE THE MOST TOLERANT SENTIENT I'VE EVER MET, OR THERE'S MORE TO THIS STORY.
SHE IS A SOLO. I MADE A PROMISE TO A SOLO ONCE.
THAT'S REALLY ALL THERE IS TO KNOW.

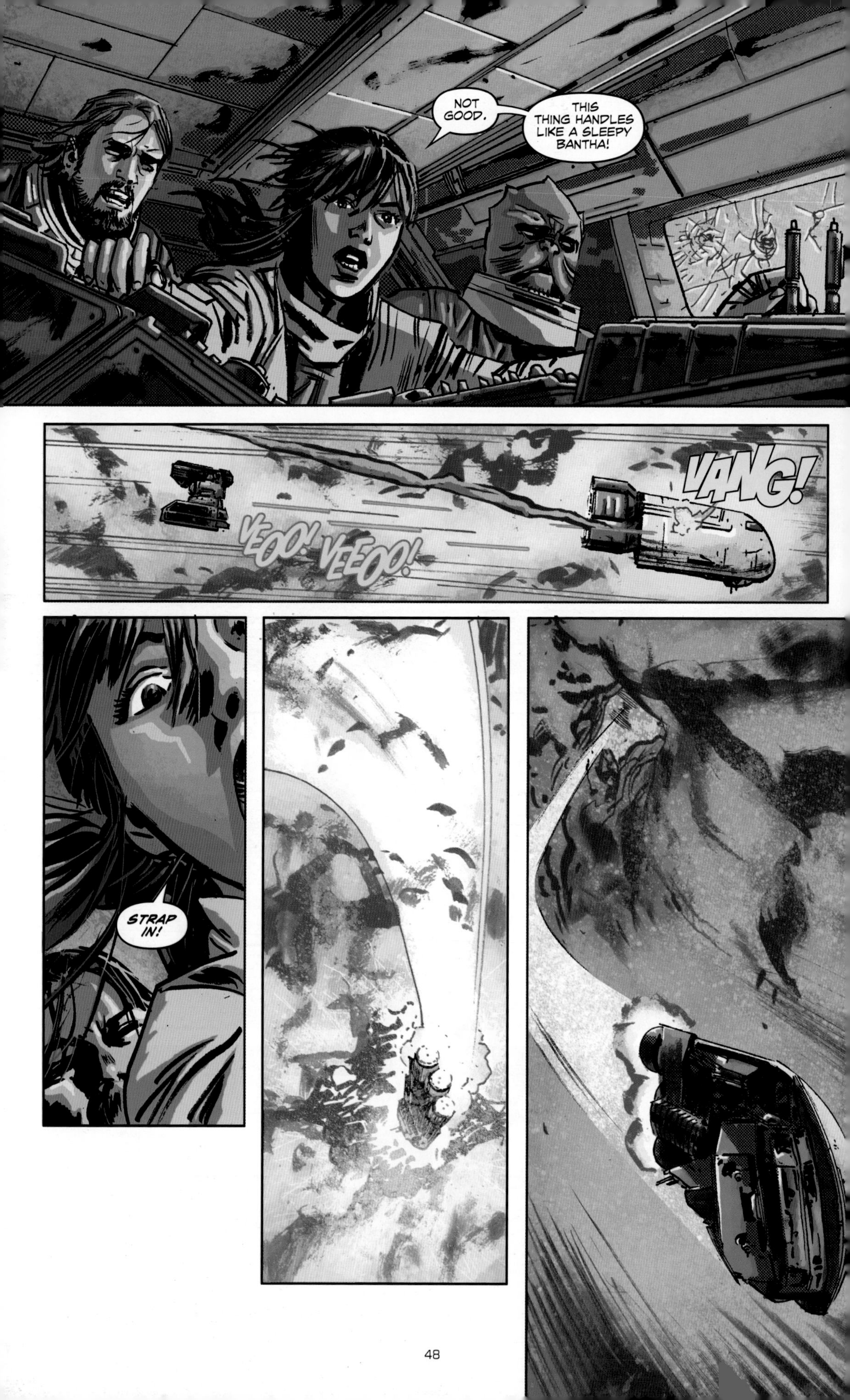
NOT GOOD.
THIS THING HANDLES LIKE A SLEEPY BANTHA!
VEEOO! VEEOO!
VANG!
STRAP IN!

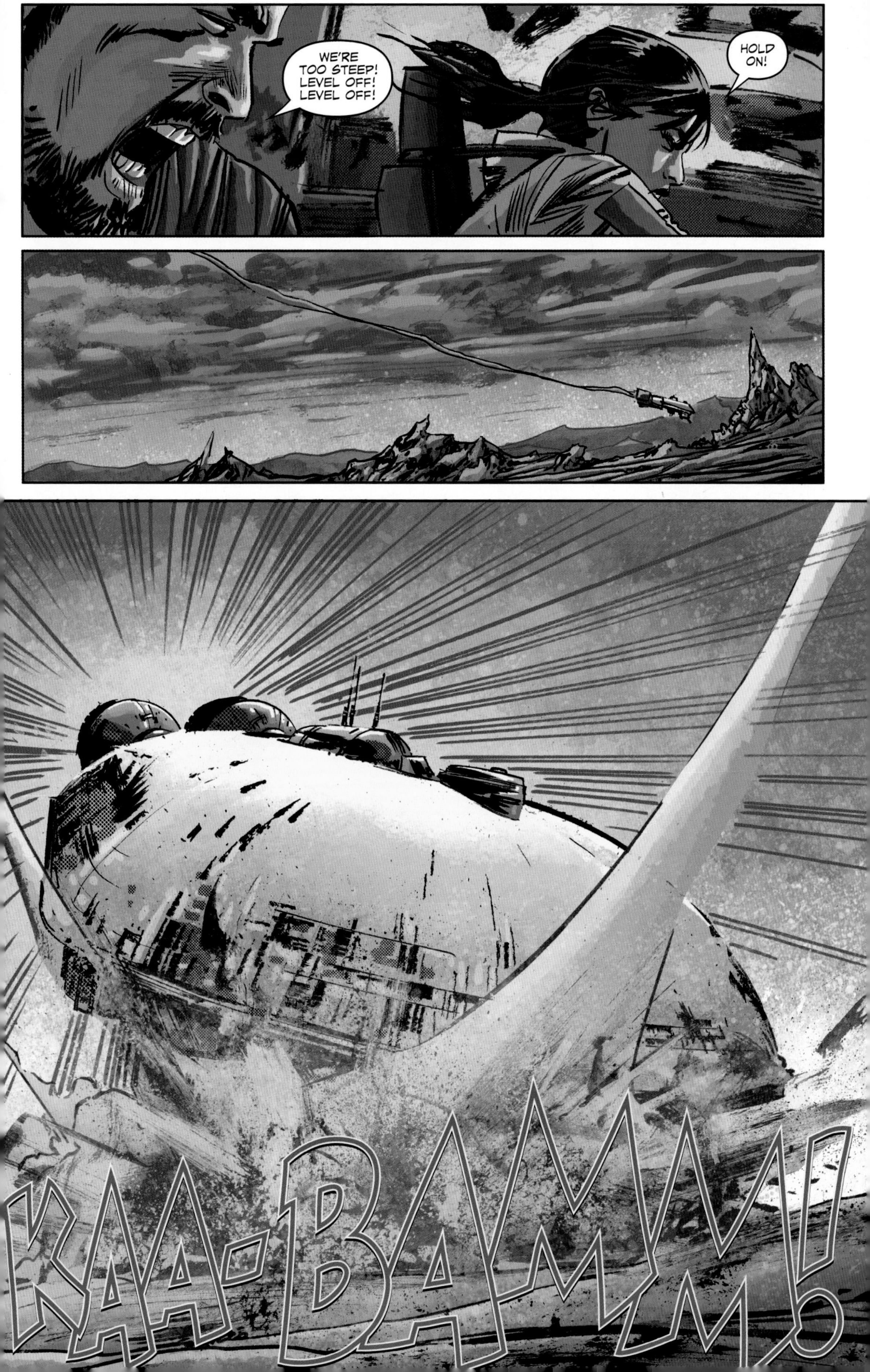
WE'RE TOO STEEP! LEVEL OFF! LEVEL OFF!
HOLD ON!
KA-BAMM!

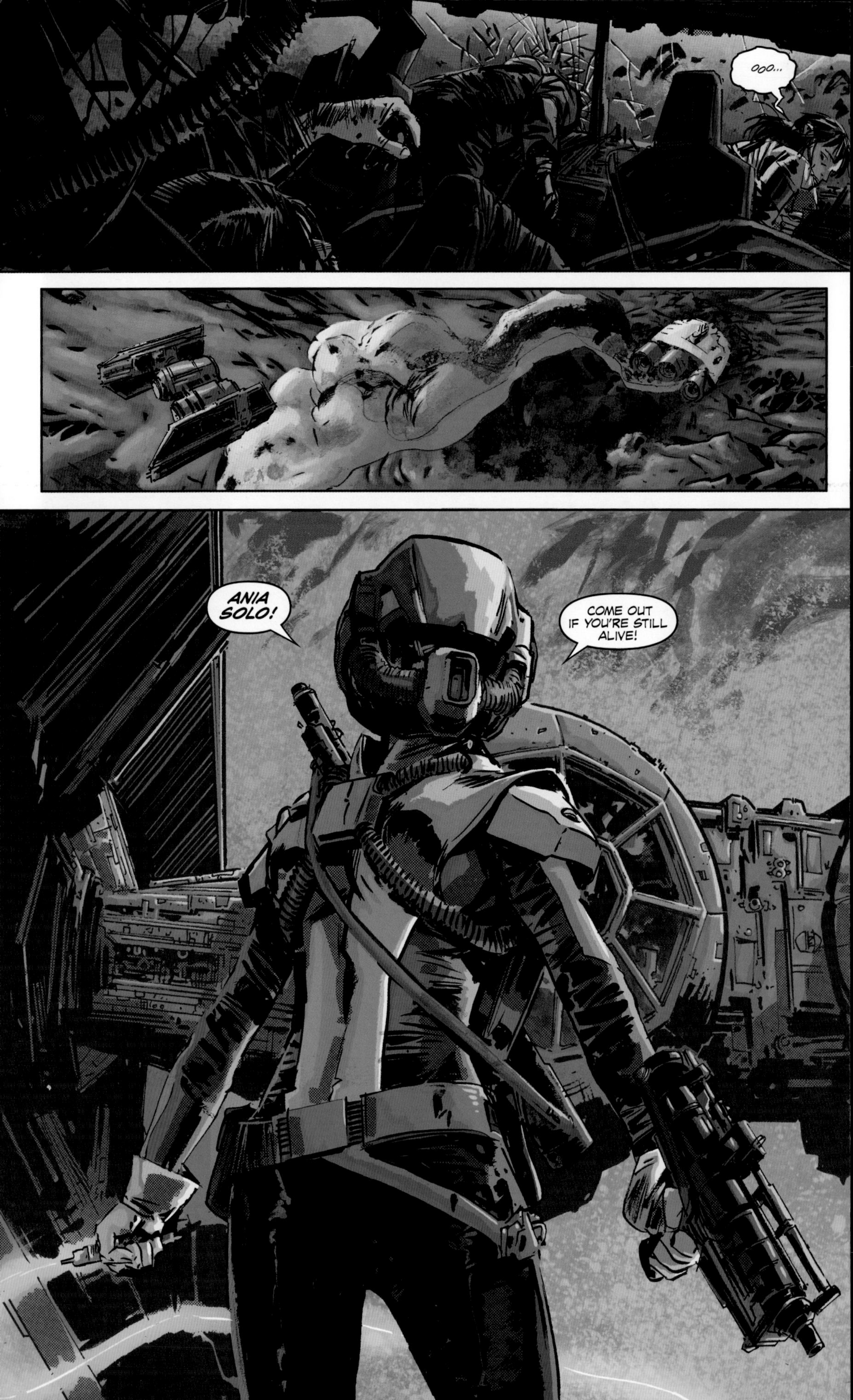
OOO...
ANIA SOLO!
COME OUT IF YOU'RE STILL ALIVE!

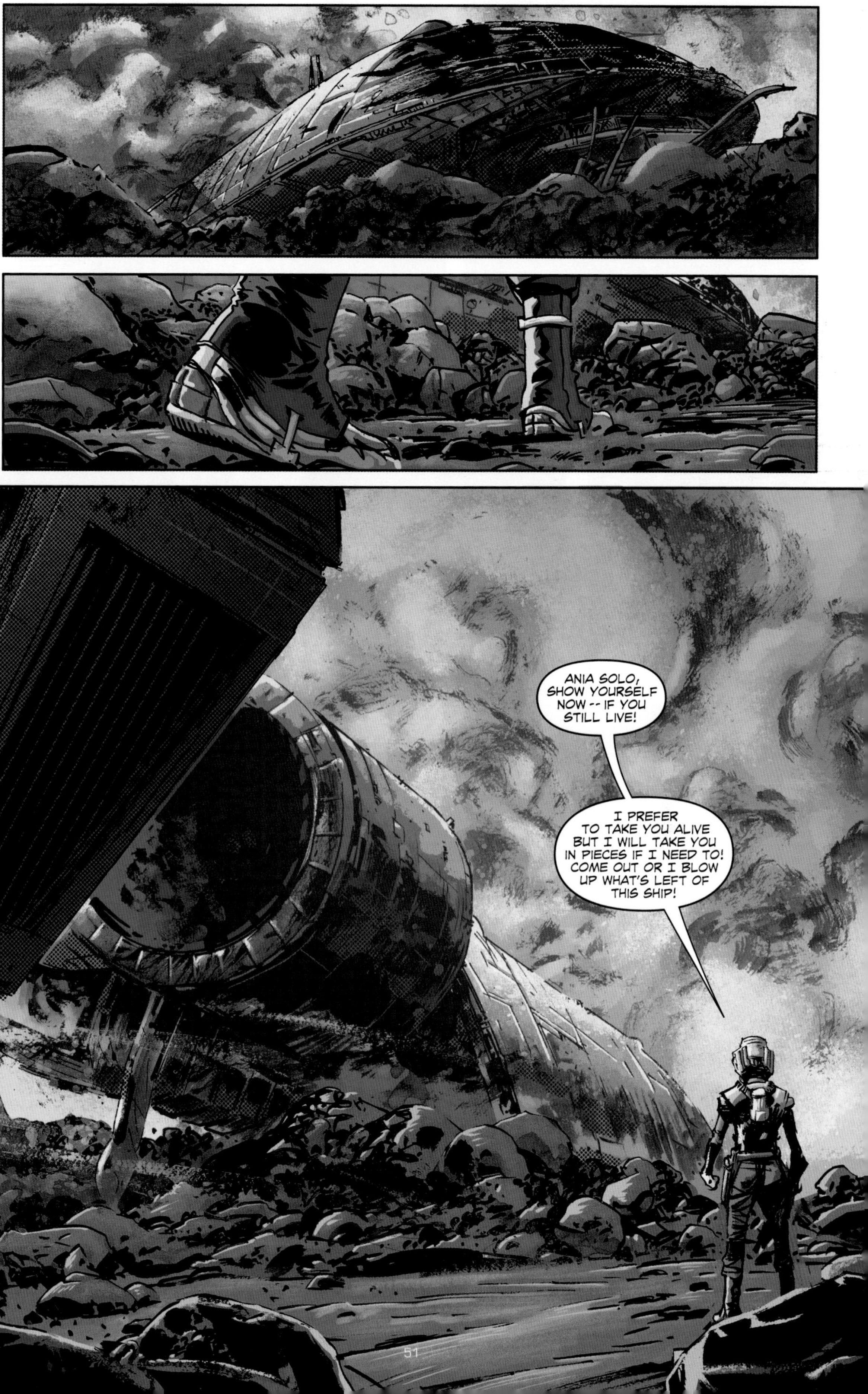
ANIA SOLO, SHOW YOURSELF NOW -- IF YOU STILL LIVE!
I PREFER TO TAKE YOU ALIVE BUT I WILL TAKE YOU IN PIECES IF I NEED TO! COME OUT OR I BLOW UP WHAT'S LEFT OF THIS SHIP!

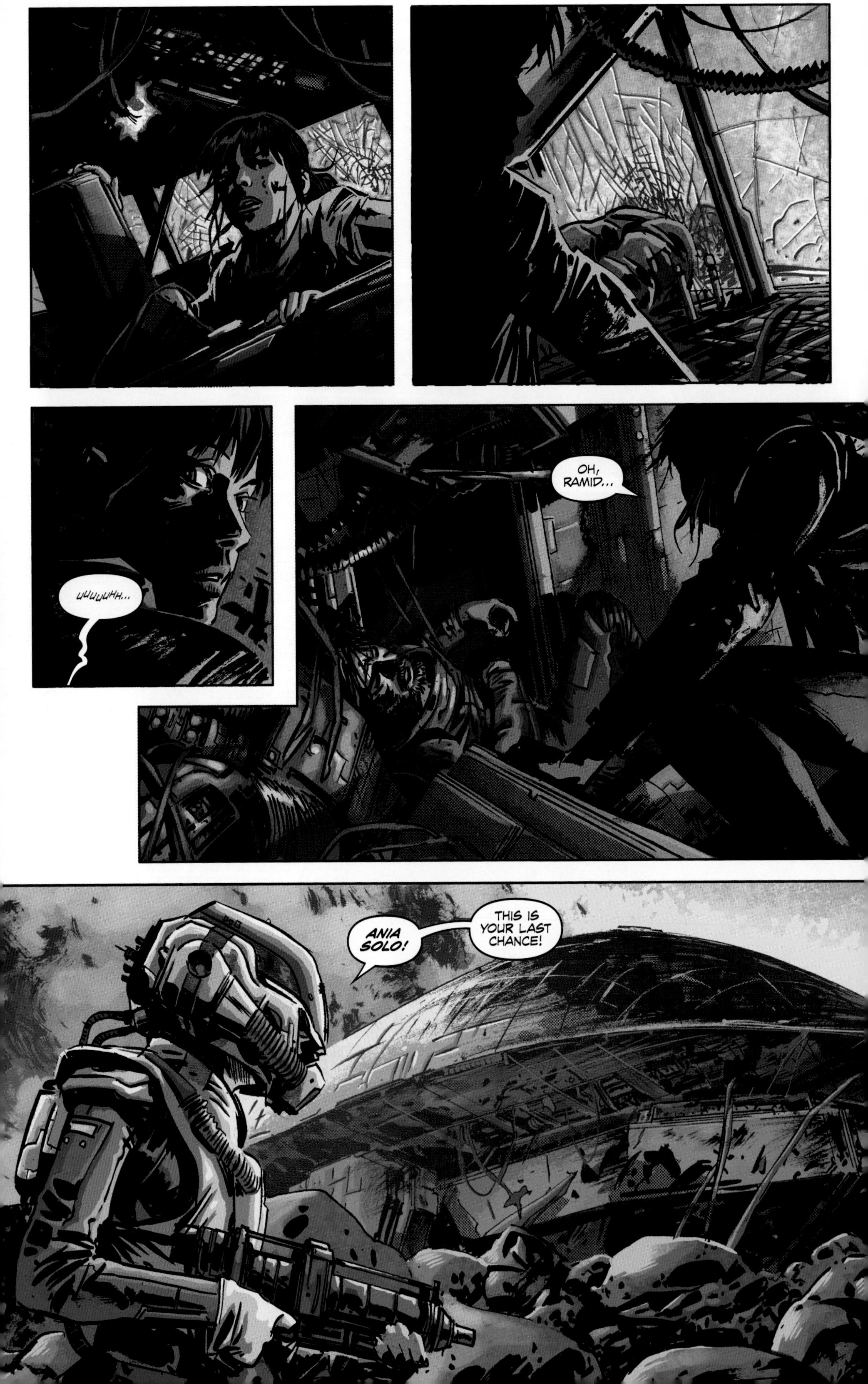
UUUUUHH...
OH, RAMID...
ANIA SOLO!
THIS IS YOUR LAST CHANCE!

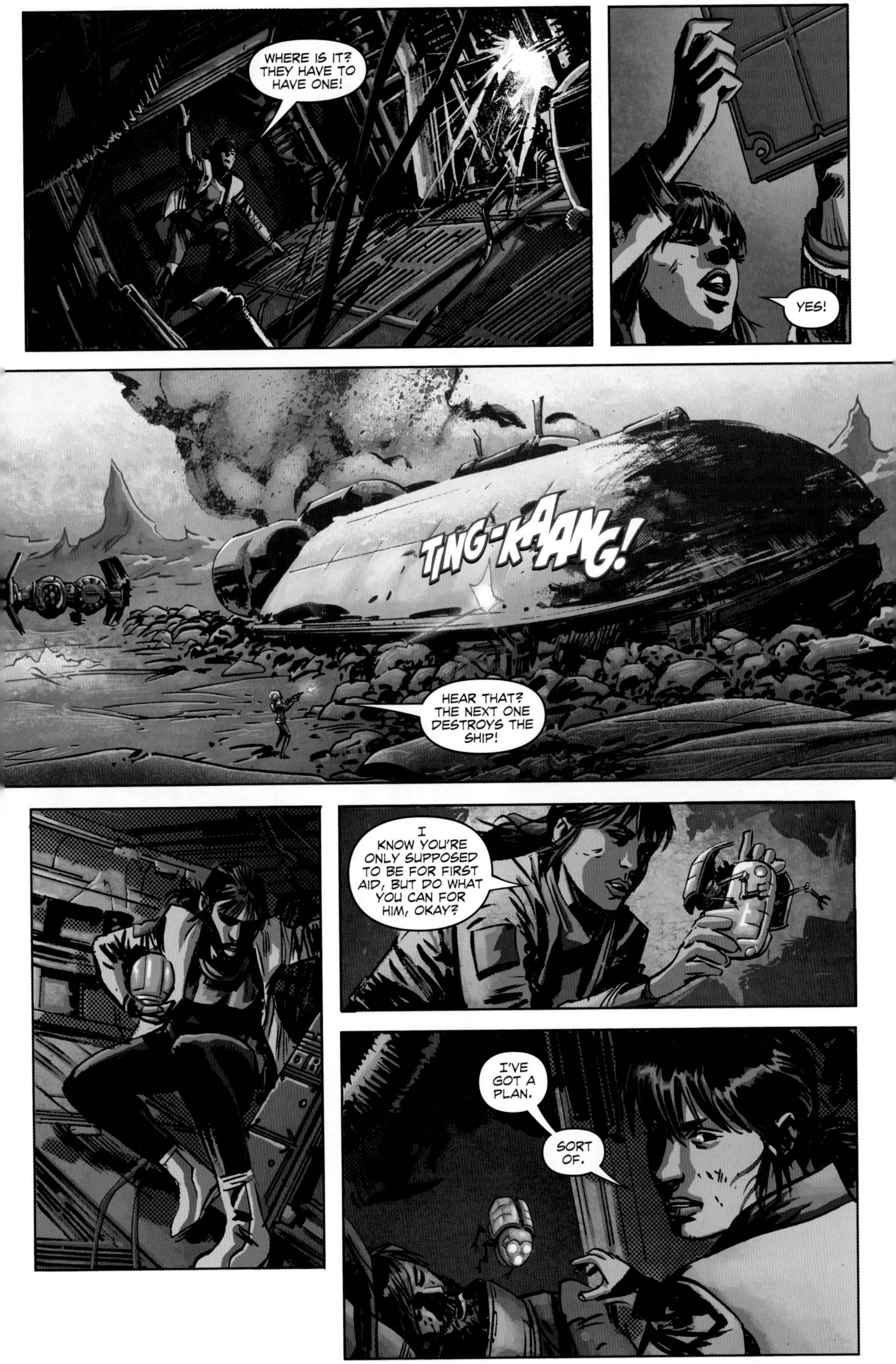
WHERE IS IT? THEY HAVE TO HAVE ONE!
YES!
TING-KAAANG!
HEAR THAT? THE NEXT ONE DESTROYS THE SHIP!
I KNOW YOU'RE ONLY SUPPOSED TO BE FOR FIRST AID, BUT DO WHAT YOU CAN FOR HIM, OKAY?
I'VE GOT A PLAN.
SORT OF.

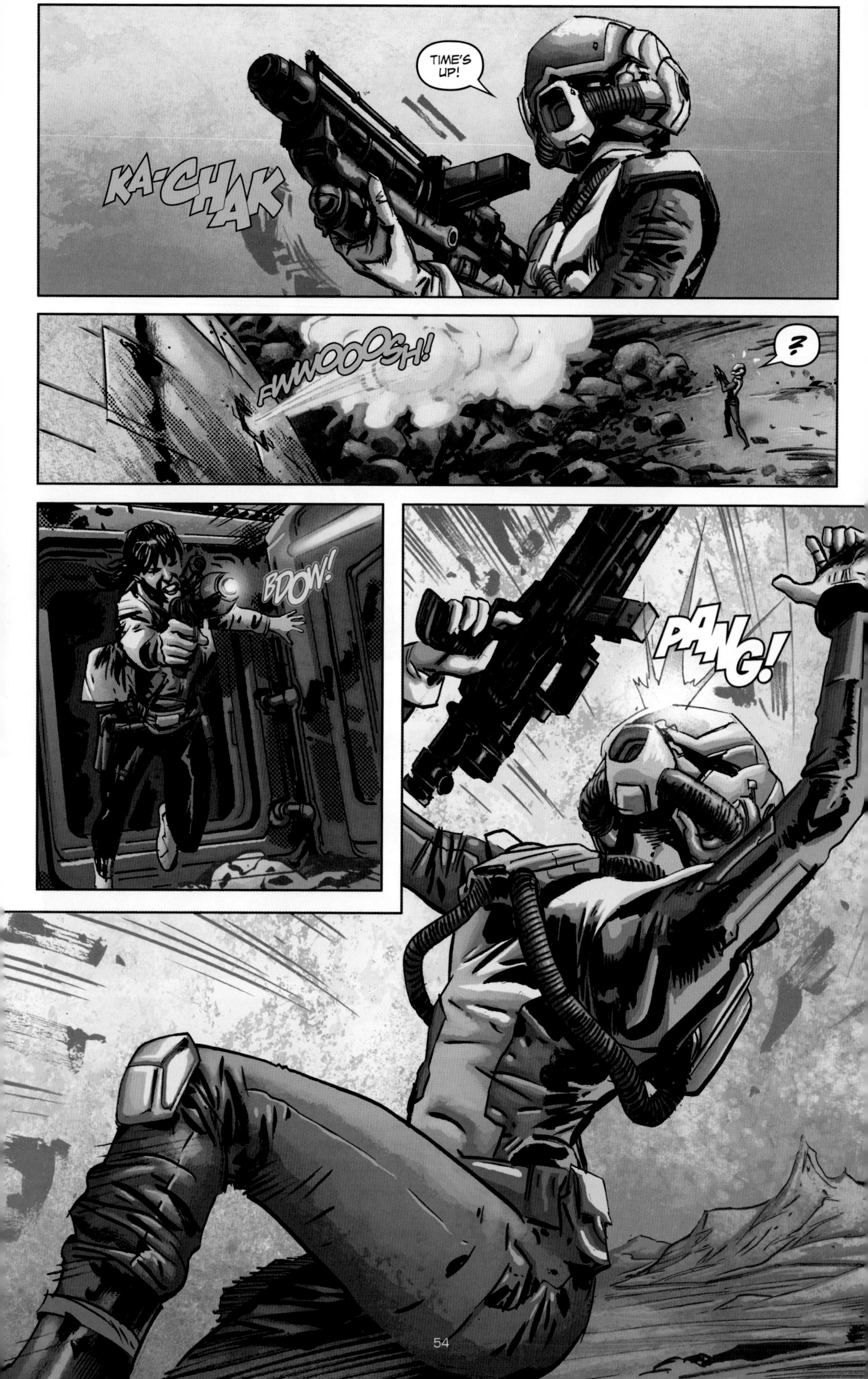
TIME'S UP!
KA-CHAK
FWWOOOSH!
?
BDOW!
PANG!

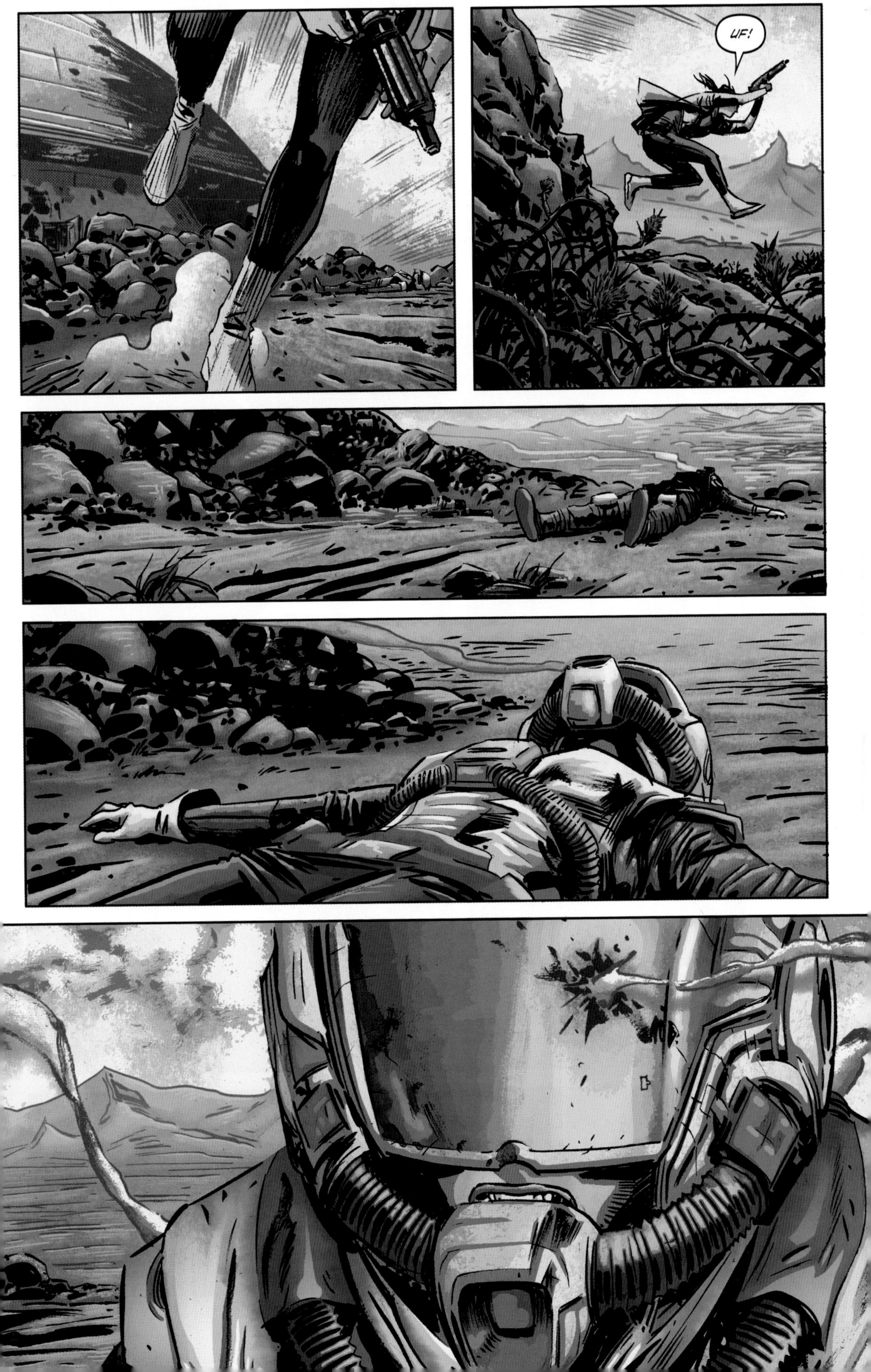
UF!

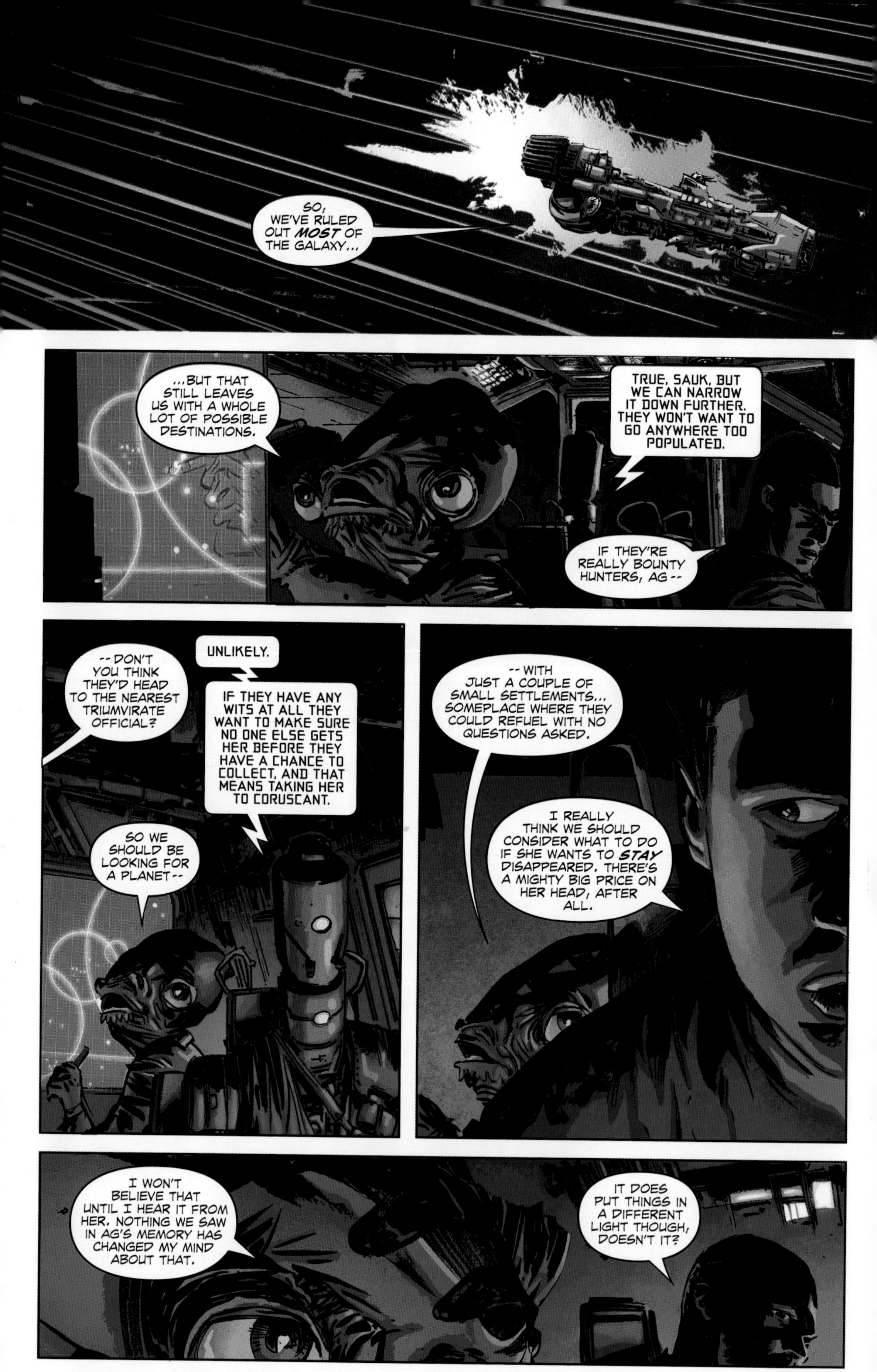

SO, WE'VE RULED OUT MOST OF THE GALAXY...
...BUT THAT STILL LEAVES US WITH A WHOLE LOT OF POSSIBLE DESTINATIONS.
TRUE, SAUK, BUT WE CAN NARROW IT DOWN FURTHER. THEY WON'T WANT TO GO ANYWHERE TOO POPULATED.
IF THEY'RE REALLY BOUNTY HUNTERS, AG --
-- DON'T YOU THINK THEY'D HEAD TO THE NEAREST TRIUMVIRATE OFFICIAL?
UNLIKELY.
IF THEY HAVE ANY WITS AT ALL THEY WANT TO MAKE SURE NO ONE ELSE GETS HER BEFORE THEY HAVE A CHANCE TO COLLECT, AND THAT MEANS TAKING HER TO CORUSCANT.
SO WE SHOULD BE LOOKING FOR A PLANET --
-- WITH JUST A COUPLE OF SMALL SETTLEMENTS... SOMEPLACE WHERE THEY COULD REFUEL WITH NO QUESTIONS ASKED.
I REALLY THINK WE SHOULD CONSIDER WHAT TO DO IF SHE WANTS TO STAY DISAPPEARED. THERE'S A MIGHTY BIG PRICE ON HER HEAD, AFTER ALL.
I WON'T BELIEVE THAT UNTIL I HEAR IT FROM HER. NOTHING WE SAW IN AG'S MEMORY HAS CHANGED MY MIND ABOUT THAT.
IT DOES PUT THINGS IN A DIFFERENT LIGHT THOUGH, DOESN'T IT?

I DON'T THINK SO, NO.

WHY ARE YOU SO UNWOUND BY THIS, JAO? YOU LEFT THE IMPERIAL KNIGHTS BEHIND.

THE FORCE IS LEADING ME IN UNEXPECTED DIRECTIONS, BUT THAT DOESN'T MEAN I'VE FORGOTTEN MY VOWS.

THE MAN THAT ANIA SUPPOSEDLY KILLED IS JUST *"A KNIGHT"* TO YOU. BUT TO ME, *TEEMEN ALTON* WAS SOMEONE I LOOKED UP TO AND RESPECTED.

THAT'S HARD TO IGNORE.

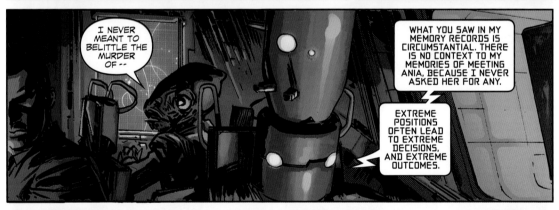

I NEVER MEANT TO BELITTLE THE MURDER OF --

WHAT YOU SAW IN MY MEMORY RECORDS IS CIRCUMSTANTIAL. THERE IS NO CONTEXT TO MY MEMORIES OF MEETING ANIA, BECAUSE I NEVER ASKED HER FOR ANY.

EXTREME POSITIONS OFTEN LEAD TO EXTREME DECISIONS, AND EXTREME OUTCOMES.

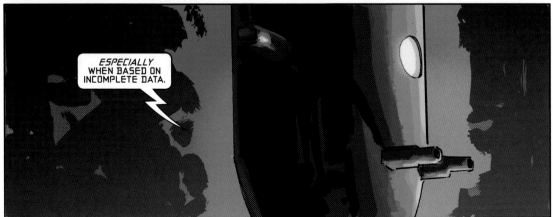

*ESPECIALLY* WHEN BASED ON INCOMPLETE DATA.

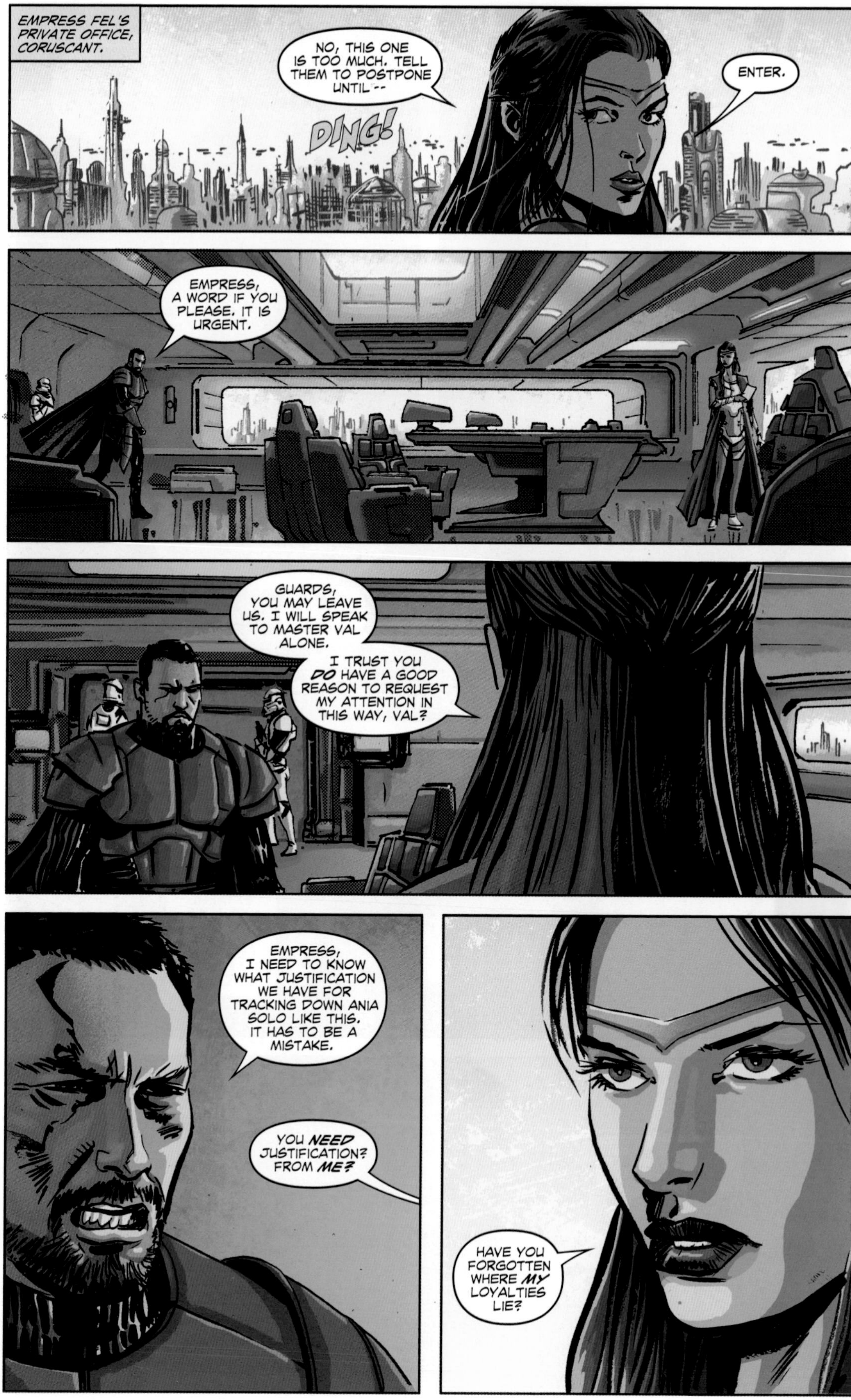
EMPRESS FEL'S PRIVATE OFFICE, CORUSCANT.
NO, THIS ONE IS TOO MUCH. TELL THEM TO POSTPONE UNTIL--
DING!
ENTER.
EMPRESS, A WORD IF YOU PLEASE. IT IS URGENT.
GUARDS, YOU MAY LEAVE US. I WILL SPEAK TO MASTER VAL ALONE.
I TRUST YOU *DO* HAVE A GOOD REASON TO REQUEST MY ATTENTION IN THIS WAY, VAL?
EMPRESS, I NEED TO KNOW WHAT JUSTIFICATION WE HAVE FOR TRACKING DOWN ANIA SOLO LIKE THIS. IT HAS TO BE A MISTAKE.
YOU *NEED* JUSTIFICATION? FROM *ME?*
HAVE YOU FORGOTTEN WHERE *MY* LOYALTIES LIE?

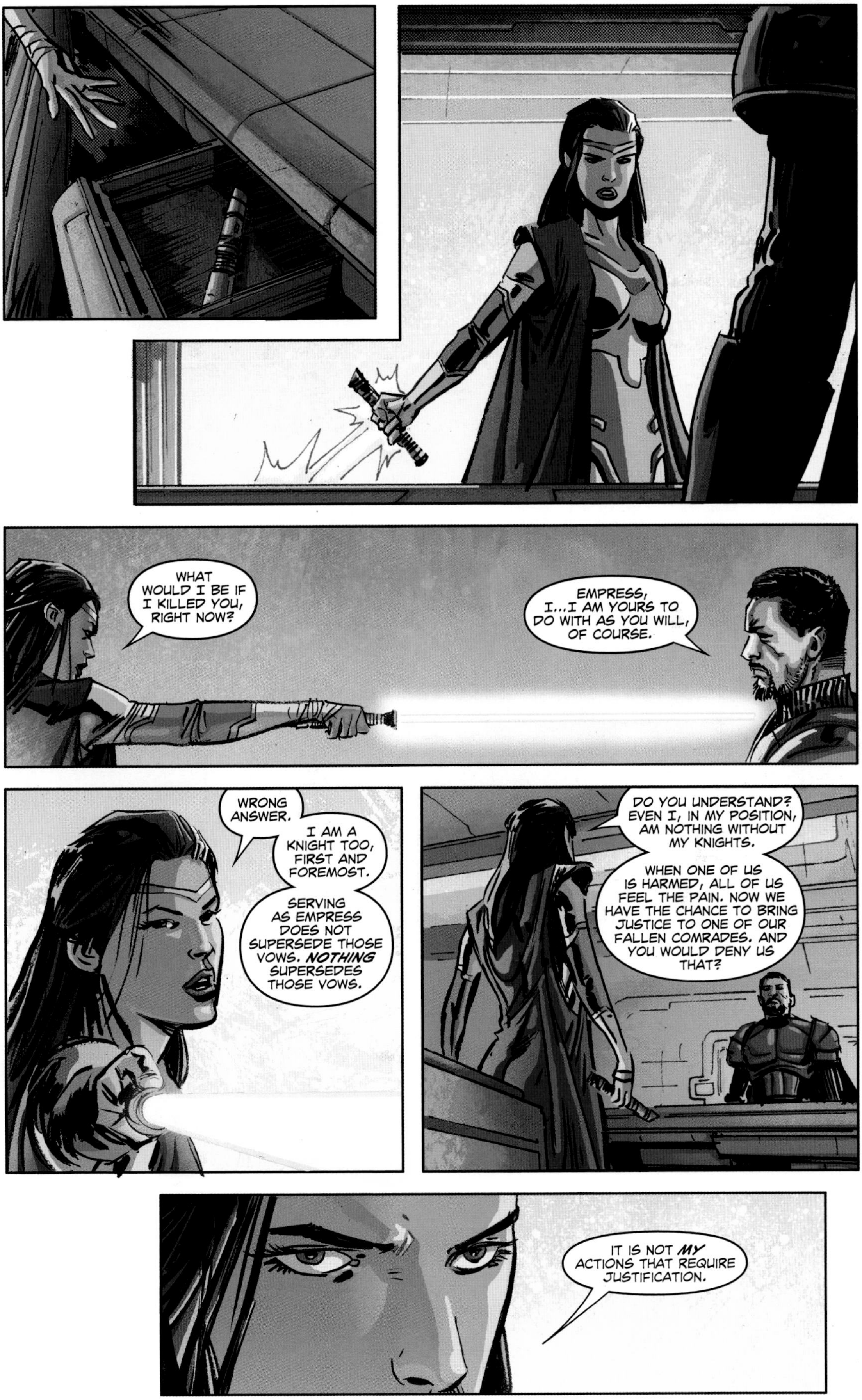
WHAT WOULD I BE IF I KILLED YOU, RIGHT NOW?
EMPRESS, I...I AM YOURS TO DO WITH AS YOU WILL, OF COURSE.
WRONG ANSWER.
I AM A KNIGHT TOO, FIRST AND FOREMOST.
SERVING AS EMPRESS DOES NOT SUPERSEDE THOSE VOWS. NOTHING SUPERSEDES THOSE VOWS.
DO YOU UNDERSTAND? EVEN I, IN MY POSITION, AM NOTHING WITHOUT MY KNIGHTS.
WHEN ONE OF US IS HARMED, ALL OF US FEEL THE PAIN. NOW WE HAVE THE CHANCE TO BRING JUSTICE TO ONE OF OUR FALLEN COMRADES. AND YOU WOULD DENY US THAT?
IT IS NOT MY ACTIONS THAT REQUIRE JUSTIFICATION.

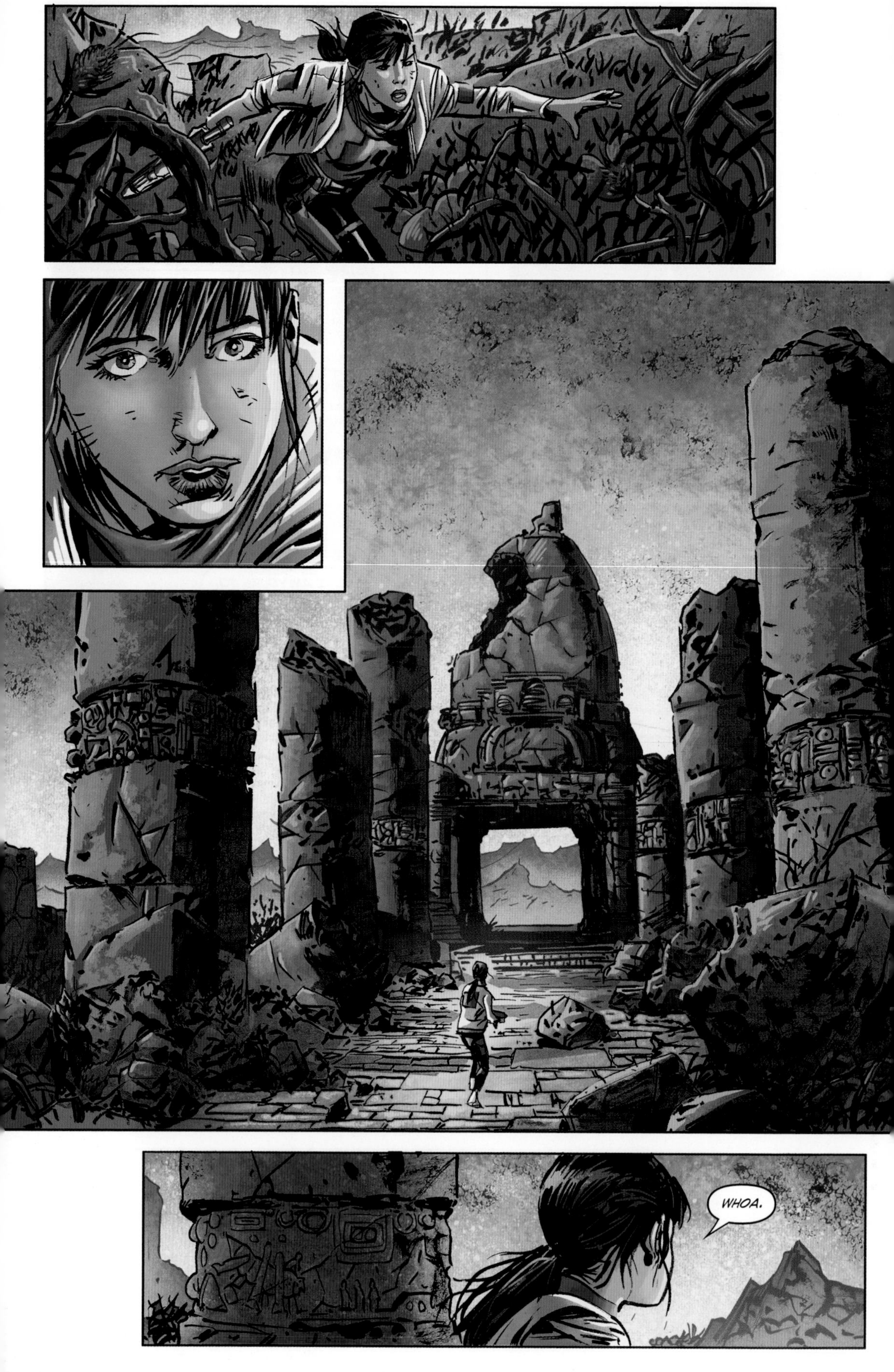
WHOA.

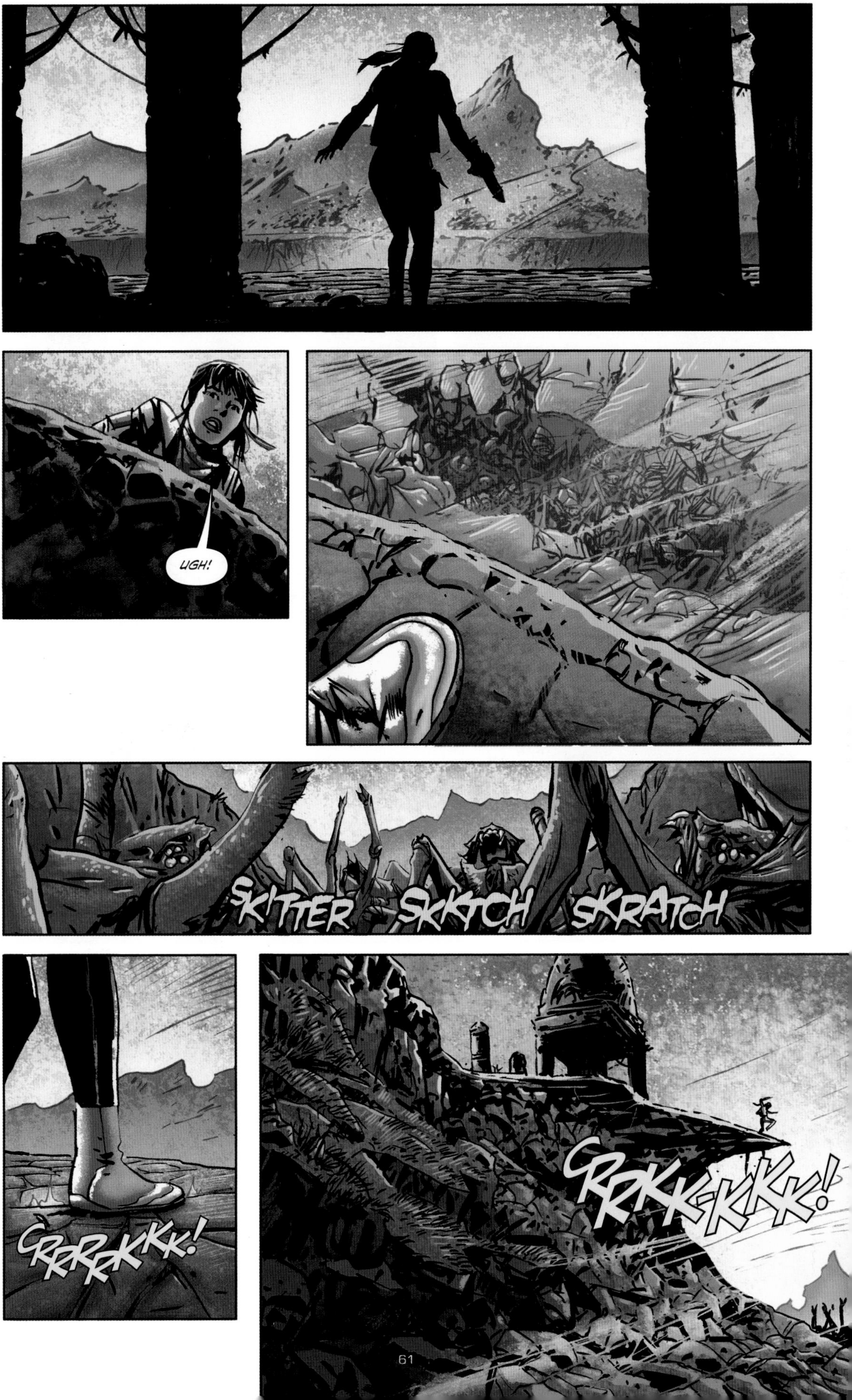
UGH!
SKITTER SKKTCH SKRATCH
CRRRRKKKK!
CRKKK-KKKK!

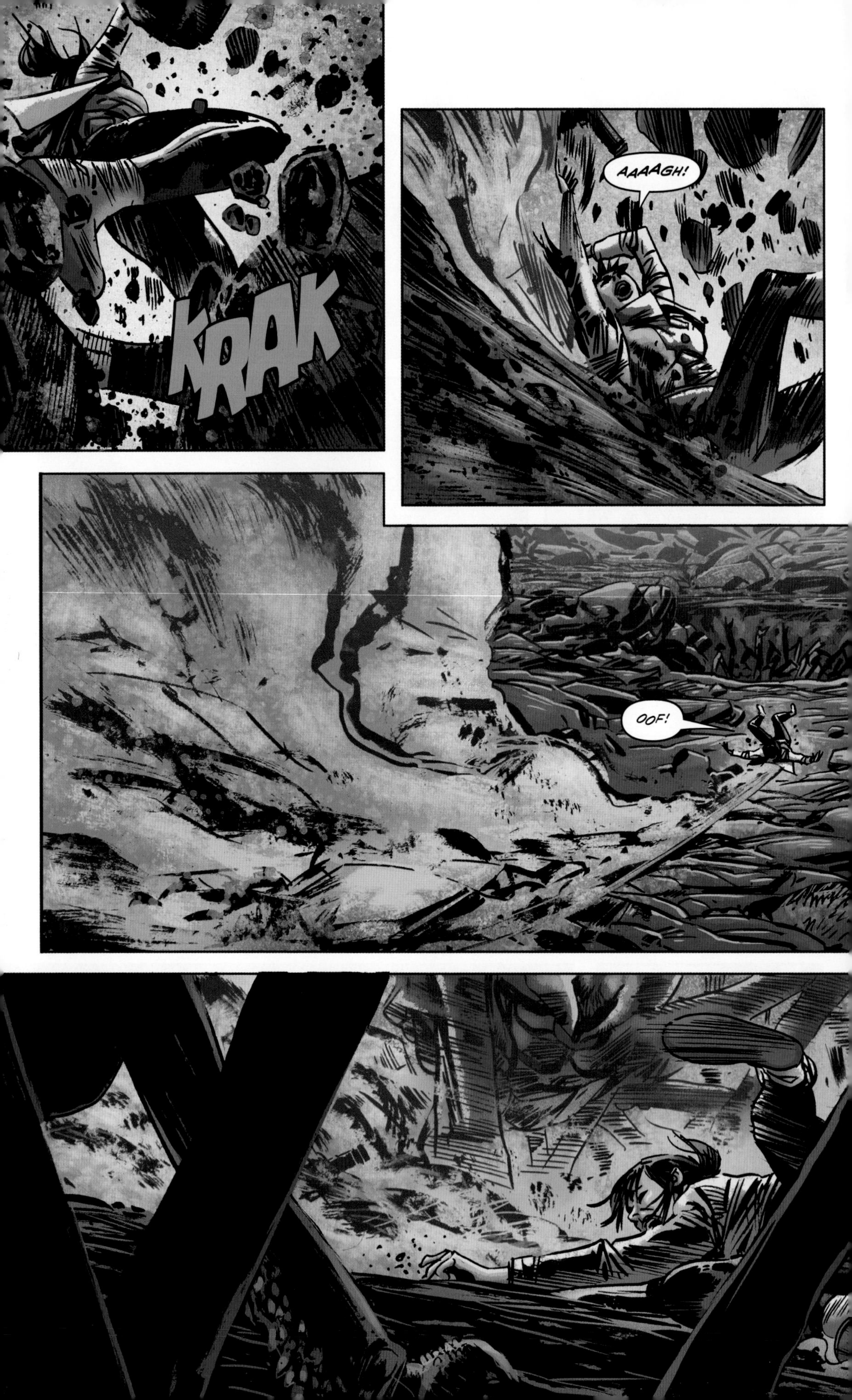
KRAK
AAAAGH!
OOF!

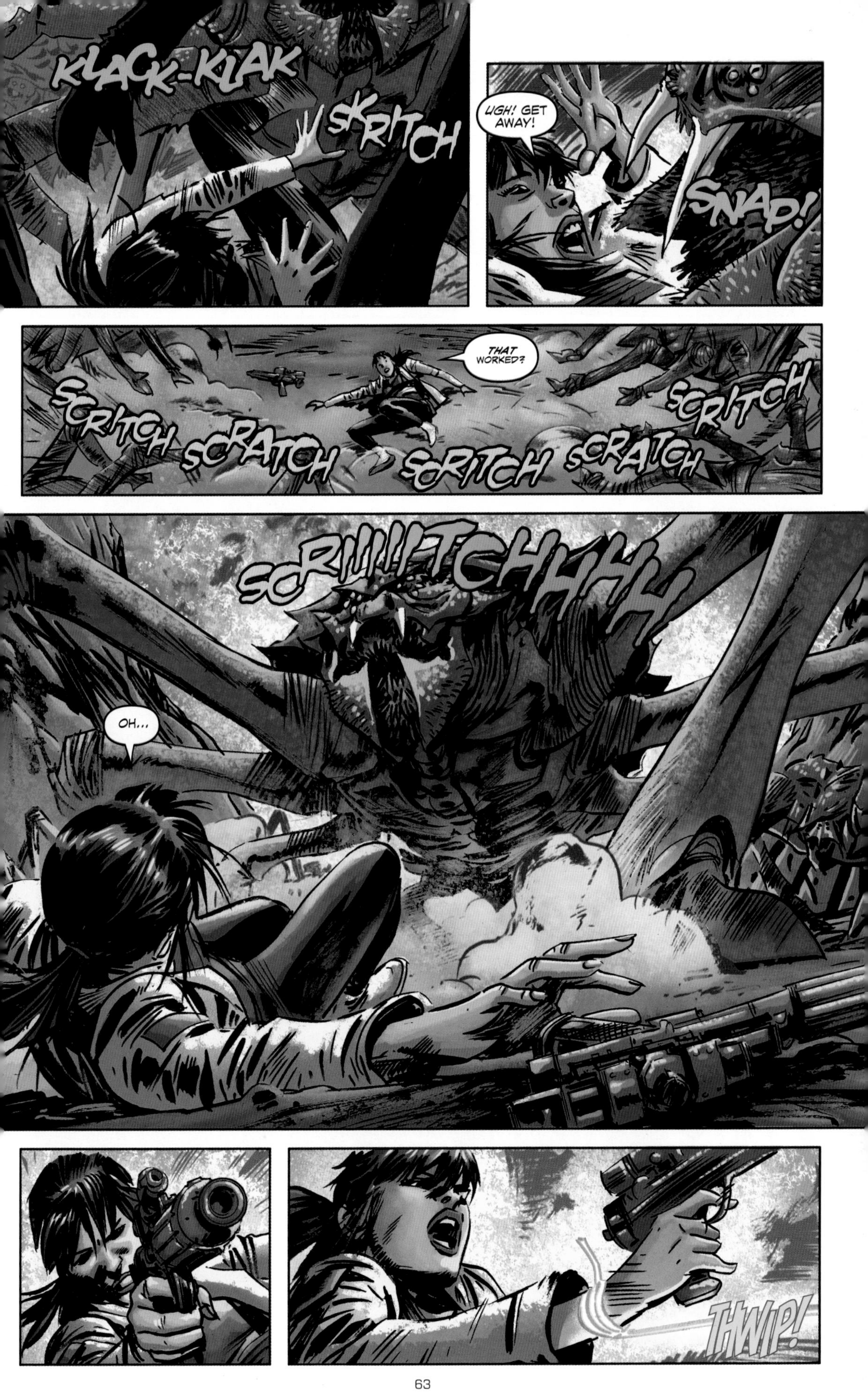
KLACK-KLAK
SKRITCH
UGH! GET AWAY!
SNAP!
THAT WORKED?
SCRITCH SCRATCH SCRITCH SCRATCH SCRITCH
SCRIIIIITCHHHH
OH...
THWIP!

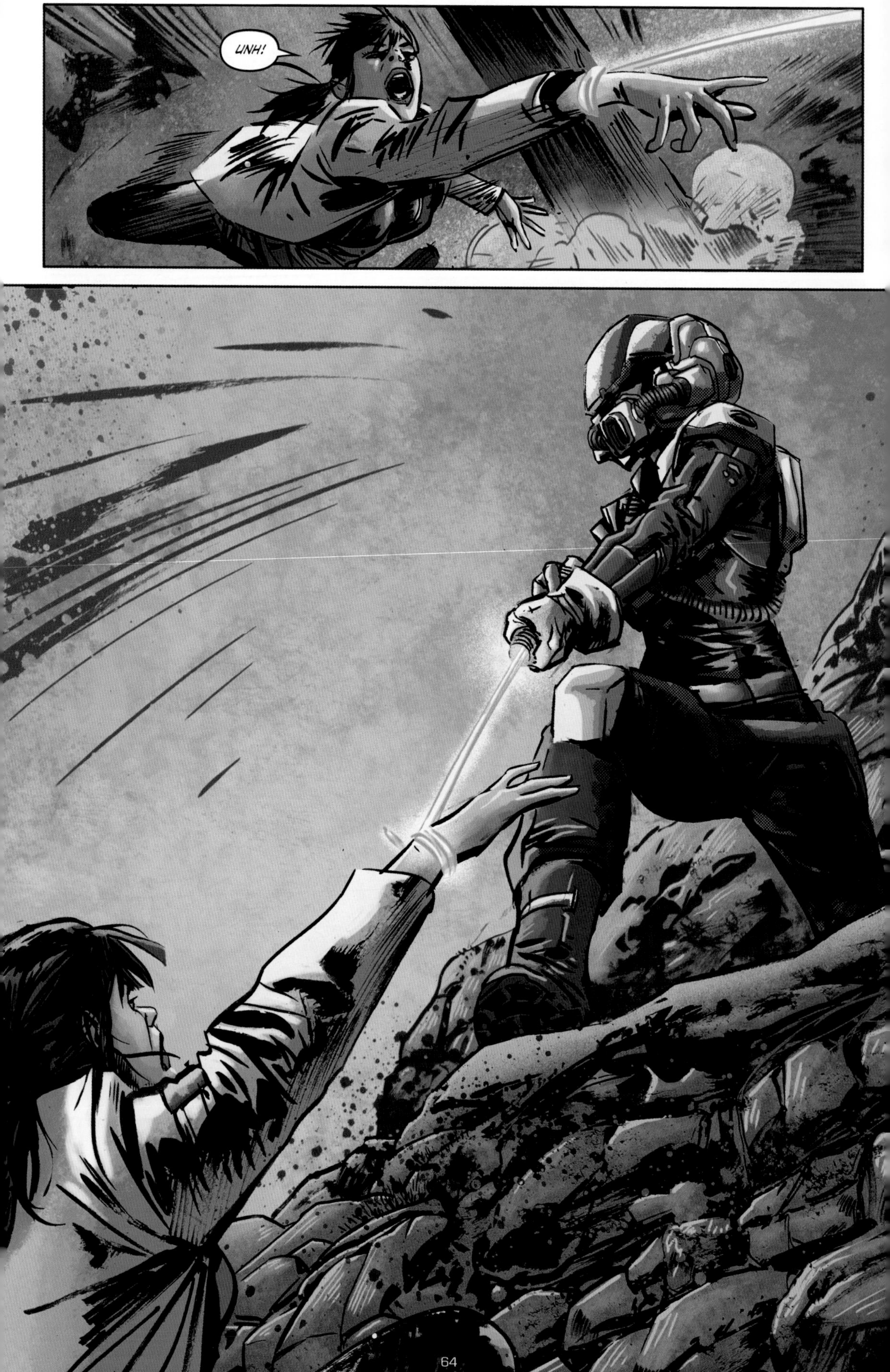
UNH!

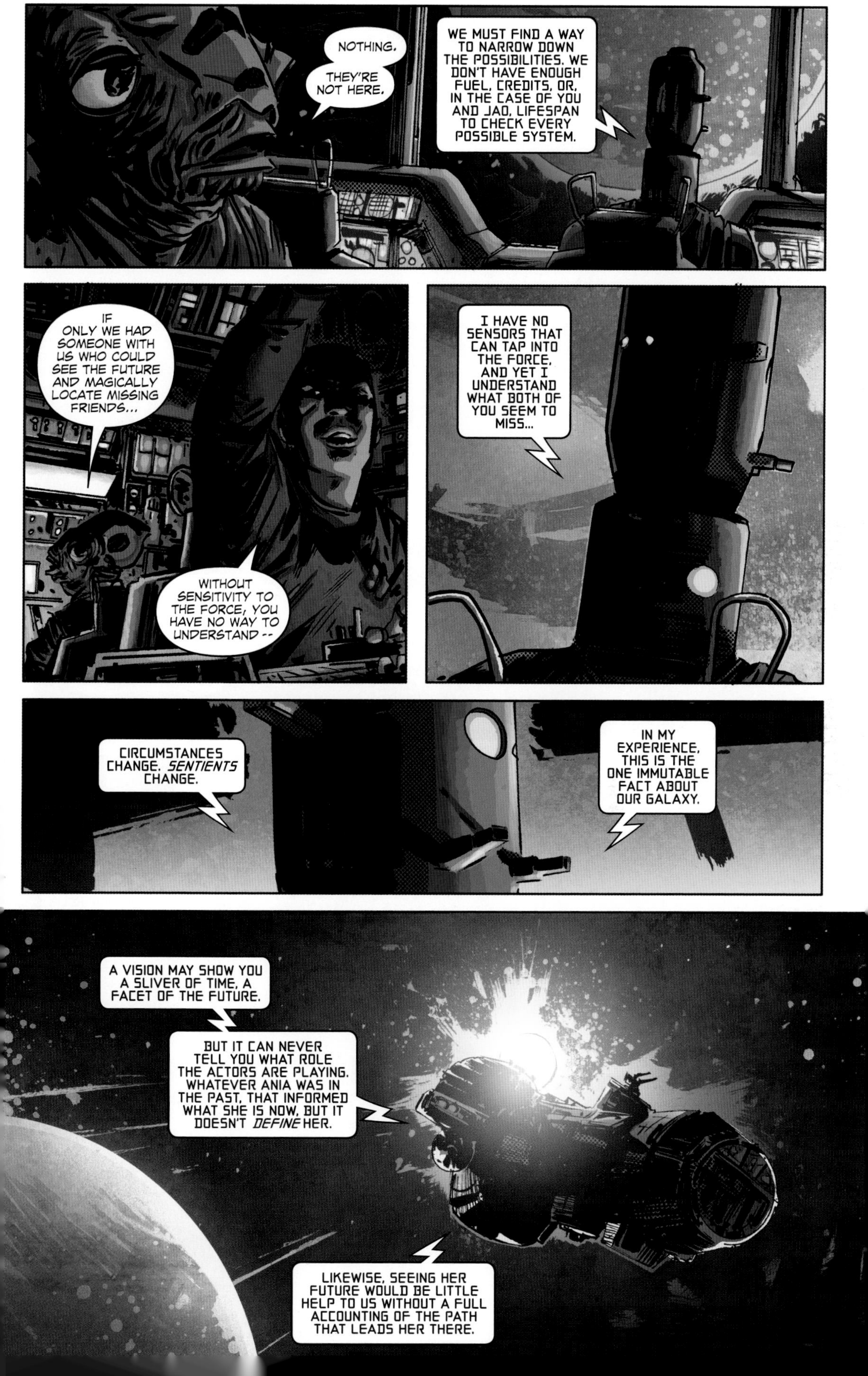
NOTHING.
THEY'RE NOT HERE.
WE MUST FIND A WAY TO NARROW DOWN THE POSSIBILITIES. WE DON'T HAVE ENOUGH FUEL, CREDITS, OR, IN THE CASE OF YOU AND JAO, LIFESPAN TO CHECK EVERY POSSIBLE SYSTEM.
IF ONLY WE HAD SOMEONE WITH US WHO COULD SEE THE FUTURE AND MAGICALLY LOCATE MISSING FRIENDS...
WITHOUT SENSITIVITY TO THE FORCE, YOU HAVE NO WAY TO UNDERSTAND --
I HAVE NO SENSORS THAT CAN TAP INTO THE FORCE, AND YET I UNDERSTAND WHAT BOTH OF YOU SEEM TO MISS...
CIRCUMSTANCES CHANGE. *SENTIENTS* CHANGE.
IN MY EXPERIENCE, THIS IS THE ONE IMMUTABLE FACT ABOUT OUR GALAXY.
A VISION MAY SHOW YOU A SLIVER OF TIME, A FACET OF THE FUTURE.
BUT IT CAN NEVER TELL YOU WHAT ROLE THE ACTORS ARE PLAYING. WHATEVER ANIA WAS IN THE PAST, THAT INFORMED WHAT SHE IS NOW, BUT IT DOESN'T *DEFINE* HER.
LIKEWISE, SEEING HER FUTURE WOULD BE LITTLE HELP TO US WITHOUT A FULL ACCOUNTING OF THE PATH THAT LEADS HER THERE.

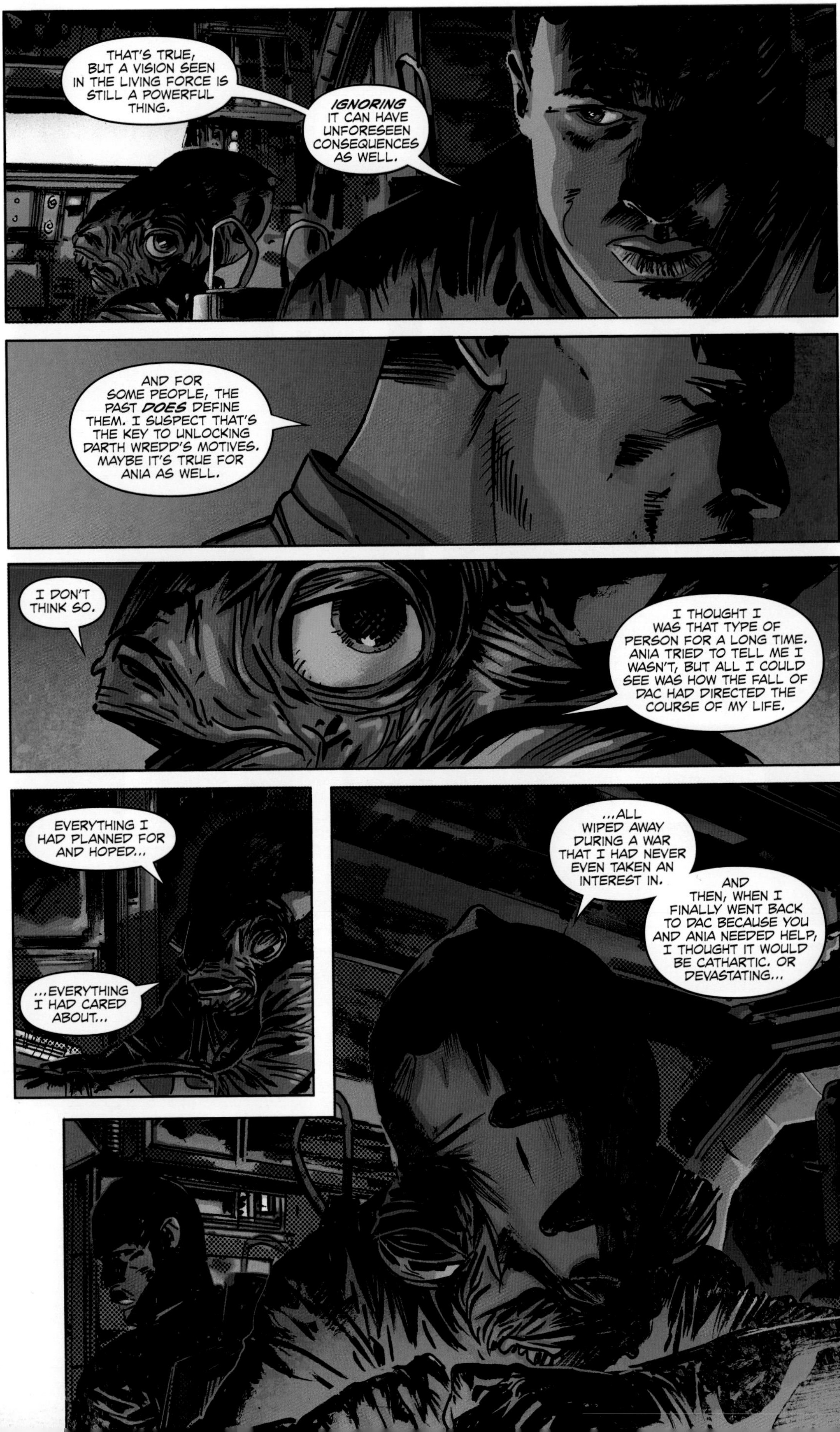
THAT'S TRUE, BUT A VISION SEEN IN THE LIVING FORCE IS STILL A POWERFUL THING.
*IGNORING* IT CAN HAVE UNFORESEEN CONSEQUENCES AS WELL.
AND FOR SOME PEOPLE, THE PAST ***DOES*** DEFINE THEM. I SUSPECT THAT'S THE KEY TO UNLOCKING DARTH WREDD'S MOTIVES. MAYBE IT'S TRUE FOR ANIA AS WELL.
I DON'T THINK SO.
I THOUGHT I WAS THAT TYPE OF PERSON FOR A LONG TIME. ANIA TRIED TO TELL ME I WASN'T, BUT ALL I COULD SEE WAS HOW THE FALL OF DAC HAD DIRECTED THE COURSE OF MY LIFE.
EVERYTHING I HAD PLANNED FOR AND HOPED...
...EVERYTHING I HAD CARED ABOUT...
...ALL WIPED AWAY DURING A WAR THAT I HAD NEVER EVEN TAKEN AN INTEREST IN.
AND THEN, WHEN I FINALLY WENT BACK TO DAC BECAUSE YOU AND ANIA NEEDED HELP, I THOUGHT IT WOULD BE CATHARTIC. OR DEVASTATING...

YOU CERTAINLY HELD YOUR OWN DURING THE RESCUE, ACCORDING TO ANIA. YOU SHOULD BE PROUD OF YOUR ROLE IN THE LIBERATION OF THE RING.

OH, YOU KNOW HOW ANIA EXAGGERATES THINGS LIKE THAT...

POINT IS, I *DIDN'T* HAVE A BIG REVELATION.

I'VE SEEN ENOUGH OF THE GALAXY NOW TO KNOW THAT ALL SORTS OF SENTIENTS SUFFERED DURING THE WAR. SURE, DAC GOT JUST ABOUT THE WORST OF IT...

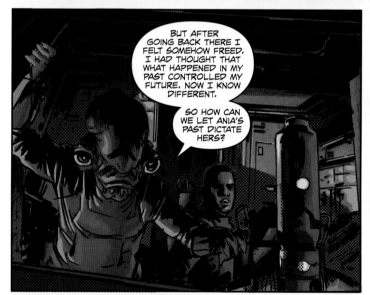

BUT AFTER GOING BACK THERE I FELT SOMEHOW FREED. I HAD THOUGHT THAT WHAT HAPPENED IN MY PAST CONTROLLED MY FUTURE. NOW I KNOW DIFFERENT.

SO HOW CAN WE LET ANIA'S PAST DICTATE HERS?

NOW, LET'S CHECK OUT THIS SYSTEM AND SEE WHAT WE CAN FIND OUT. IT'S A BIG GALAXY, BUT ANIA'S HERE *SOMEWHERE*.

IMPECCABLE LOGIC, MY FRIEND.

I DON'T KNOW WHAT HAPPENED BACK IN THAT PRISON CAMP, BUT I KNOW WE OWE IT TO ANIA TO LET HER TELL US HERSELF.

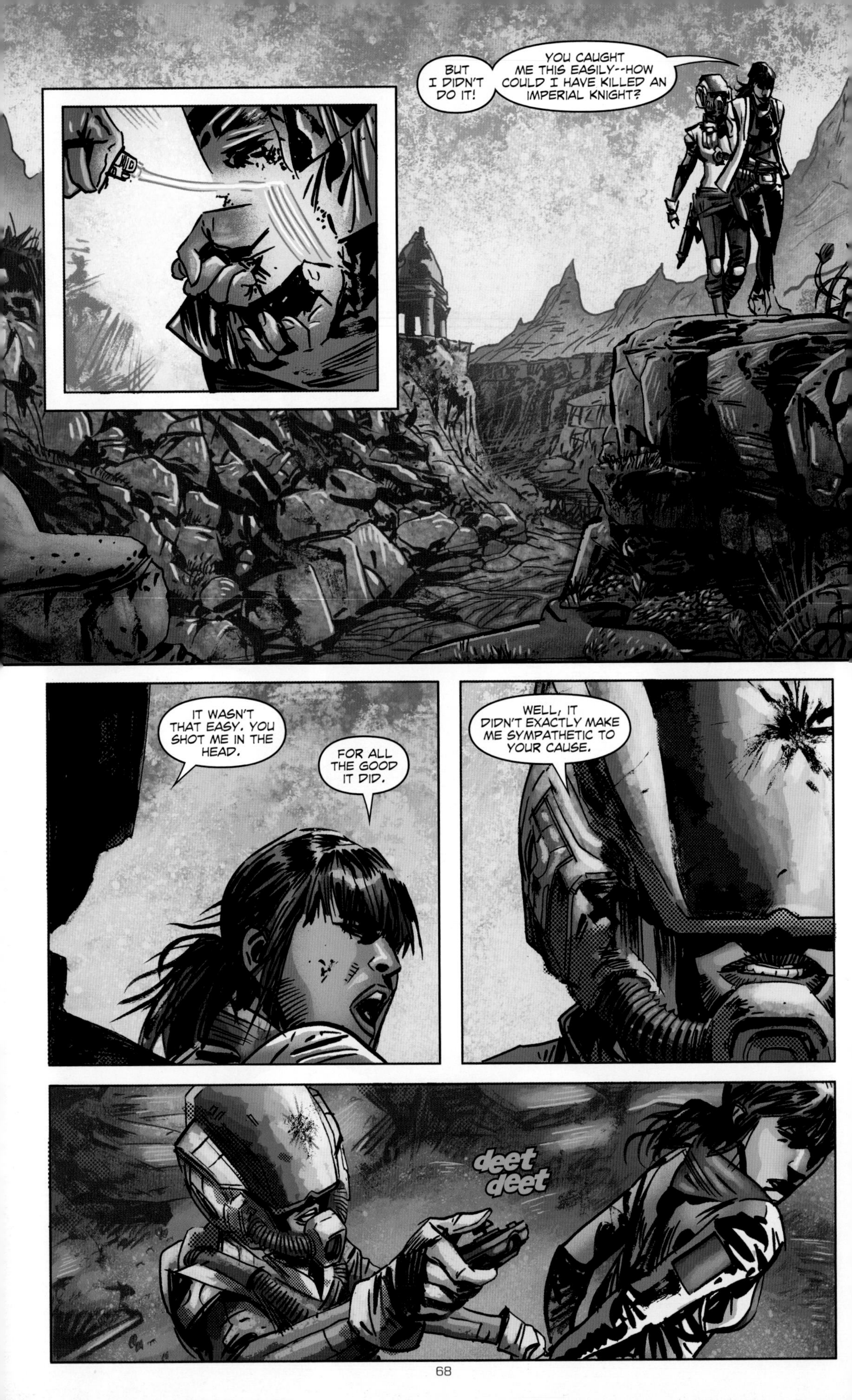
BUT I DIDN'T DO IT!
YOU CAUGHT ME THIS EASILY--HOW COULD I HAVE KILLED AN IMPERIAL KNIGHT?
IT WASN'T THAT EASY. YOU SHOT ME IN THE HEAD.
FOR ALL THE GOOD IT DID.
WELL, IT DIDN'T EXACTLY MAKE ME SYMPATHETIC TO YOUR CAUSE.
deet deet

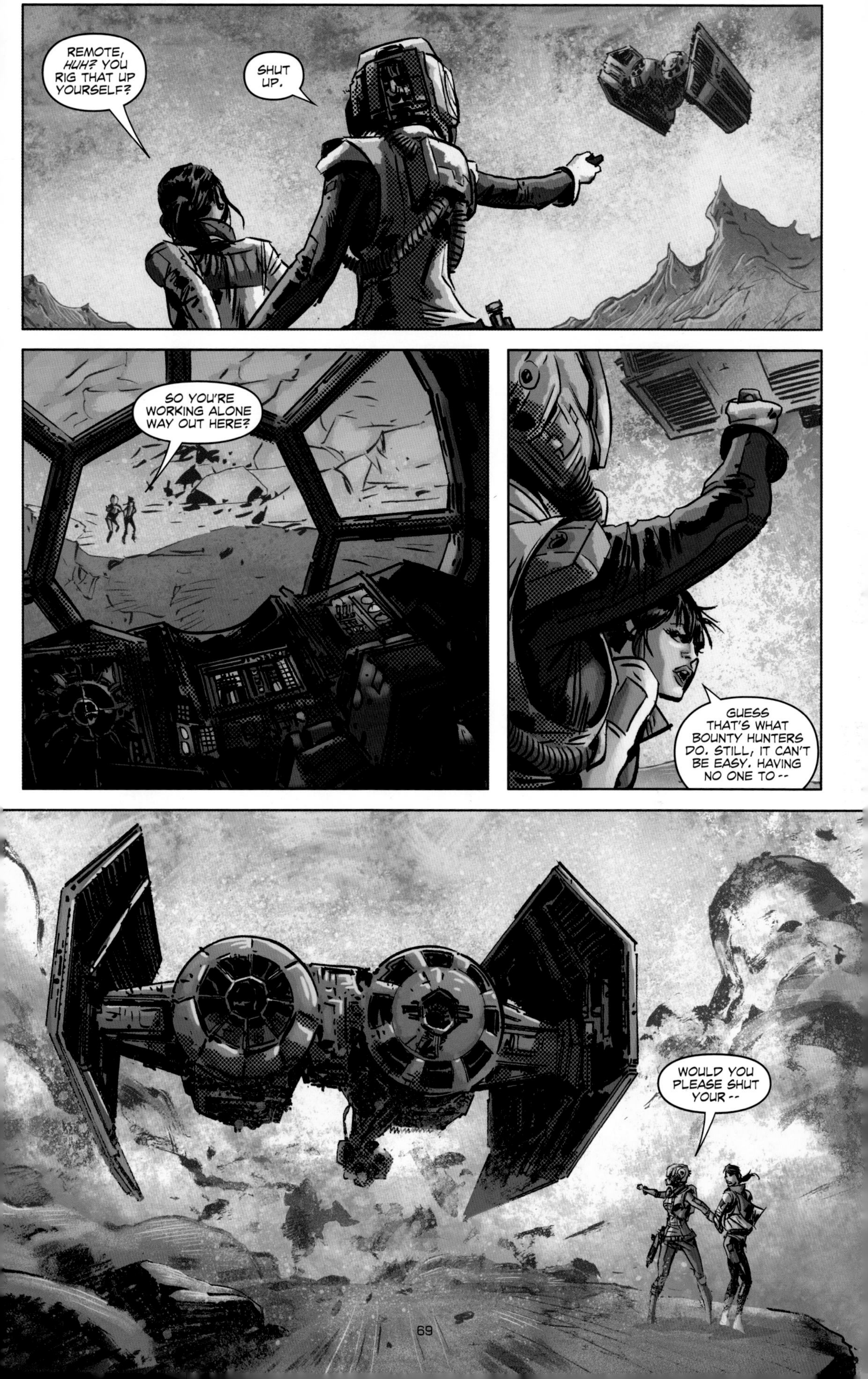
REMOTE, HUH? YOU RIG THAT UP YOURSELF?
SHUT UP.
SO YOU'RE WORKING ALONE WAY OUT HERE?
GUESS THAT'S WHAT BOUNTY HUNTERS DO. STILL, IT CAN'T BE EASY. HAVING NO ONE TO --
WOULD YOU PLEASE SHUT YOUR --

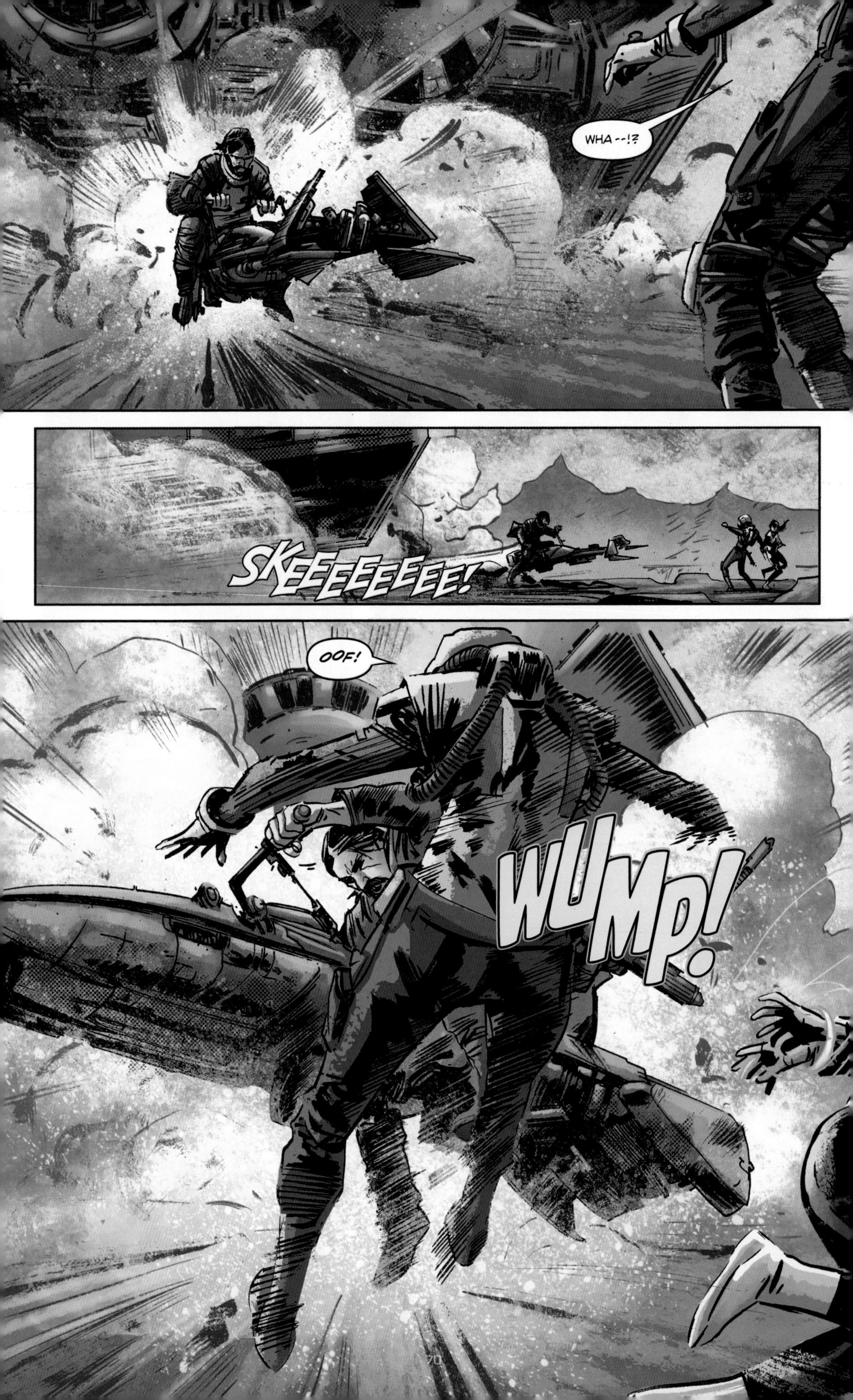
WHA--!?
SKEEEEEEEEE!
OOF!
WUMP!

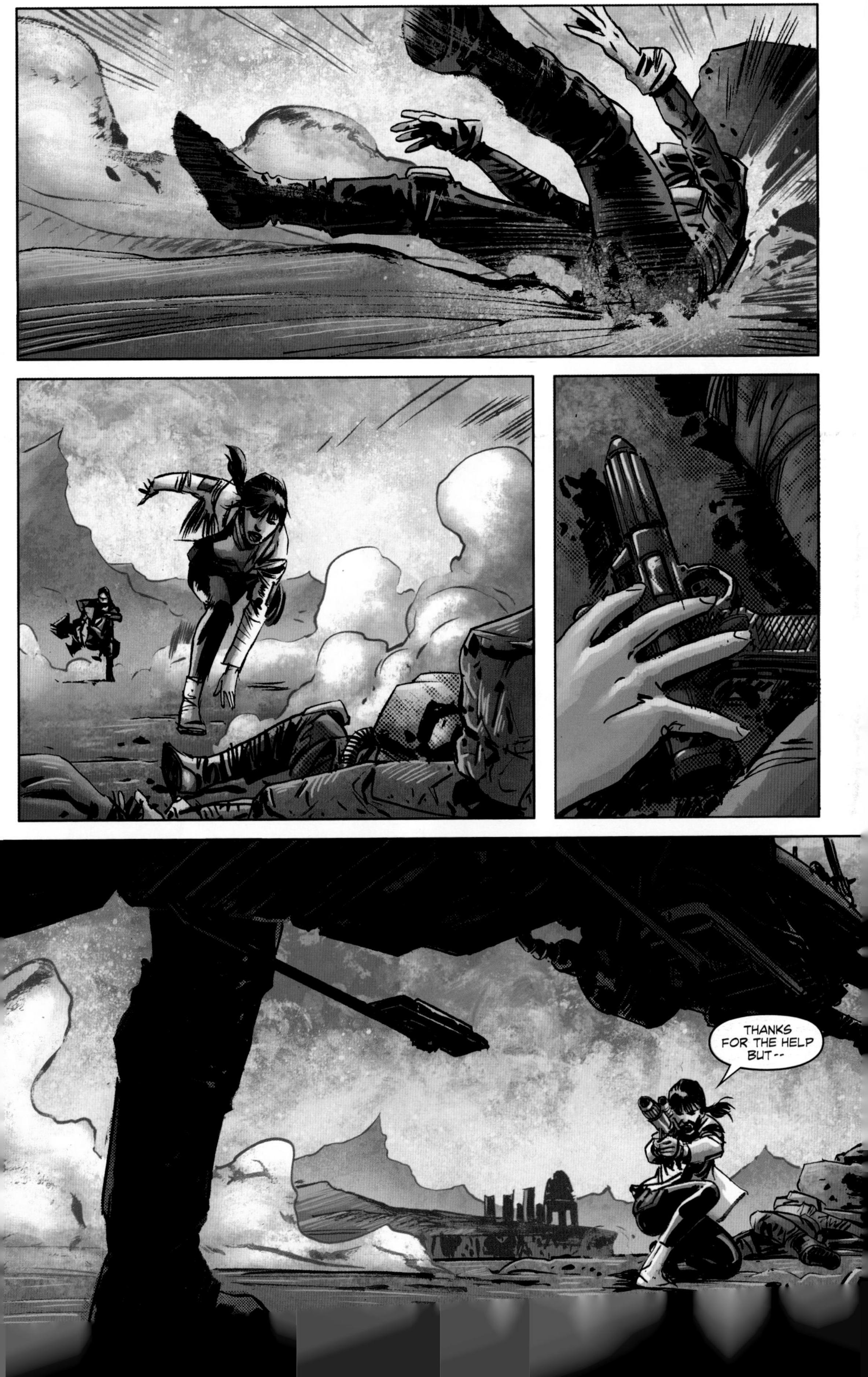
THANKS
FOR THE HELP
BUT--

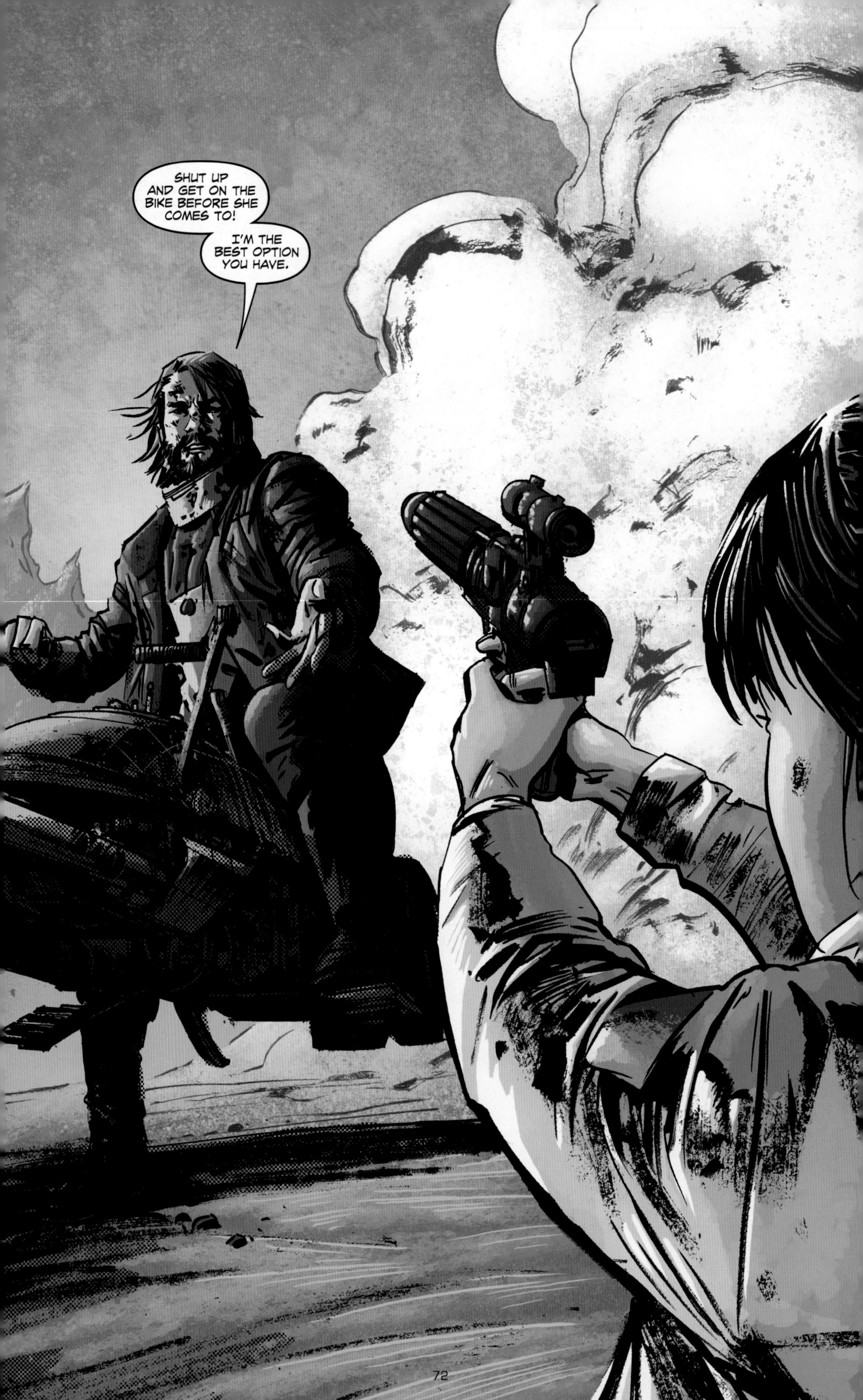
SHUT UP AND GET ON THE BIKE BEFORE SHE COMES TO!
I'M THE BEST OPTION YOU HAVE.

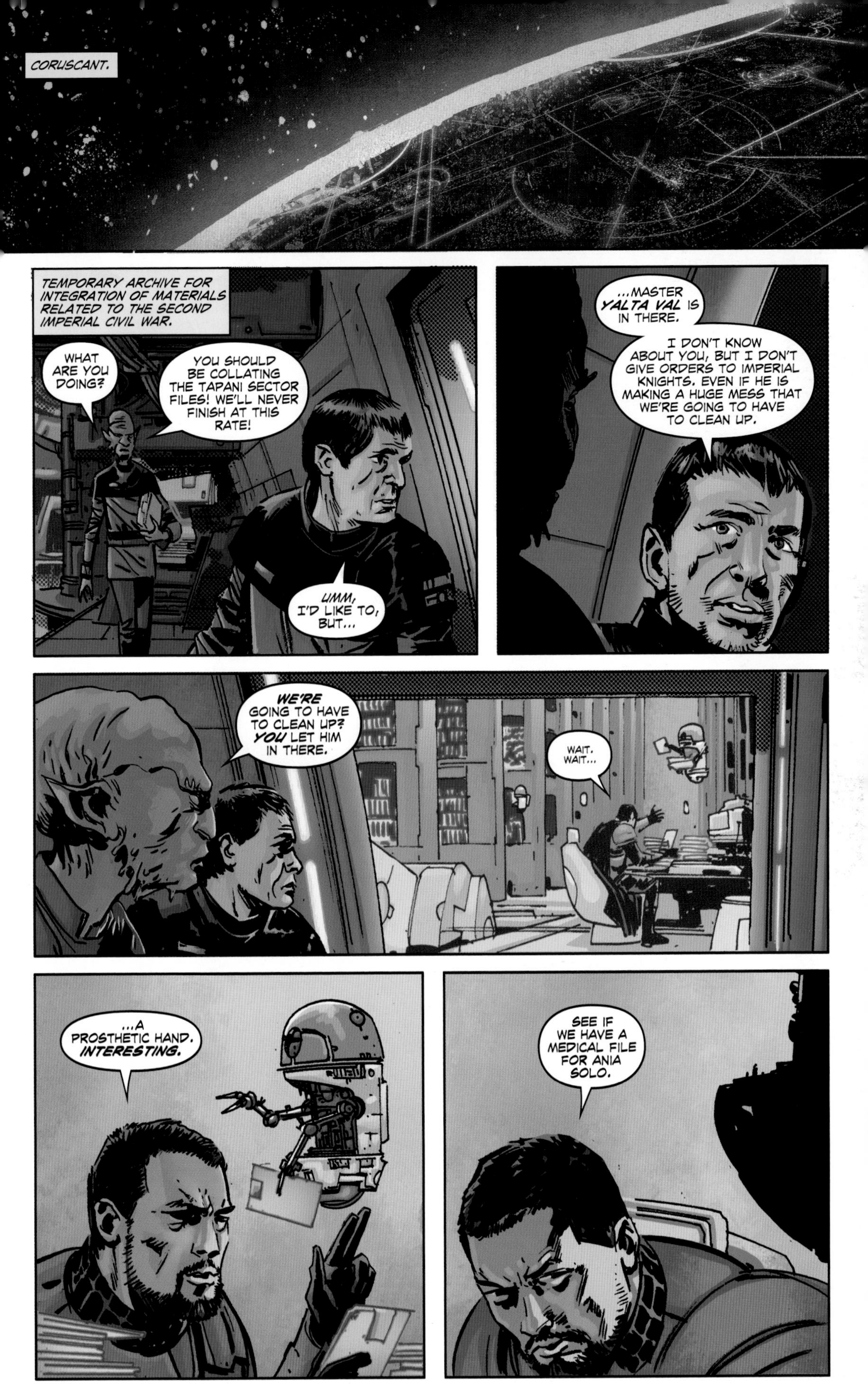
CORUSCANT.
TEMPORARY ARCHIVE FOR INTEGRATION OF MATERIALS RELATED TO THE SECOND IMPERIAL CIVIL WAR.
WHAT ARE YOU DOING?
YOU SHOULD BE COLLATING THE TAPANI SECTOR FILES! WE'LL NEVER FINISH AT THIS RATE!
UMM, I'D LIKE TO, BUT...
...MASTER YALTA VAL IS IN THERE.
I DON'T KNOW ABOUT YOU, BUT I DON'T GIVE ORDERS TO IMPERIAL KNIGHTS. EVEN IF HE IS MAKING A HUGE MESS THAT WE'RE GOING TO HAVE TO CLEAN UP.
WE'RE GOING TO HAVE TO CLEAN UP? YOU LET HIM IN THERE.
WAIT. WAIT...
...A PROSTHETIC HAND. INTERESTING.
SEE IF WE HAVE A MEDICAL FILE FOR ANIA SOLO.

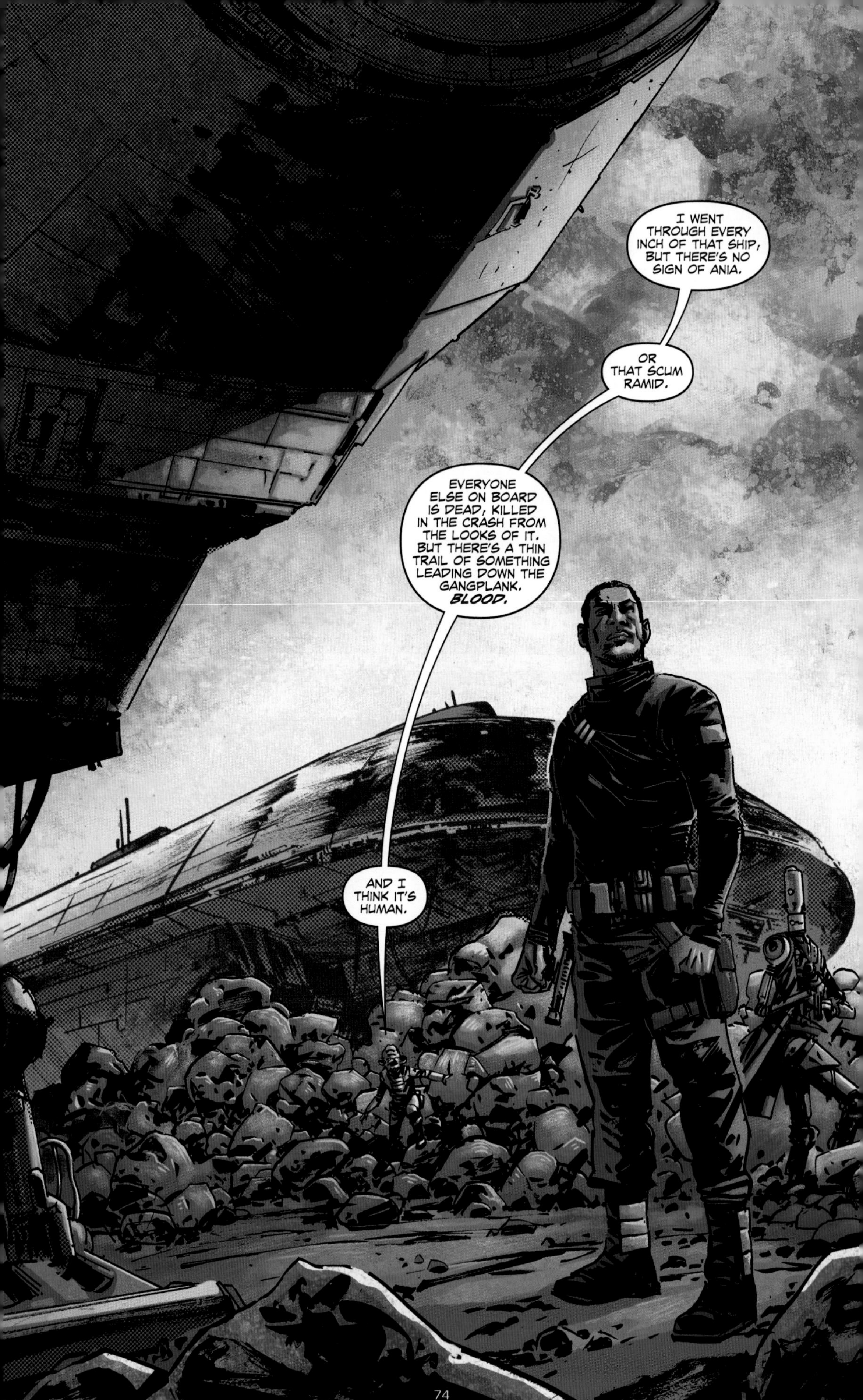
I WENT THROUGH EVERY INCH OF THAT SHIP, BUT THERE'S NO SIGN OF ANIA.
OR THAT SCUM RAMID.
EVERYONE ELSE ON BOARD IS DEAD, KILLED IN THE CRASH FROM THE LOOKS OF IT. BUT THERE'S A THIN TRAIL OF SOMETHING LEADING DOWN THE GANGPLANK. BLOOD.
AND I THINK IT'S HUMAN.

THEY COULDN'T HAVE GONE FAR ON FOOT. ESPECIALLY NOT IF ONE OF THEM WAS INJURED.

WELL, THAT'S THE THING...

...I FOUND STORAGE FOR A SPEEDER, BUT NO BIKE. THOSE THINGS CAN COVER A LOT OF TERRITORY PRETTY FAST.

WE ARE WASTING TIME. OUR INDECISION WILL NOT BRING THEM CLOSER.

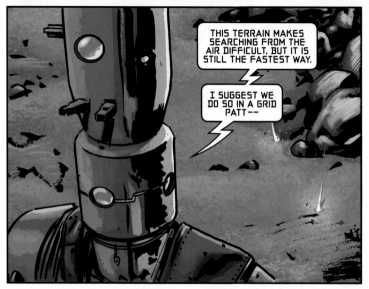

THIS TERRAIN MAKES SEARCHING FROM THE AIR DIFFICULT, BUT IT IS STILL THE FASTEST WAY.

I SUGGEST WE DO SO IN A GRID PATT--

AGH!

SOMETHING CUT ME!

IT'S RAINING... GLASS!

QUICK! GET BACK IN THE SHIP!

TINK!

TINK!

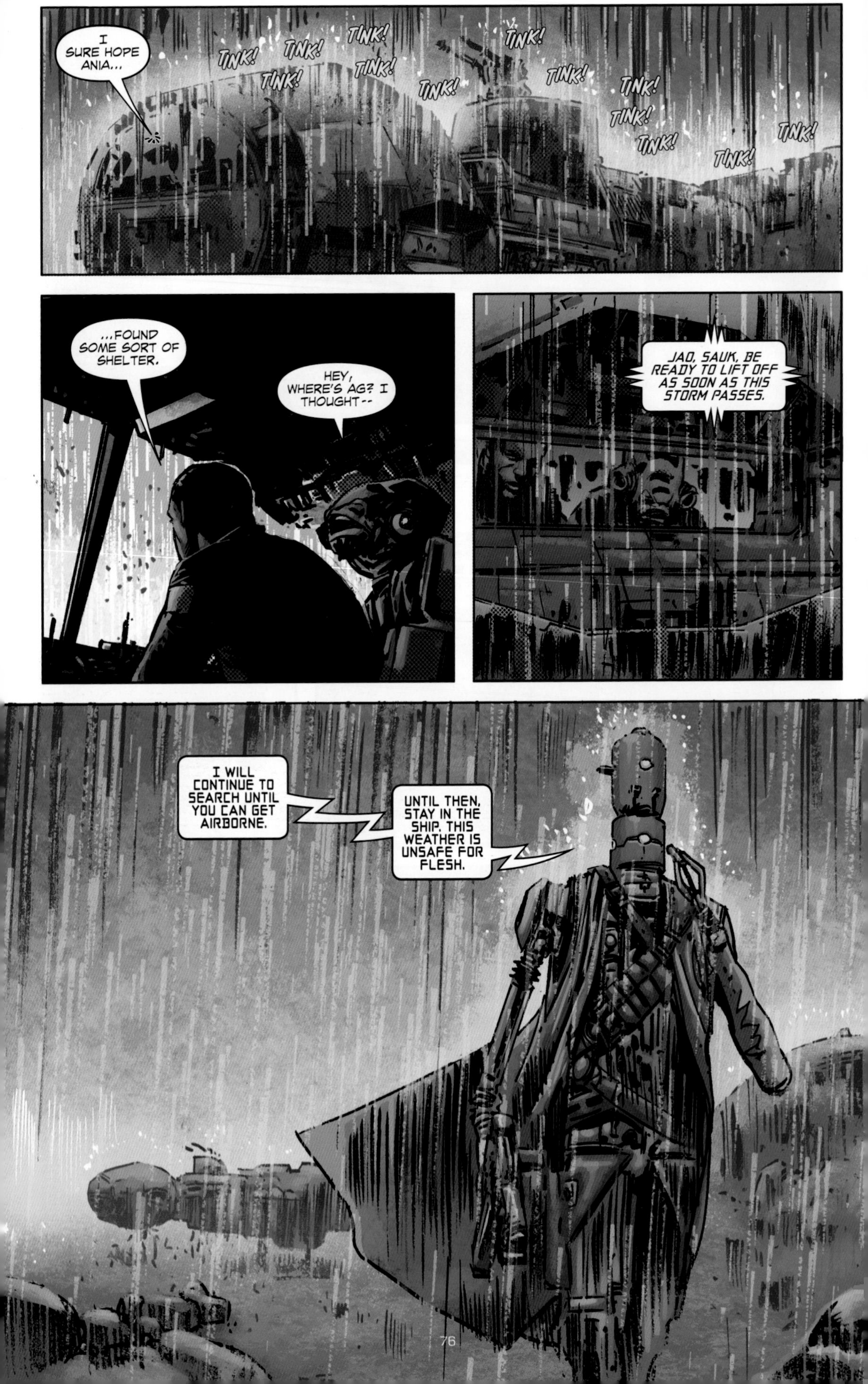
I SURE HOPE ANIA...
TINK! TINK! TINK! TINK! TINK! TINK! TINK! TINK! TINK! TINK! TINK! TINK! TINK!
...FOUND SOME SORT OF SHELTER.
HEY, WHERE'S AG? I THOUGHT--
JAO, SAUK, BE READY TO LIFT OFF AS SOON AS THIS STORM PASSES.
I WILL CONTINUE TO SEARCH UNTIL YOU CAN GET AIRBORNE.
UNTIL THEN, STAY IN THE SHIP. THIS WEATHER IS UNSAFE FOR FLESH.

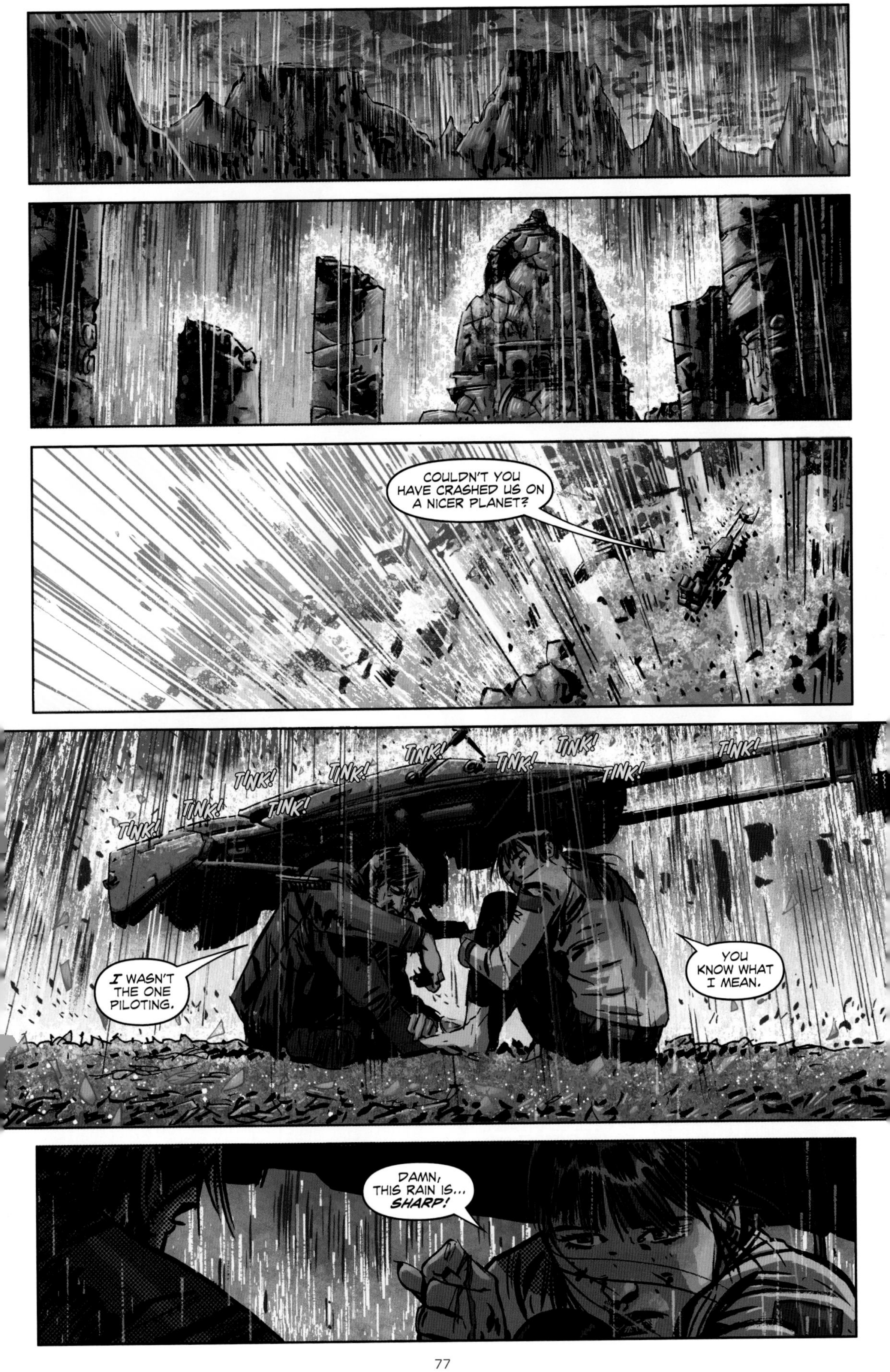
COULDN'T YOU HAVE CRASHED US ON A NICER PLANET?
TINK! TINK! TINK! TINK! TINK! TINK! TINK! TINK! TINK! TINK!
I WASN'T THE ONE PILOTING.
YOU KNOW WHAT I MEAN.
DAMN, THIS RAIN IS... SHARP!

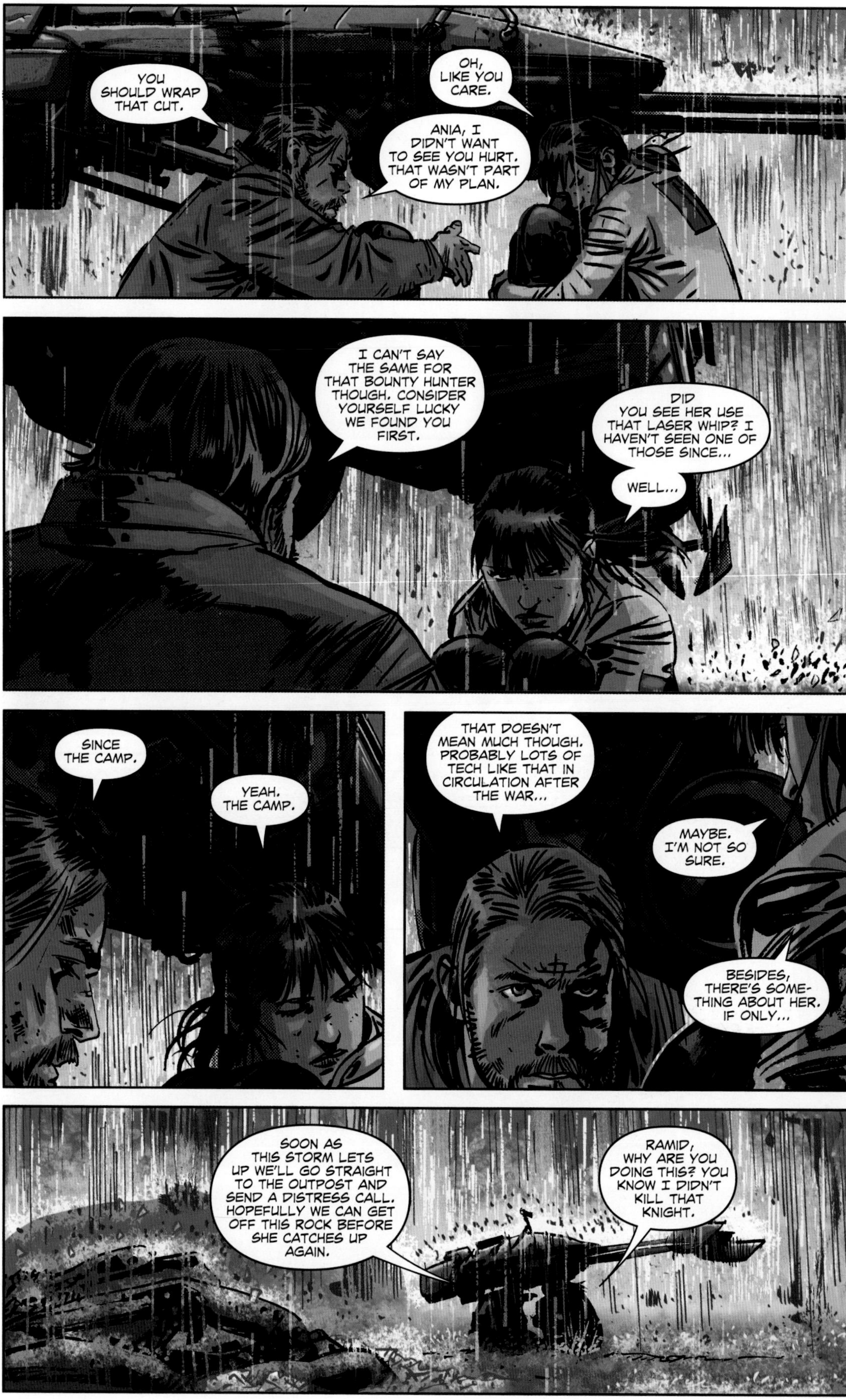
YOU SHOULD WRAP THAT CUT.
OH, LIKE YOU CARE.
ANIA, I DIDN'T WANT TO SEE YOU HURT. THAT WASN'T PART OF MY PLAN.
I CAN'T SAY THE SAME FOR THAT BOUNTY HUNTER THOUGH. CONSIDER YOURSELF LUCKY WE FOUND YOU FIRST.
DID YOU SEE HER USE THAT LASER WHIP? I HAVEN'T SEEN ONE OF THOSE SINCE...
WELL...
SINCE THE CAMP.
YEAH. THE CAMP.
THAT DOESN'T MEAN MUCH THOUGH. PROBABLY LOTS OF TECH LIKE THAT IN CIRCULATION AFTER THE WAR...
MAYBE. I'M NOT SO SURE.
BESIDES, THERE'S SOME-THING ABOUT HER. IF ONLY...
SOON AS THIS STORM LETS UP WE'LL GO STRAIGHT TO THE OUTPOST AND SEND A DISTRESS CALL. HOPEFULLY WE CAN GET OFF THIS ROCK BEFORE SHE CATCHES UP AGAIN.
RAMID, WHY ARE YOU DOING THIS? YOU KNOW I DIDN'T KILL THAT KNIGHT.

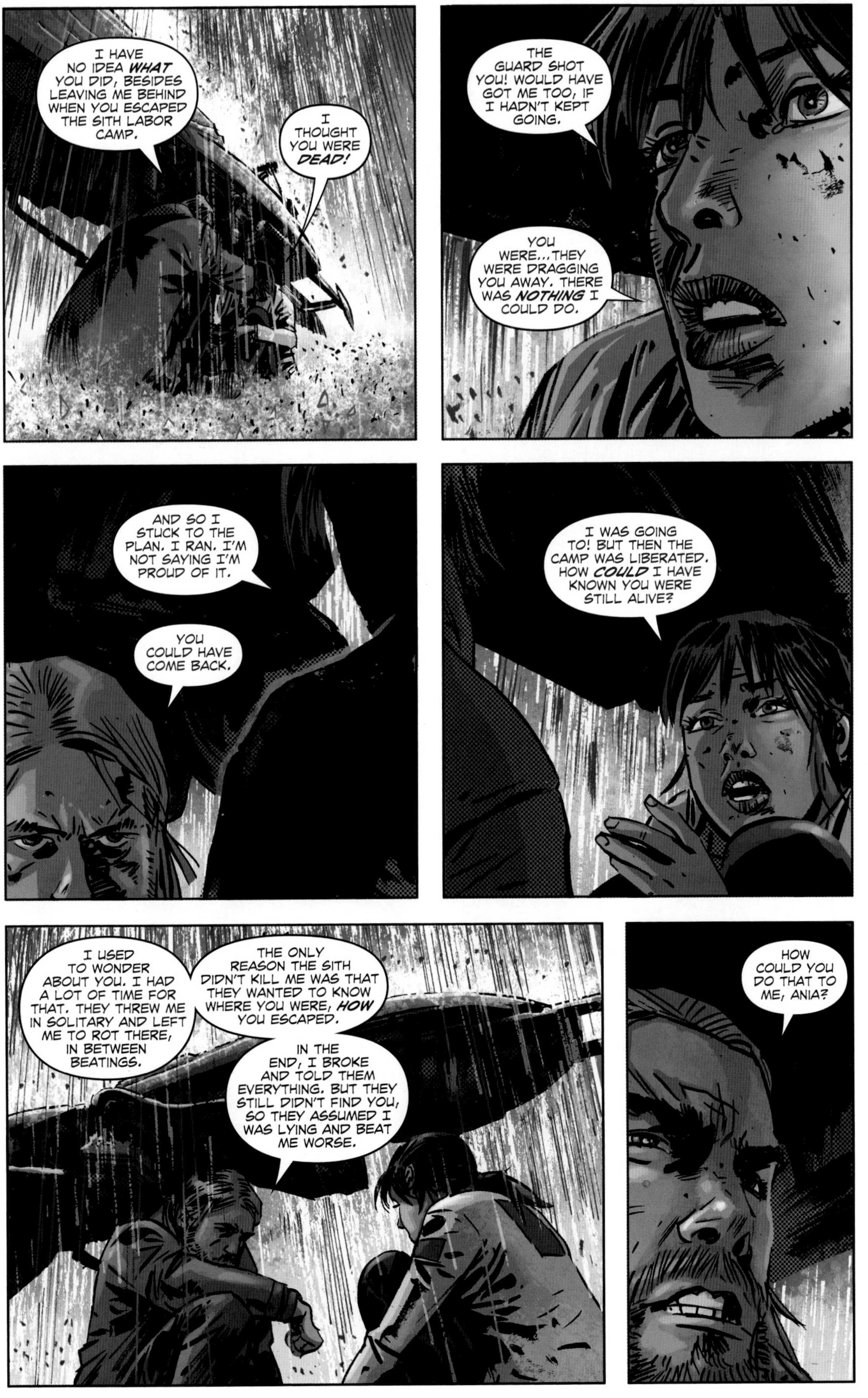
I HAVE NO IDEA *WHAT* YOU DID, BESIDES LEAVING ME BEHIND WHEN YOU ESCAPED THE SITH LABOR CAMP.
I THOUGHT YOU WERE *DEAD!*
THE GUARD SHOT YOU! WOULD HAVE GOT ME TOO, IF I HADN'T KEPT GOING.
YOU WERE...THEY WERE DRAGGING YOU AWAY. THERE WAS *NOTHING* I COULD DO.
AND SO I STUCK TO THE PLAN. I RAN. I'M NOT SAYING I'M PROUD OF IT.
YOU COULD HAVE COME BACK.
I WAS GOING TO! BUT THEN THE CAMP WAS LIBERATED. HOW *COULD* I HAVE KNOWN YOU WERE STILL ALIVE?
I USED TO WONDER ABOUT YOU. I HAD A LOT OF TIME FOR THAT. THEY THREW ME IN SOLITARY AND LEFT ME TO ROT THERE, IN BETWEEN BEATINGS.
THE ONLY REASON THE SITH DIDN'T KILL ME WAS THAT THEY WANTED TO KNOW WHERE YOU WERE, *HOW* YOU ESCAPED.
IN THE END, I BROKE AND TOLD THEM EVERYTHING. BUT THEY STILL DIDN'T FIND YOU, SO THEY ASSUMED I WAS LYING AND BEAT ME WORSE.
HOW COULD YOU DO THAT TO ME, ANIA?

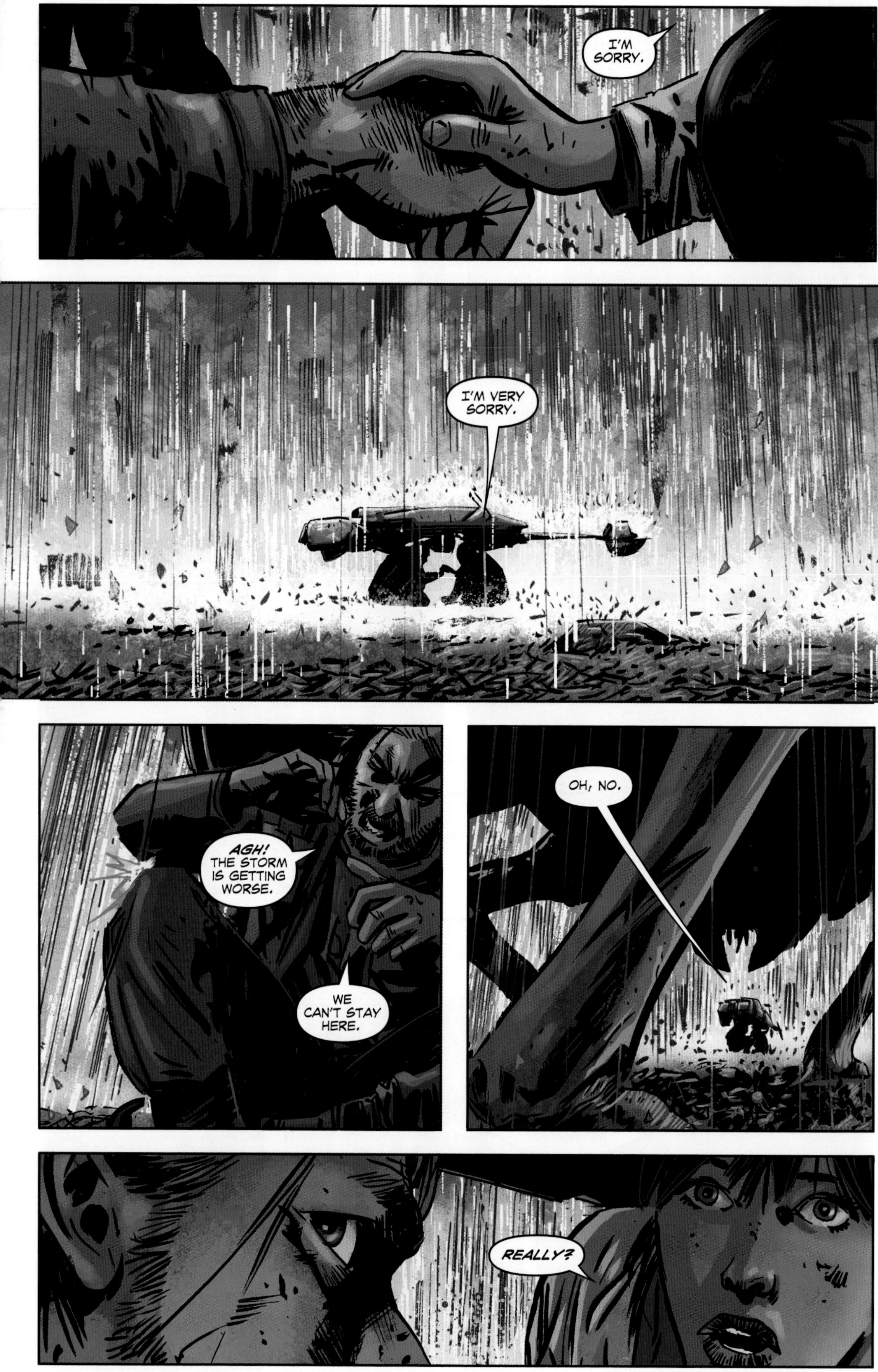
I'M SORRY.
I'M VERY SORRY.
AGH! THE STORM IS GETTING WORSE.
WE CAN'T STAY HERE.
OH, NO.
REALLY?

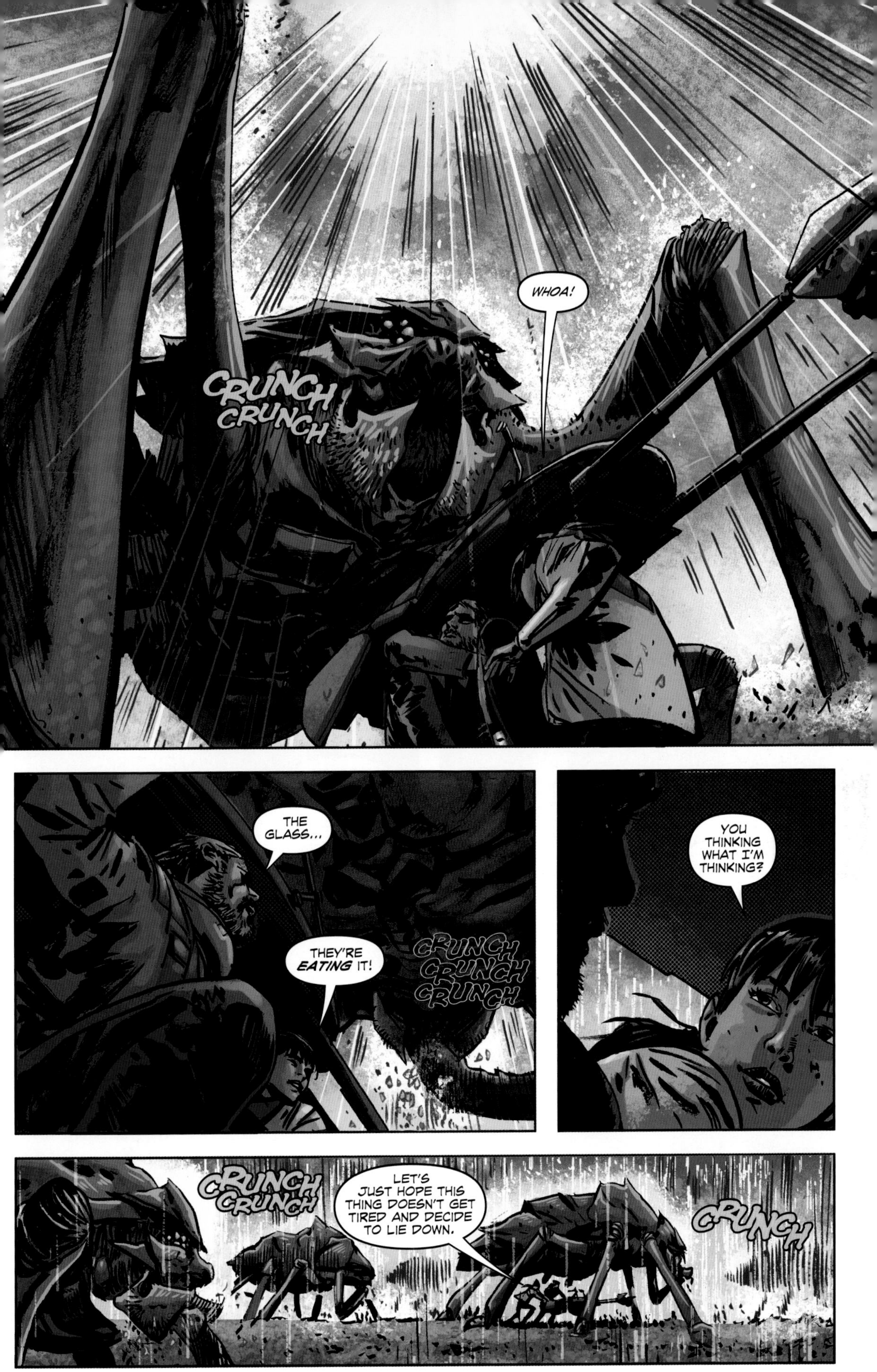
WHOA!
CRUNCH CRUNCH
THE GLASS...
THEY'RE *EATING* IT!
CRUNCH CRUNCH CRUNCH
YOU THINKING WHAT I'M THINKING?
CRUNCH CRUNCH
LET'S JUST HOPE THIS THING DOESN'T GET TIRED AND DECIDE TO LIE DOWN.
CRUNCH

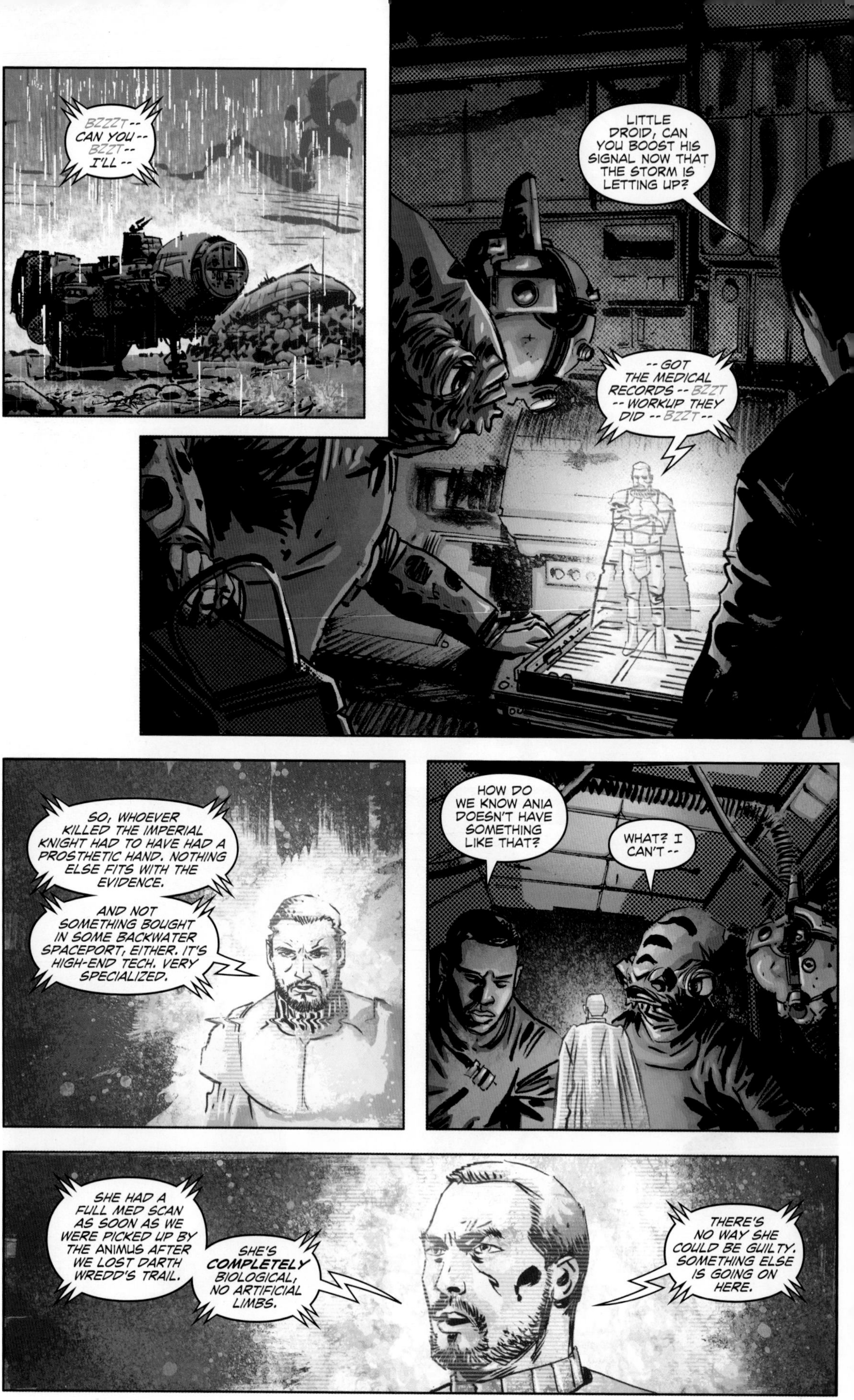
BZZZT -- CAN YOU -- BZZT -- I'LL --
LITTLE DROID, CAN YOU BOOST HIS SIGNAL NOW THAT THE STORM IS LETTING UP?
-- GOT THE MEDICAL RECORDS -- BZZT -- WORKUP THEY DID -- BZZT --
SO, WHOEVER KILLED THE IMPERIAL KNIGHT HAD TO HAVE HAD A PROSTHETIC HAND. NOTHING ELSE FITS WITH THE EVIDENCE.
AND NOT SOMETHING BOUGHT IN SOME BACKWATER SPACEPORT, EITHER. IT'S HIGH-END TECH. VERY SPECIALIZED.
HOW DO WE KNOW ANIA DOESN'T HAVE SOMETHING LIKE THAT?
WHAT? I CAN'T --
SHE HAD A FULL MED SCAN AS SOON AS WE WERE PICKED UP BY THE ANIMUS AFTER WE LOST DARTH WREDD'S TRAIL.
SHE'S **COMPLETELY** BIOLOGICAL, NO ARTIFICIAL LIMBS.
THERE'S NO WAY SHE COULD BE GUILTY. SOMETHING ELSE IS GOING ON HERE.

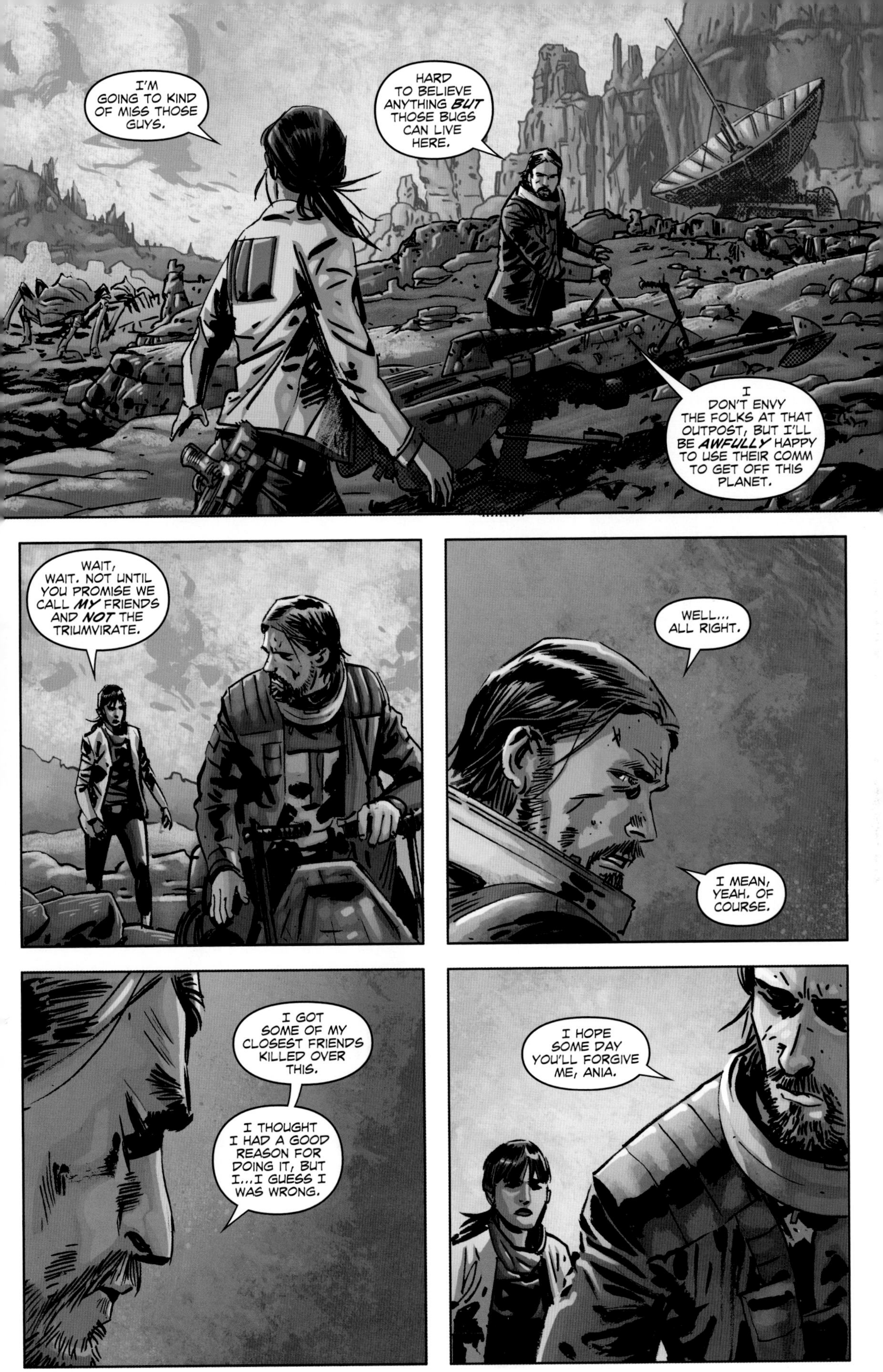
I'M GOING TO KIND OF MISS THOSE GUYS.
HARD TO BELIEVE ANYTHING BUT THOSE BUGS CAN LIVE HERE.
I DON'T ENVY THE FOLKS AT THAT OUTPOST, BUT I'LL BE AWFULLY HAPPY TO USE THEIR COMM TO GET OFF THIS PLANET.
WAIT, WAIT. NOT UNTIL YOU PROMISE WE CALL MY FRIENDS AND NOT THE TRIUMVIRATE.
WELL... ALL RIGHT.
I MEAN, YEAH. OF COURSE.
I GOT SOME OF MY CLOSEST FRIENDS KILLED OVER THIS.
I THOUGHT I HAD A GOOD REASON FOR DOING IT, BUT I...I GUESS I WAS WRONG.
I HOPE SOME DAY YOU'LL FORGIVE ME, ANIA.

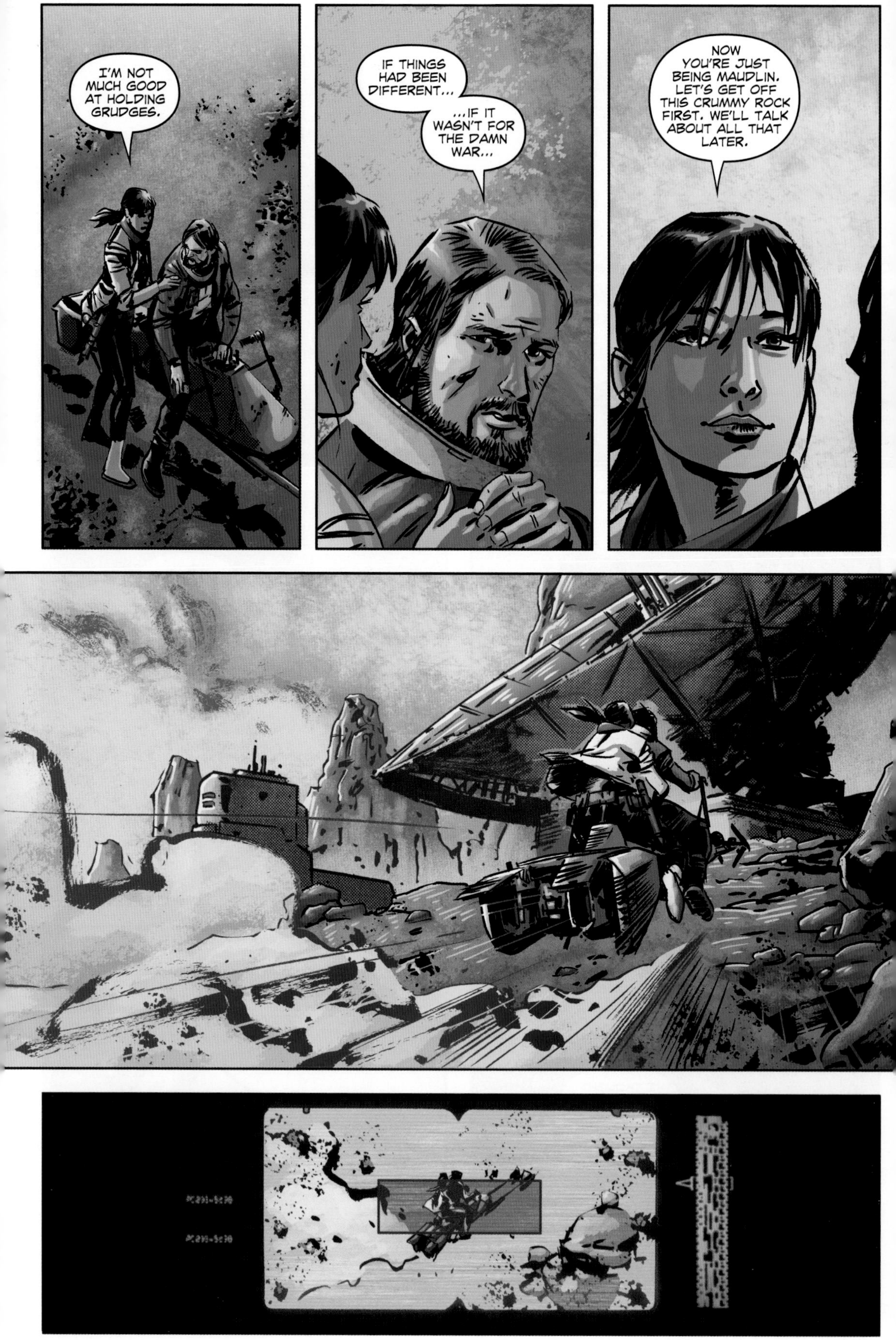
I'M NOT MUCH GOOD AT HOLDING GRUDGES.
IF THINGS HAD BEEN DIFFERENT...
...IF IT WASN'T FOR THE DAMN WAR...
NOW YOU'RE JUST BEING MAUDLIN. LET'S GET OFF THIS CRUMMY ROCK FIRST. WE'LL TALK ABOUT ALL THAT LATER.

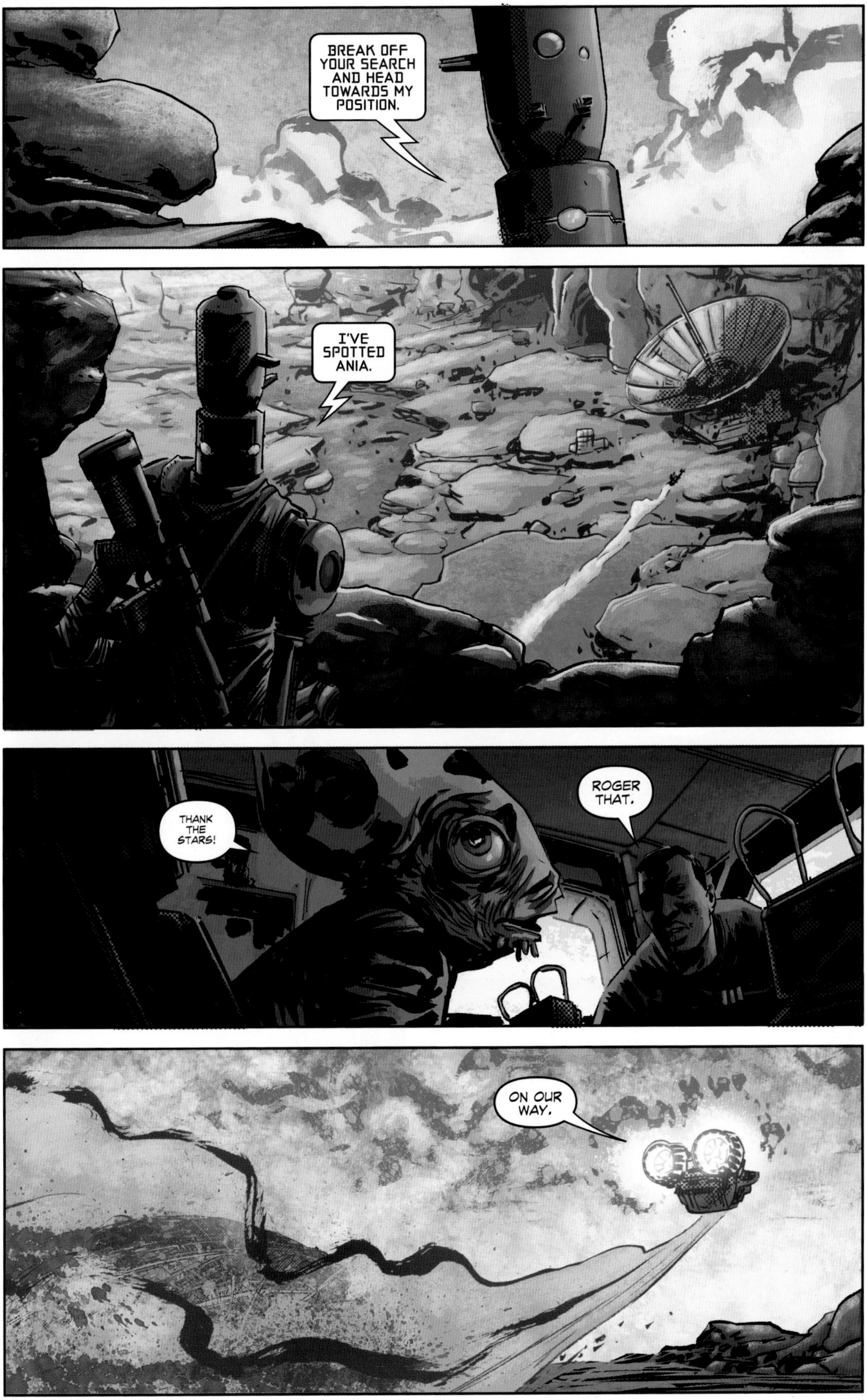
BREAK OFF YOUR SEARCH AND HEAD TOWARDS MY POSITION.
I'VE SPOTTED ANIA.
THANK THE STARS!
ROGER THAT.
ON OUR WAY.

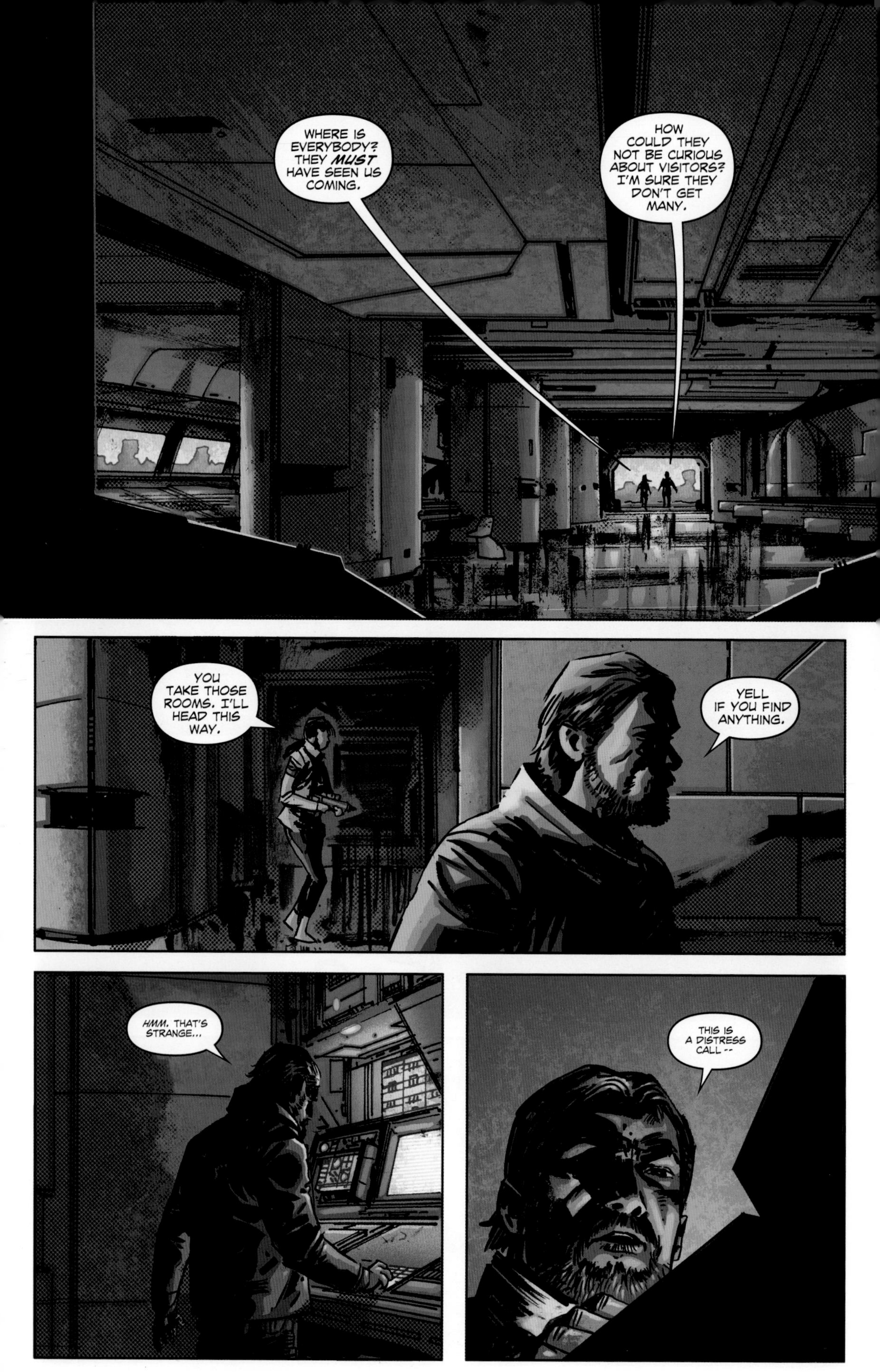
WHERE IS EVERYBODY? THEY MUST HAVE SEEN US COMING.
HOW COULD THEY NOT BE CURIOUS ABOUT VISITORS? I'M SURE THEY DON'T GET MANY.
YOU TAKE THOSE ROOMS. I'LL HEAD THIS WAY.
YELL IF YOU FIND ANYTHING.
HMM. THAT'S STRANGE...
THIS IS A DISTRESS CALL --

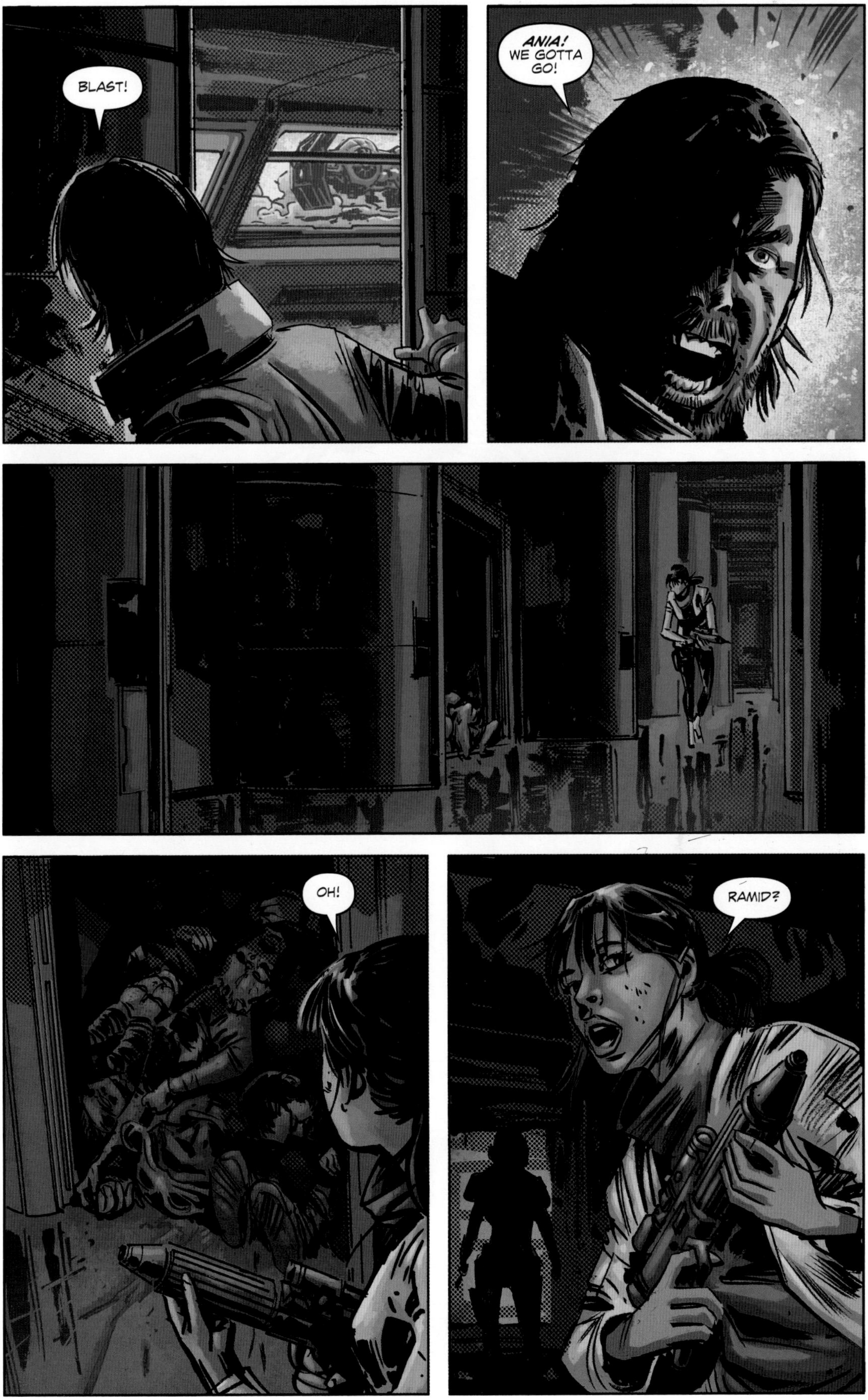
BLAST!
ANIA! WE GOTTA GO!
OH!
RAMID?

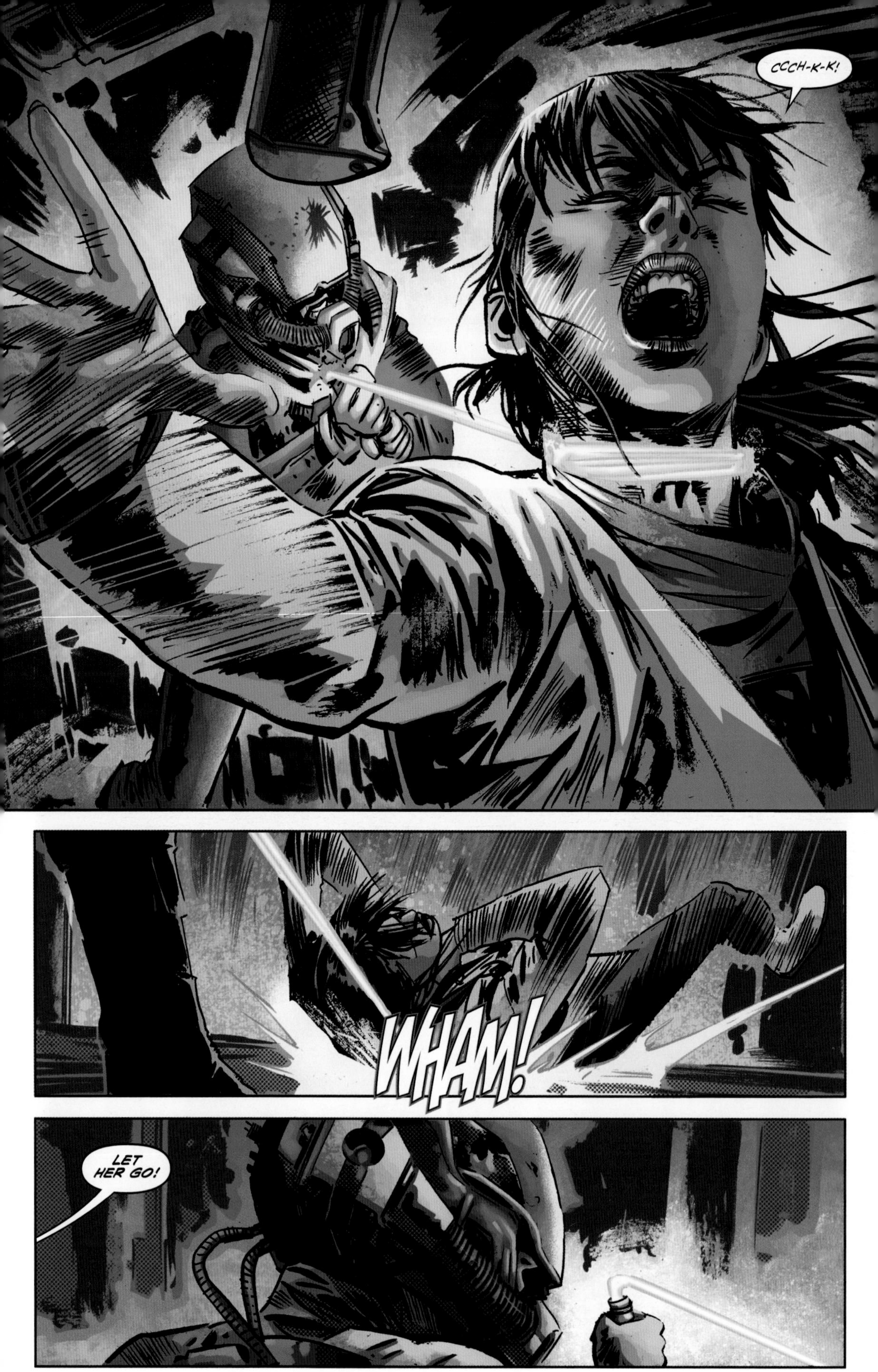
CCCH-K-K!
WHAM!
LET HER GO!

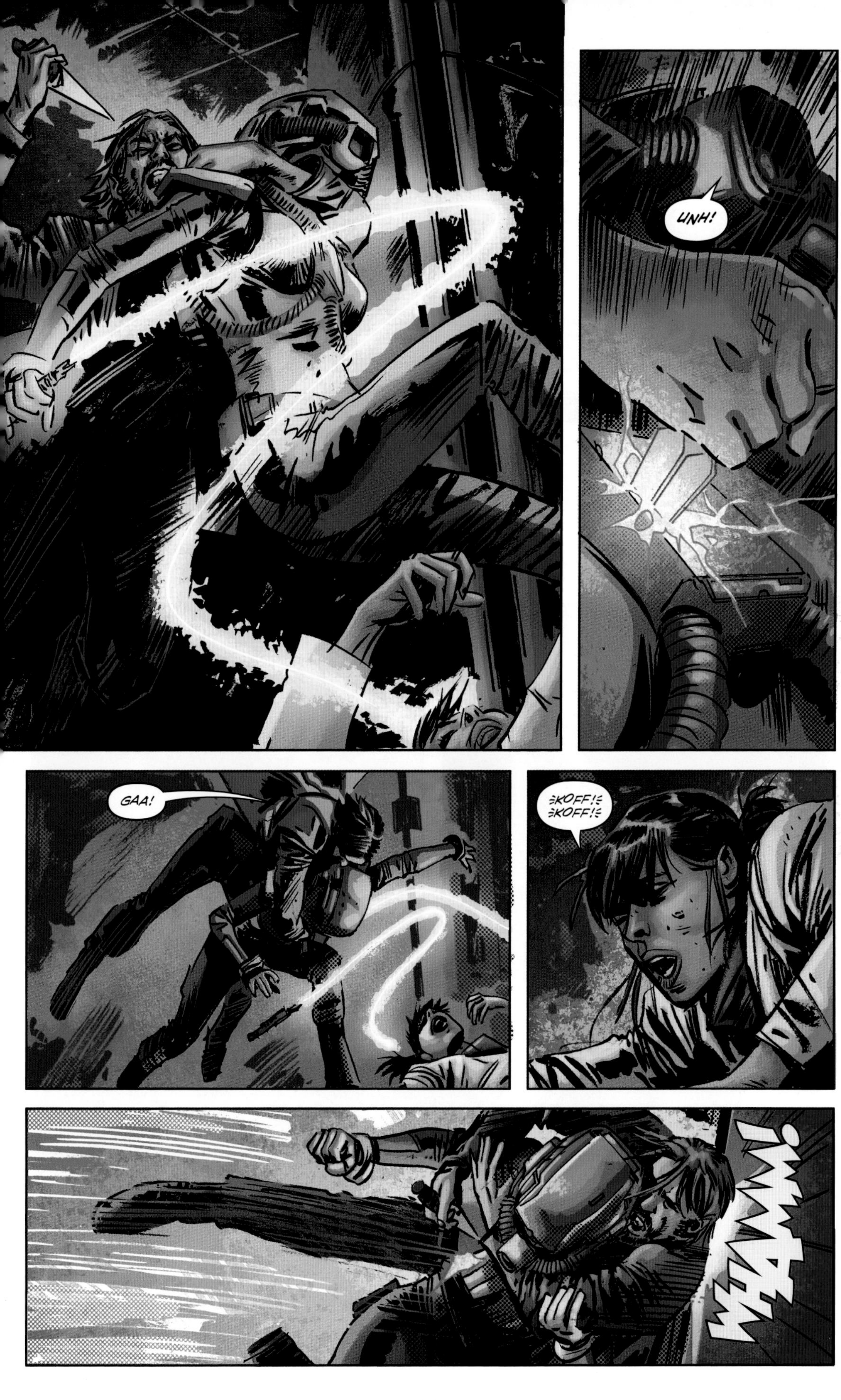
UNH!
GAA!
≶KOFF!≶
≶KOFF!≶
WHAM!

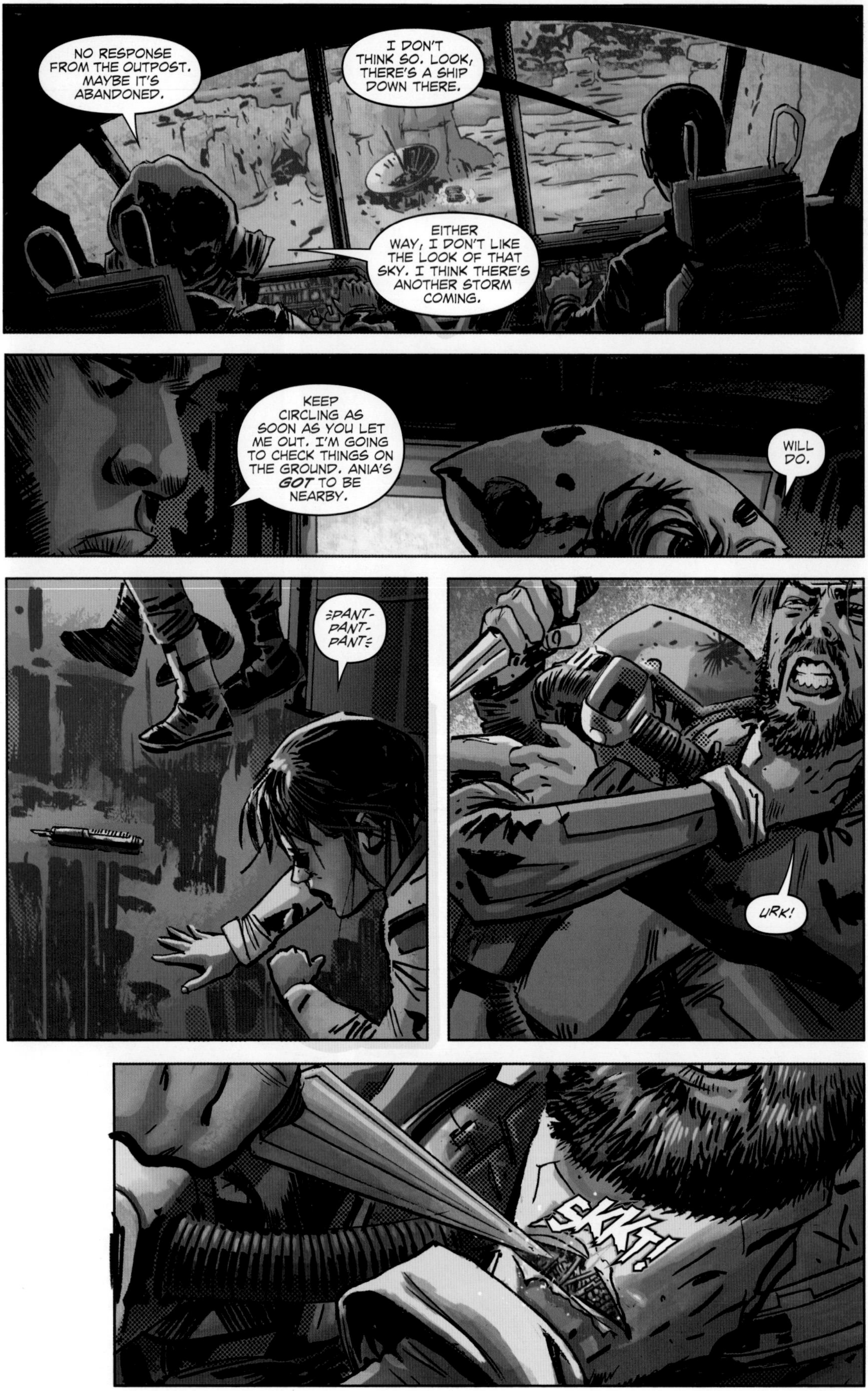
NO RESPONSE FROM THE OUTPOST. MAYBE IT'S ABANDONED.
I DON'T THINK SO. LOOK, THERE'S A SHIP DOWN THERE.
EITHER WAY, I DON'T LIKE THE LOOK OF THAT SKY. I THINK THERE'S ANOTHER STORM COMING.
KEEP CIRCLING AS SOON AS YOU LET ME OUT. I'M GOING TO CHECK THINGS ON THE GROUND. ANIA'S GOT TO BE NEARBY.
WILL DO.
PANT-PANT-PANT
URK!
SKKT!

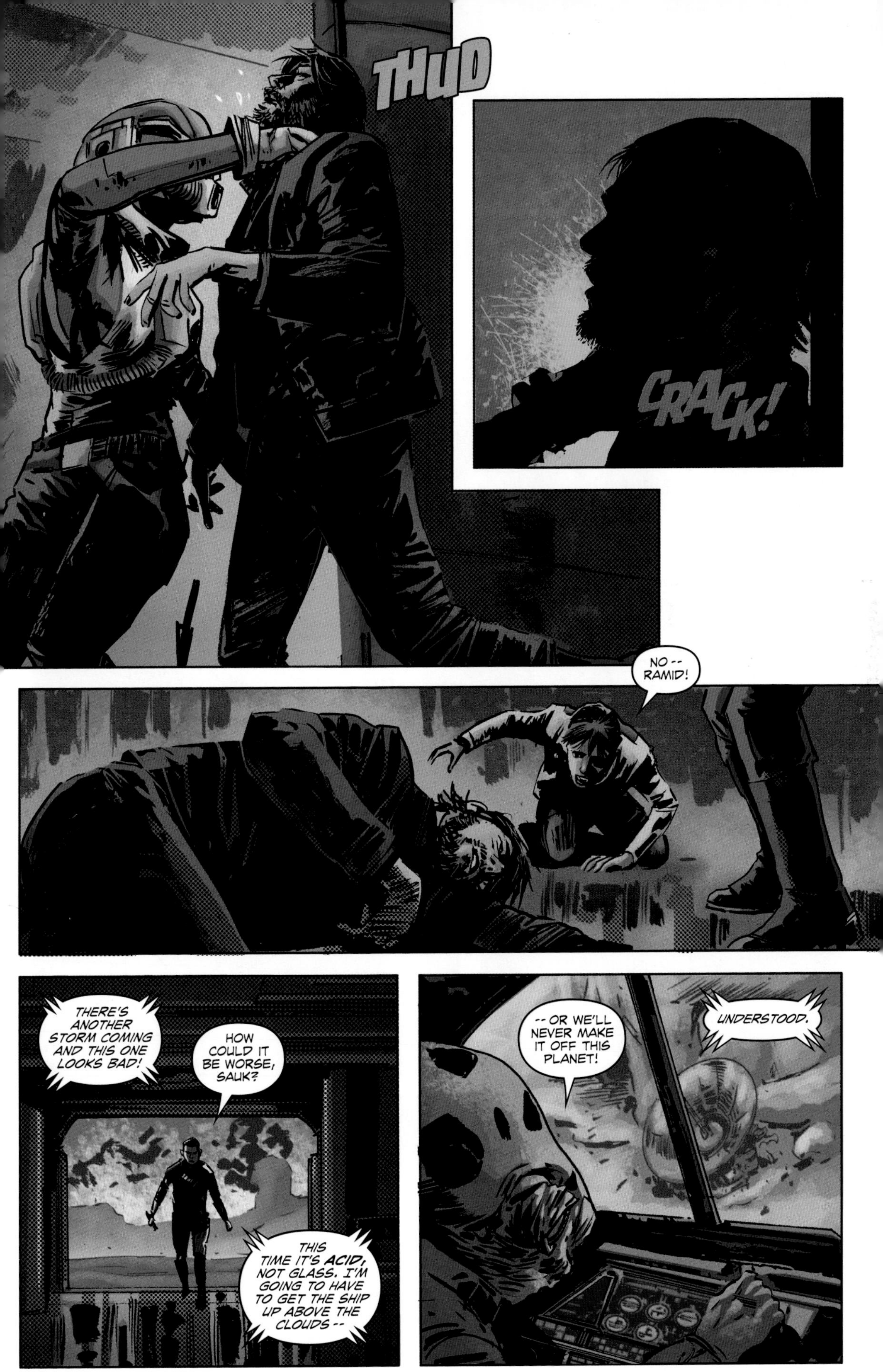
THUD
CRACK!
NO -- RAMID!
THERE'S ANOTHER STORM COMING AND THIS ONE LOOKS BAD!
HOW COULD IT BE WORSE, SAUK?
THIS TIME IT'S ACID, NOT GLASS. I'M GOING TO HAVE TO GET THE SHIP UP ABOVE THE CLOUDS --
-- OR WE'LL NEVER MAKE IT OFF THIS PLANET!
UNDERSTOOD.

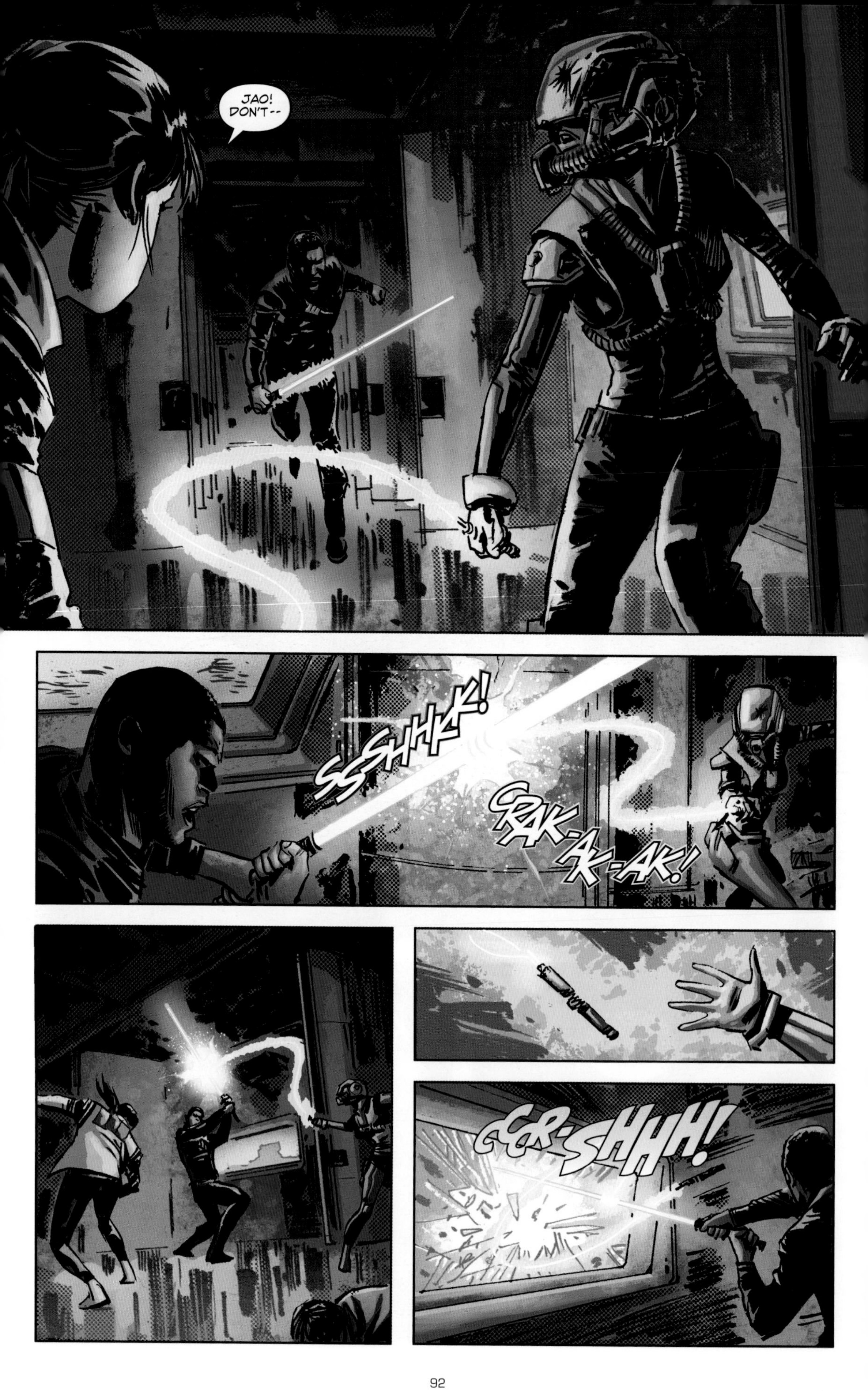

JAO! DON'T--
SSSHHKK!
CRAK-AK-AK!
CCR-SHHH!

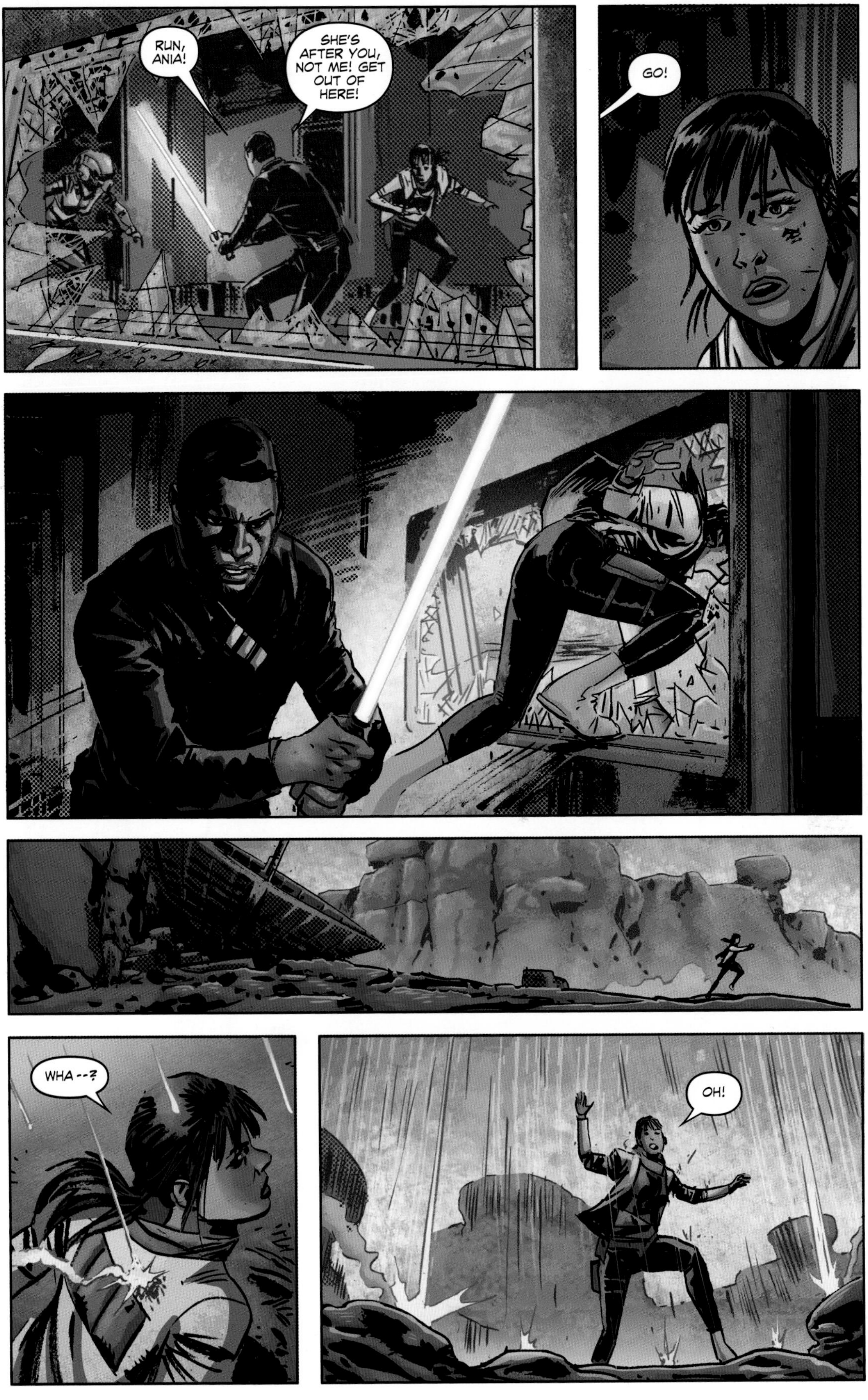
RUN, ANIA!
SHE'S AFTER YOU, NOT ME! GET OUT OF HERE!
GO!
WHA --?
OH!

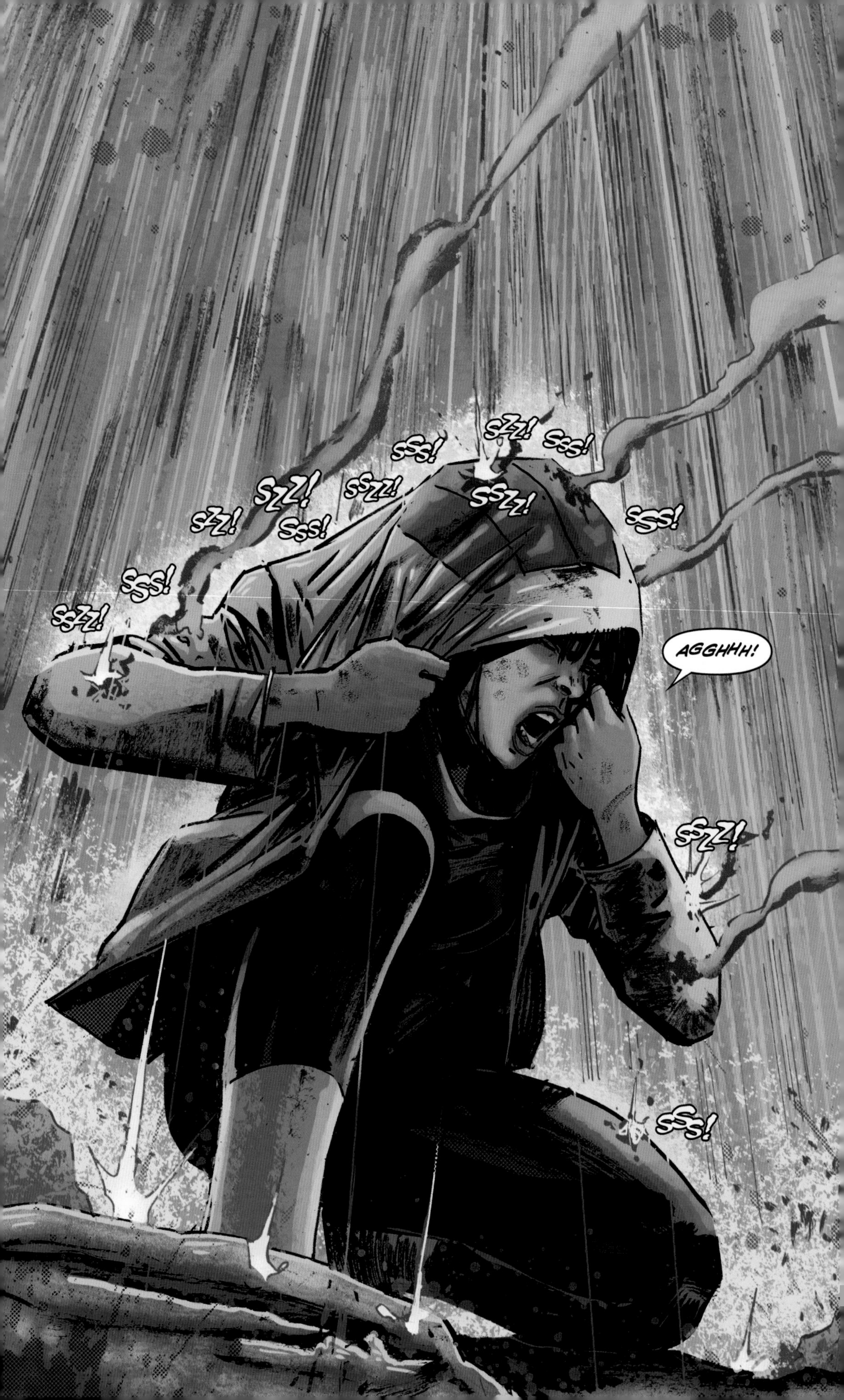
SSS!
SZZ!
SSS!
SSZZ!
SZZ!
SSSZZ!
SZZ!
SSS!
SSS!
SSS!
SSZZ!
AGGHHH!
SSZZ!
SSS!

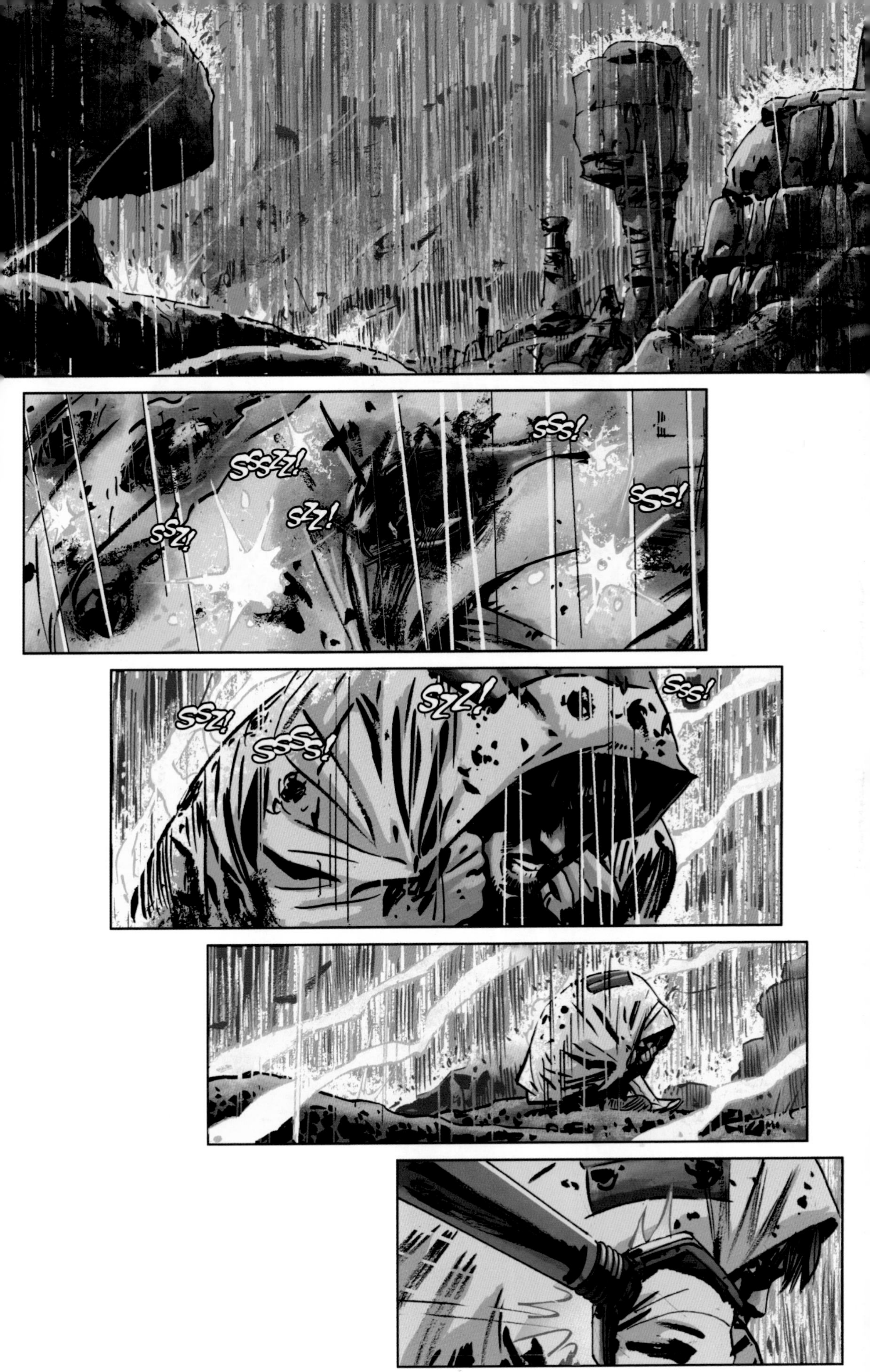
SSSZZ!
SSZ!
SZZ!
SSS!
SSS!
SSZ!
SSSS!
SZZ!
SSS!

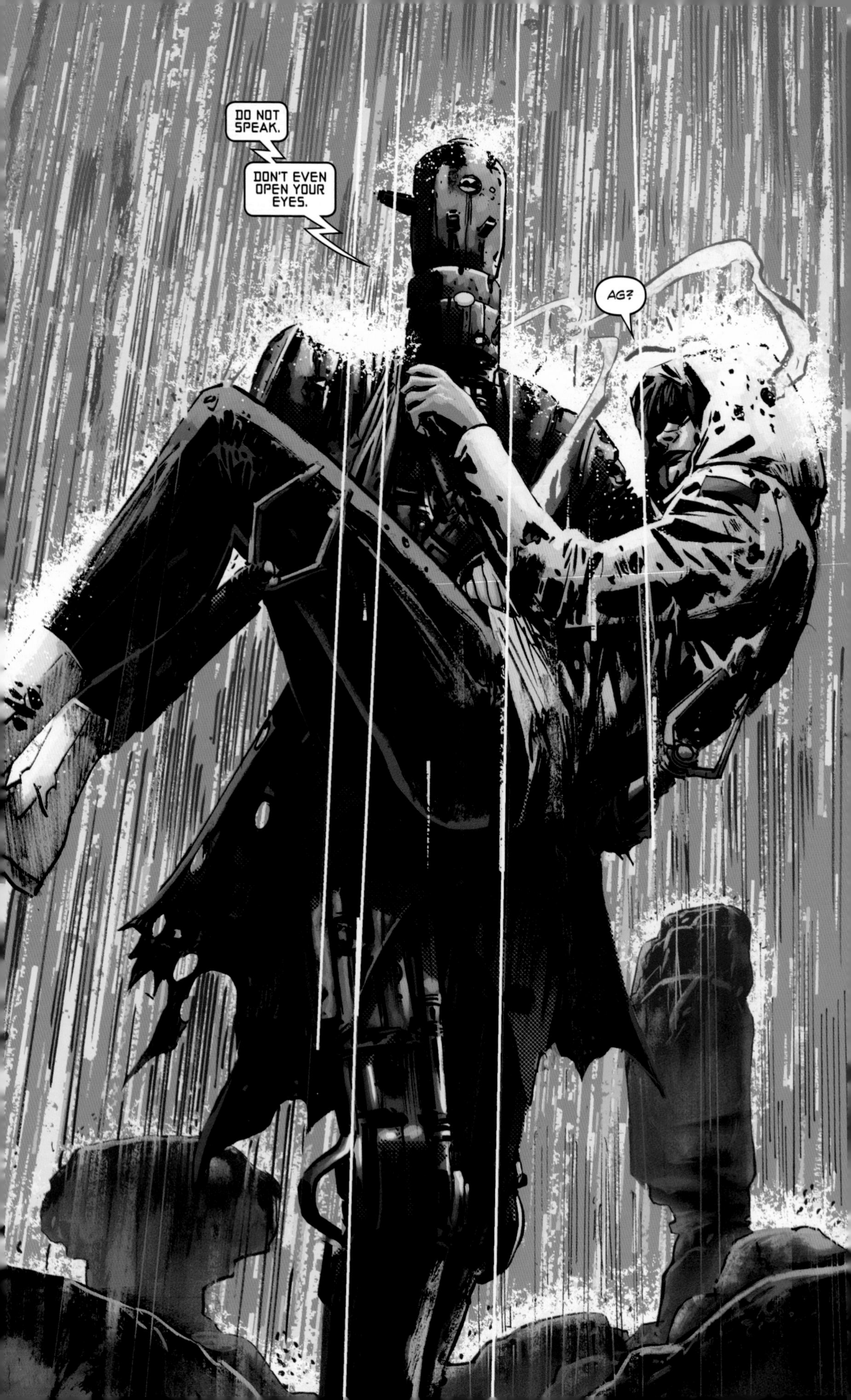
DO NOT SPEAK.
DON'T EVEN OPEN YOUR EYES.
AG?

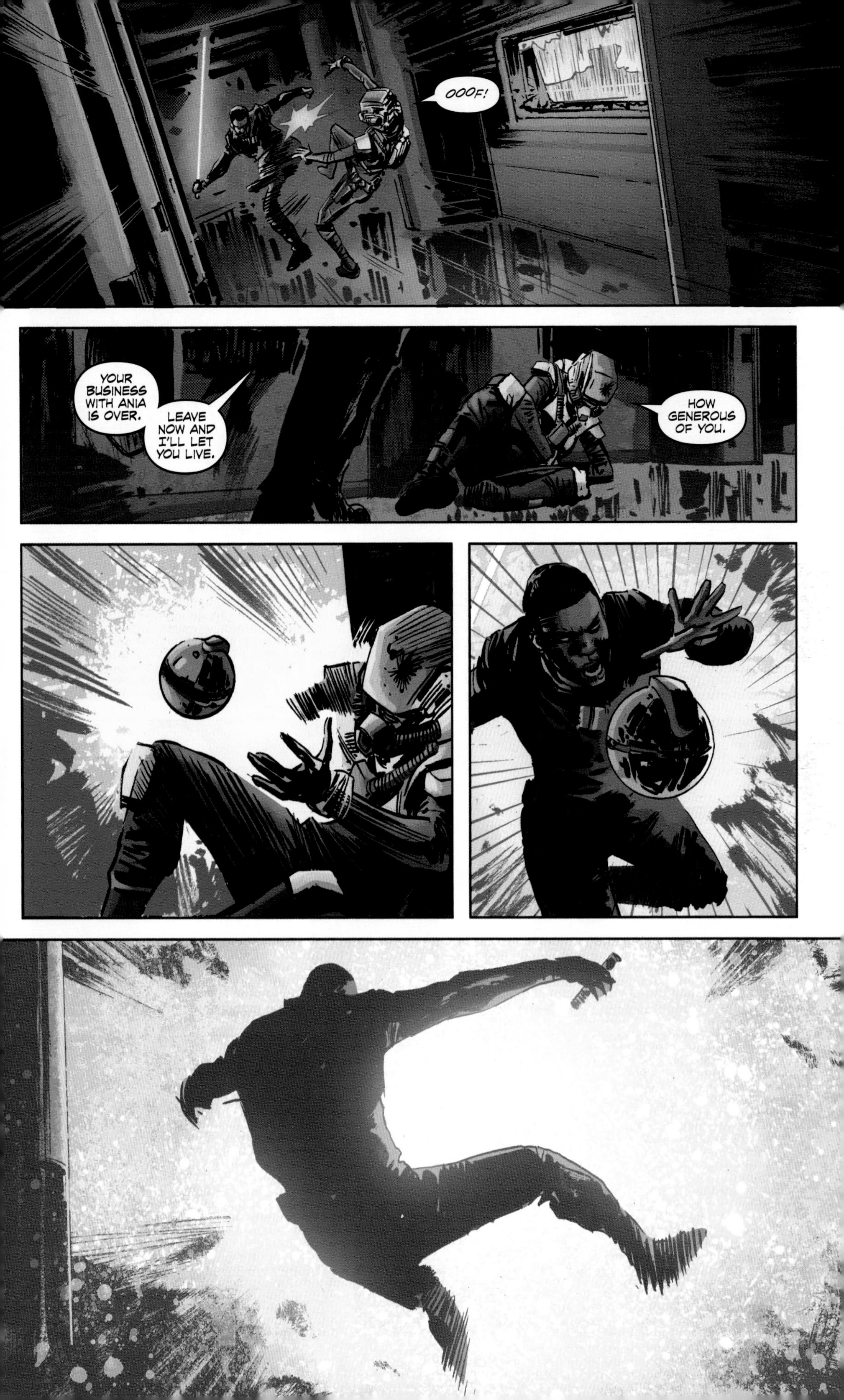
OOOF!
YOUR BUSINESS WITH ANIA IS OVER.
LEAVE NOW AND I'LL LET YOU LIVE.
HOW GENEROUS OF YOU.

YOU ARE SAFE NOW, ANIA.

DON'T OVERSTATE IT.

UGH! THIS STUFF IS KILLING ME!

LOOKS LIKE IT'S TIME FOR A NEW JACKET, IF WE EVER GET OUT OF HERE.

MY BLASTERS HAVE FARED NO BETTER. THEY ARE INOPERABLE NOW.

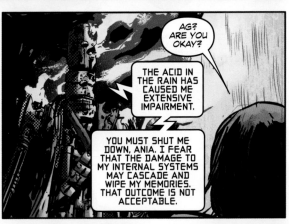

AG? ARE YOU OKAY?

THE ACID IN THE RAIN HAS CAUSED ME EXTENSIVE IMPAIRMENT.

YOU MUST SHUT ME DOWN, ANIA. I FEAR THAT THE DAMAGE TO MY INTERNAL SYSTEMS MAY CASCADE AND WIPE MY MEMORIES. THAT OUTCOME IS NOT ACCEPTABLE.

BUT...SHOULDN'T *YOU* SHUT DOWN YOUR OWN SYSTEMS? WOULDN'T THAT BE SAFER?

THE RELAY IS FRIED. I CAN'T DO IT MYSELF.

I HAVE SELDOM ASKED YOU FOR ANYTHING, ANIA, BUT I AM ASKING YOU FOR THIS.

THEET

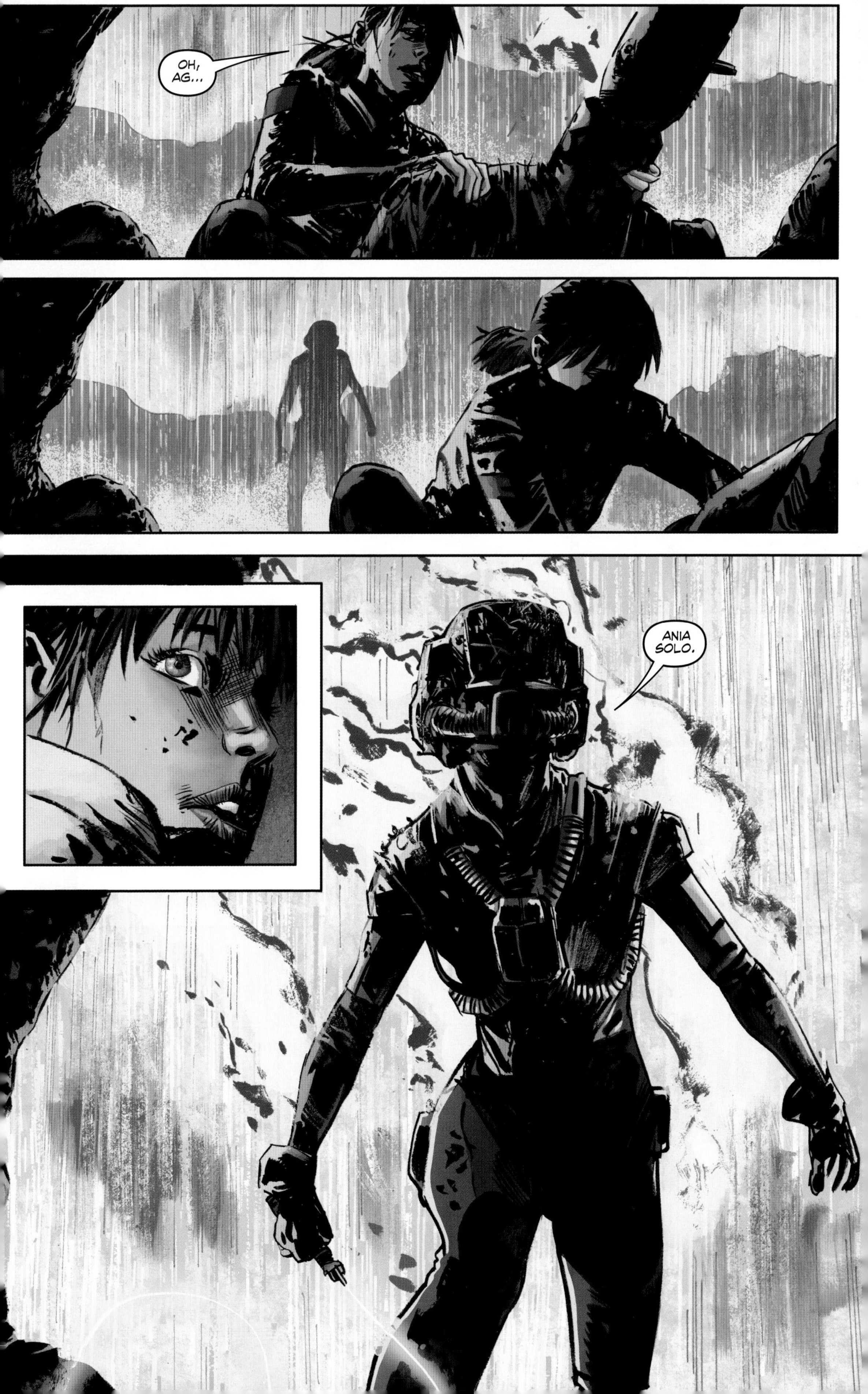
OH, AG...
ANIA SOLO.

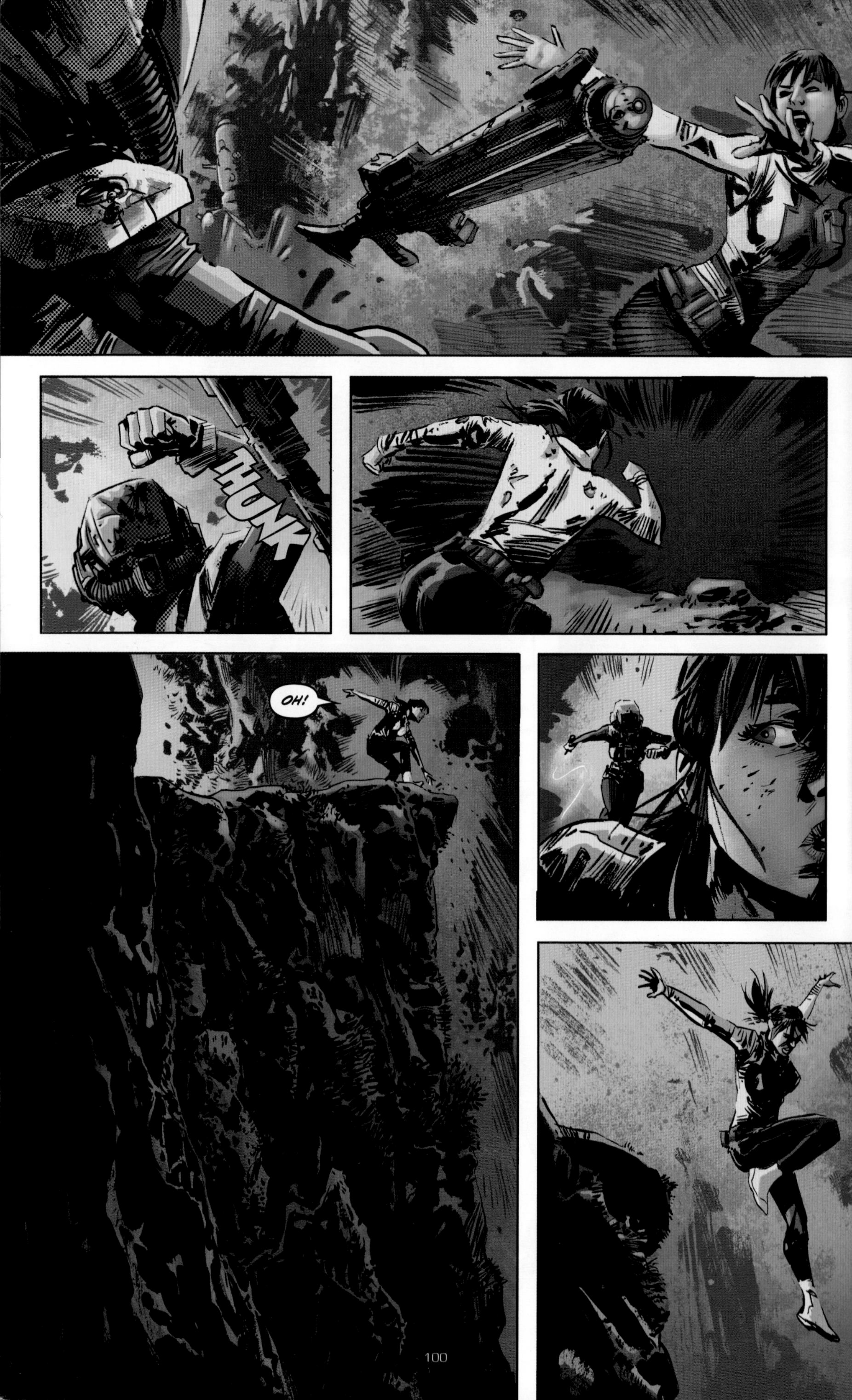
THUNK
OH!

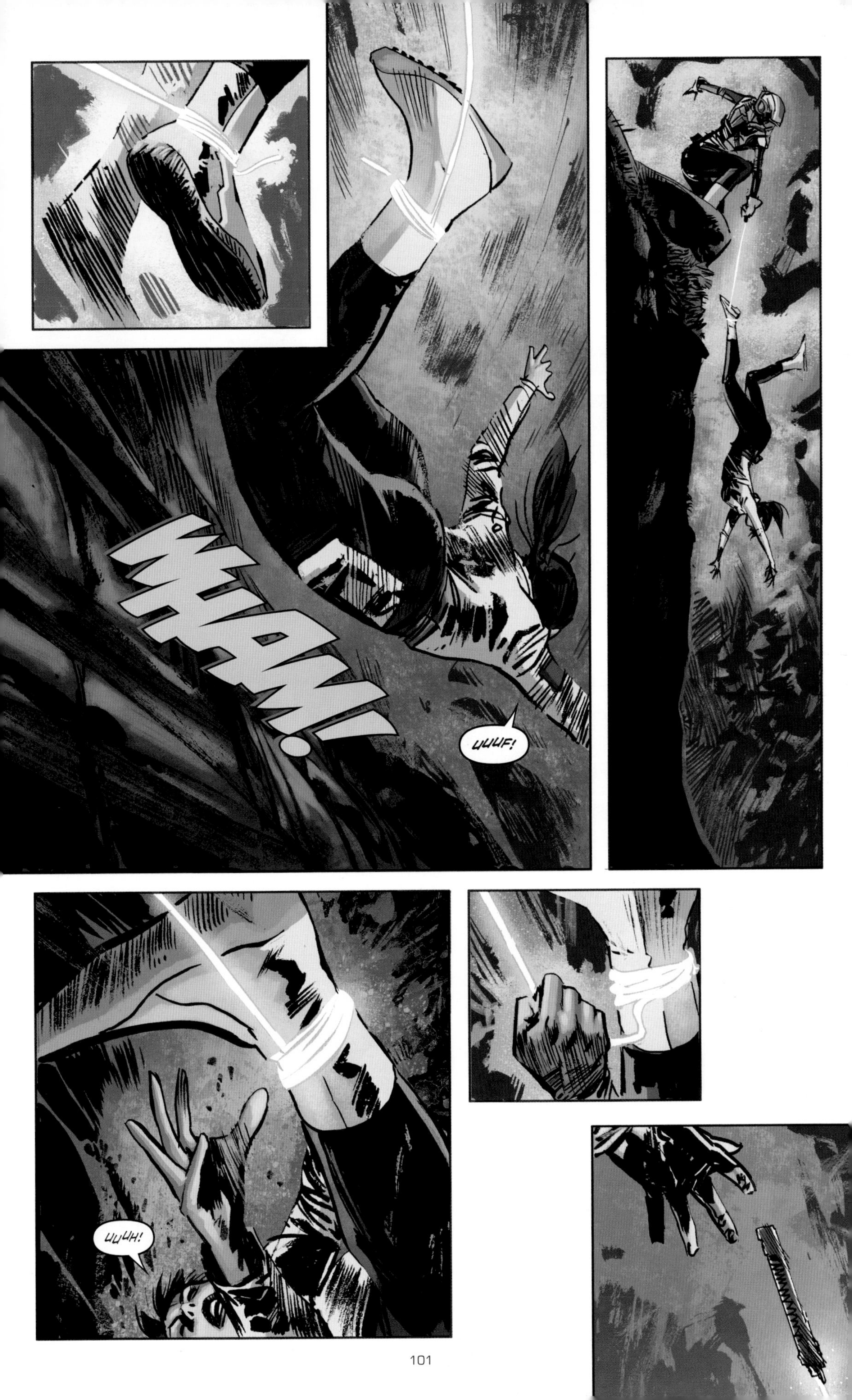
WHAM!
UUUF!
UUUH!

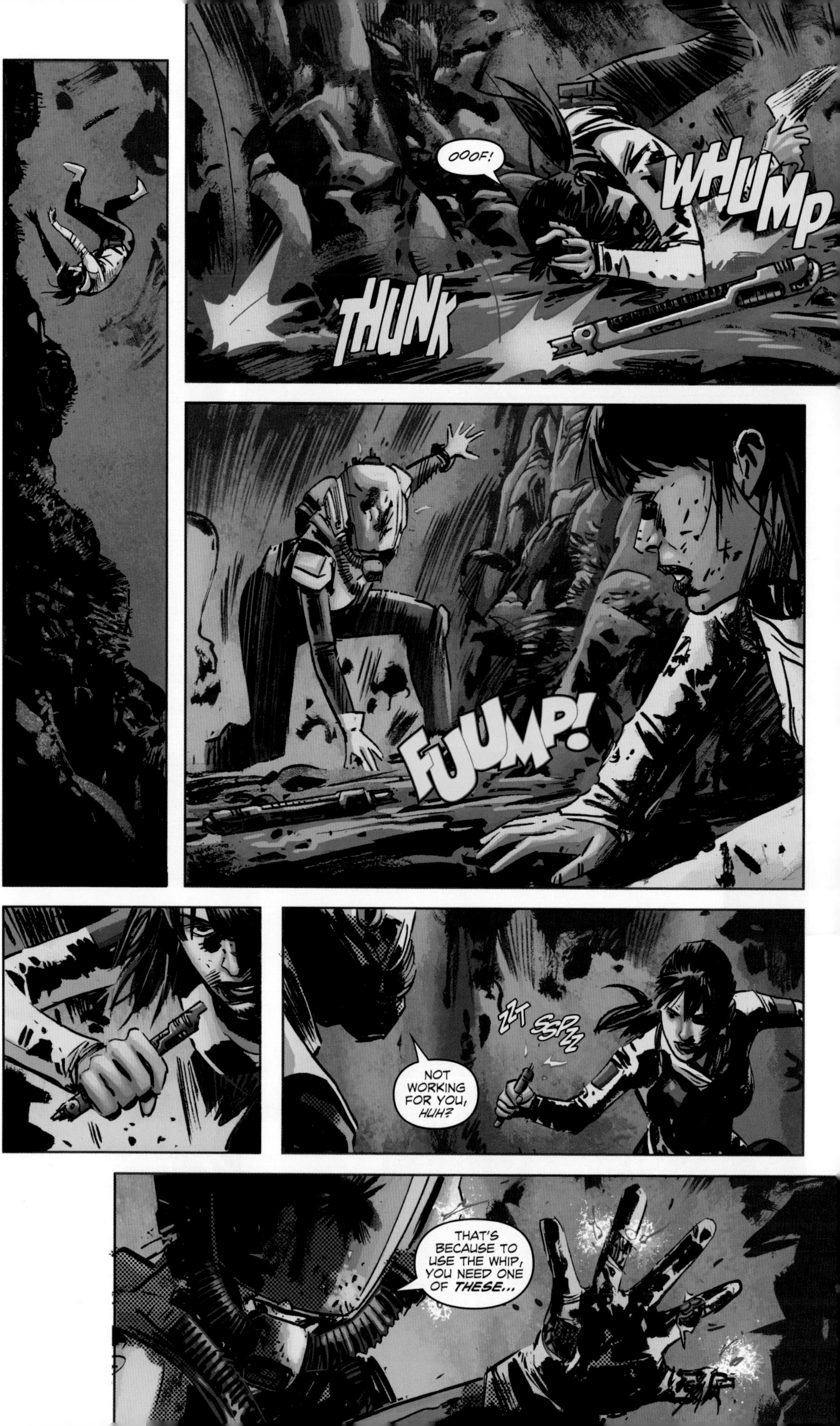
OOOF!
WHUMP
THUNK
FUUMP!
ZZT SSPZZ
NOT WORKING FOR YOU, HUH?
THAT'S BECAUSE TO USE THE WHIP, YOU NEED ONE OF THESE...

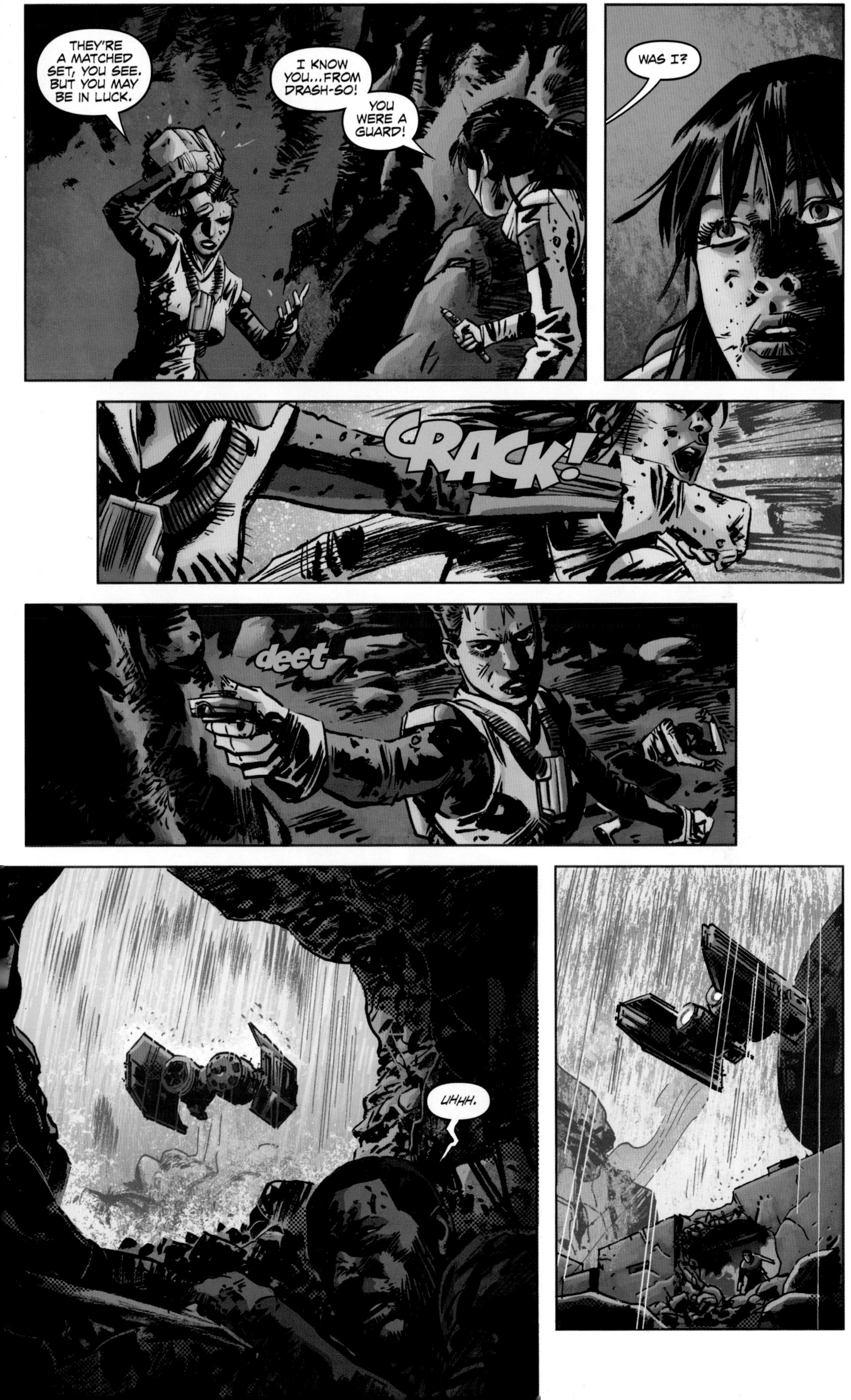
THEY'RE A MATCHED SET, YOU SEE. BUT YOU MAY BE IN LUCK.
I KNOW YOU...FROM DRASH-SO!
YOU WERE A GUARD!
WAS I?
CRACK!
deet
UHHH.

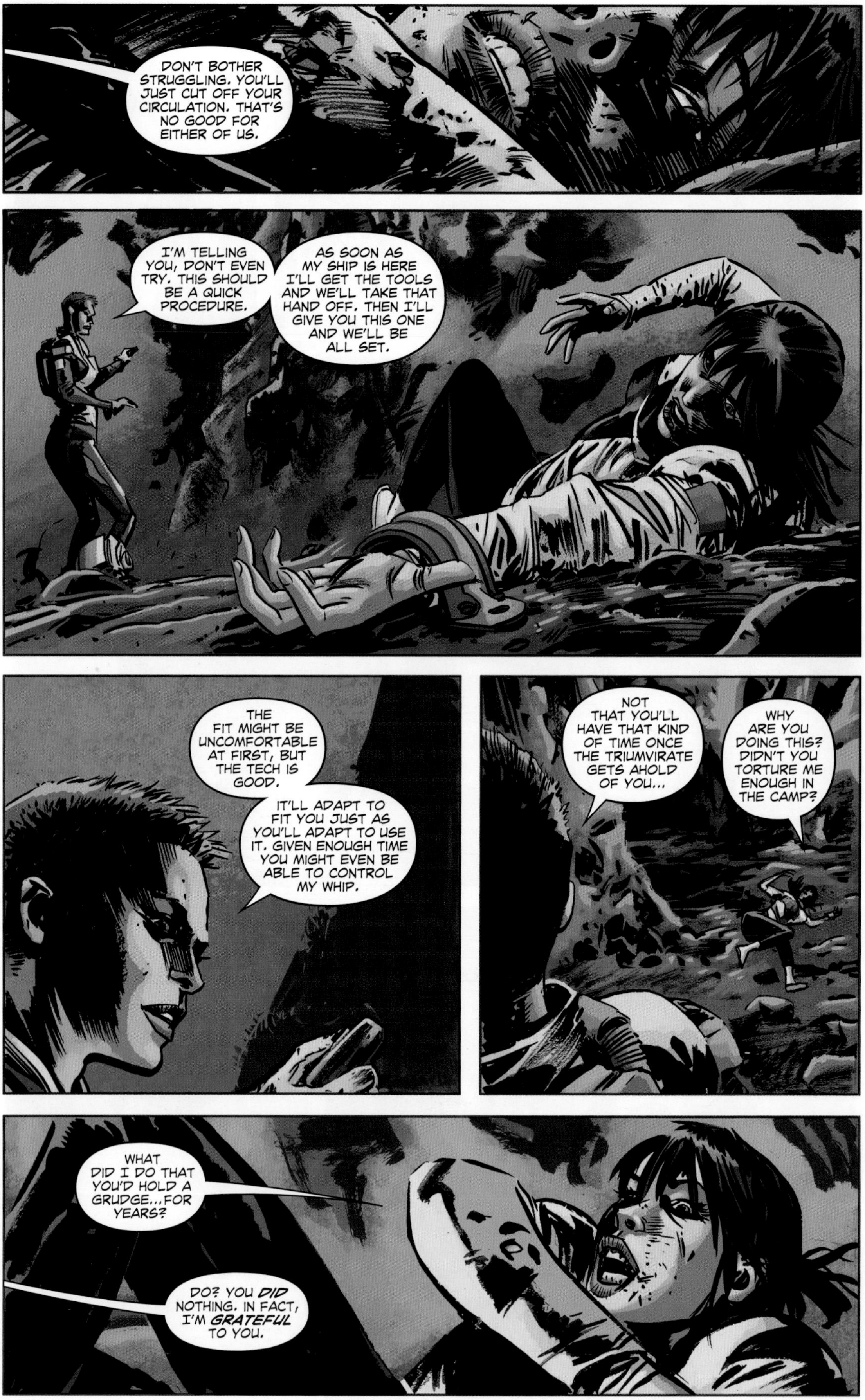
DON'T BOTHER STRUGGLING. YOU'LL JUST CUT OFF YOUR CIRCULATION. THAT'S NO GOOD FOR EITHER OF US.
I'M TELLING YOU, DON'T EVEN TRY. THIS SHOULD BE A QUICK PROCEDURE.
AS SOON AS MY SHIP IS HERE I'LL GET THE TOOLS AND WE'LL TAKE THAT HAND OFF. THEN I'LL GIVE YOU THIS ONE AND WE'LL BE ALL SET.
THE FIT MIGHT BE UNCOMFORTABLE AT FIRST, BUT THE TECH IS GOOD.
IT'LL ADAPT TO FIT YOU JUST AS YOU'LL ADAPT TO USE IT. GIVEN ENOUGH TIME YOU MIGHT EVEN BE ABLE TO CONTROL MY WHIP.
NOT THAT YOU'LL HAVE THAT KIND OF TIME ONCE THE TRIUMVIRATE GETS AHOLD OF YOU...
WHY ARE YOU DOING THIS? DIDN'T YOU TORTURE ME ENOUGH IN THE CAMP?
WHAT DID I DO THAT YOU'D HOLD A GRUDGE...FOR YEARS?
DO? YOU *DID* NOTHING. IN FACT, I'M *GRATEFUL* TO YOU.

YOU DID ME A FAVOR WHEN YOU ESCAPED. SURE, I GOT...PUNISHED FOR LOSING A PRISONER.

BUT WHEN THE CAMP WAS INVADED BY IMPERIAL RENEGADES -- "LIBERATED," IF YOU WILL -- I HAD THE PERFECT ALIBI.

I... I...WHAT DO YOU MEAN?

I SIMPLY BECAME ANIA SOLO.

YOU TOOK MY NAME? BUT --

THE SITH DON'T LIKE TO SHOW WEAKNESS, YOU KNOW. NO ONE HIGHER UP REPORTED YOU MISSING FOR FEAR OF EXECUTION.

WHEN THOSE IMPERIAL FOOLS DID A ROLL CALL BASED ON PRISON RECORDS, YOUR NAME WAS STILL THERE.

I STEPPED FORWARD, CLAIMING I WAS YOU, AND WALKED OUT OF THAT CAMP A REFUGEE, NOT A WAR CRIMINAL.

BUT --

I WOULD HAVE STAYED ANIA SOLO, TOO, BUT A PARTICULARLY ARROGANT IMPERIAL KNIGHT GOT IN MY WAY. THAT FORCED ME TO TAKE ON THIS BOUNTY HUNTER PERSONA UNTIL THINGS COOLED DOWN.

BUT NOW, WITH YOUR FACE ALL OVER THE VIDS AFTER WHAT YOU PULLED IN THE CARRERAS SYSTEM...

ANYWAY, THEY'LL FIGURE THINGS OUT AS SOON AS THEY HAVE YOU IN CUSTODY. NOT YOUR HAND, NOT YOUR CRIME.

UNLESS IT IS YOUR HAND --

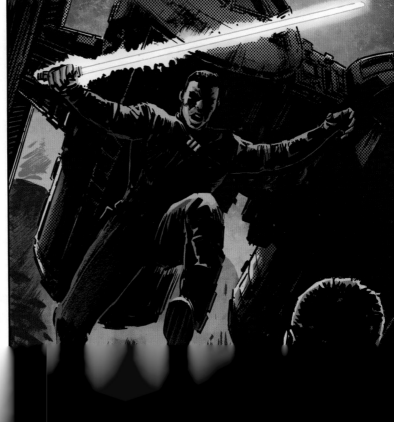

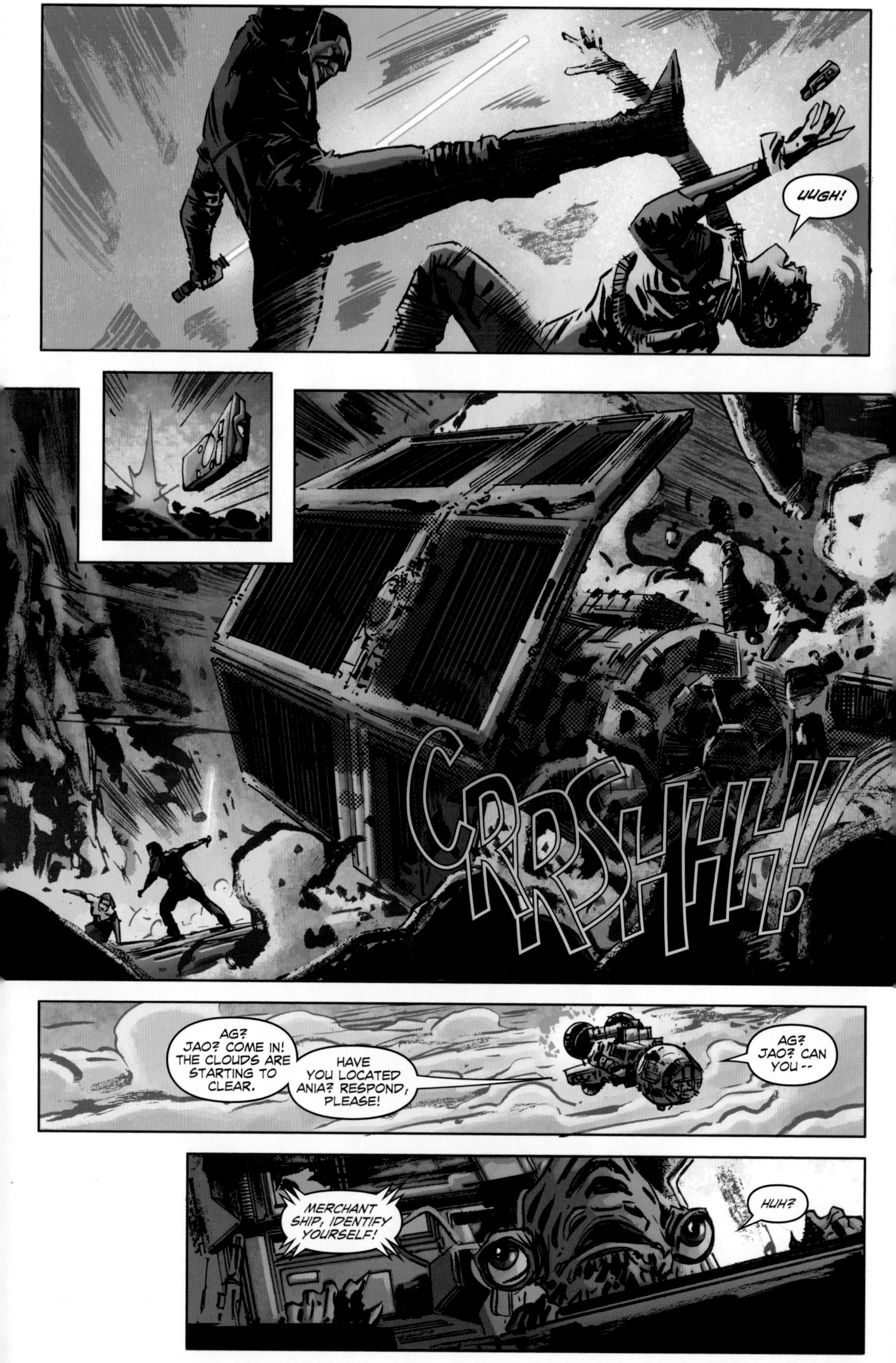
UUGH!
CRRSHHH!
AG? JAO? COME IN! THE CLOUDS ARE STARTING TO CLEAR.
HAVE YOU LOCATED ANIA? RESPOND, PLEASE!
AG? JAO? CAN YOU --
MERCHANT SHIP, IDENTIFY YOURSELF!
HUH?

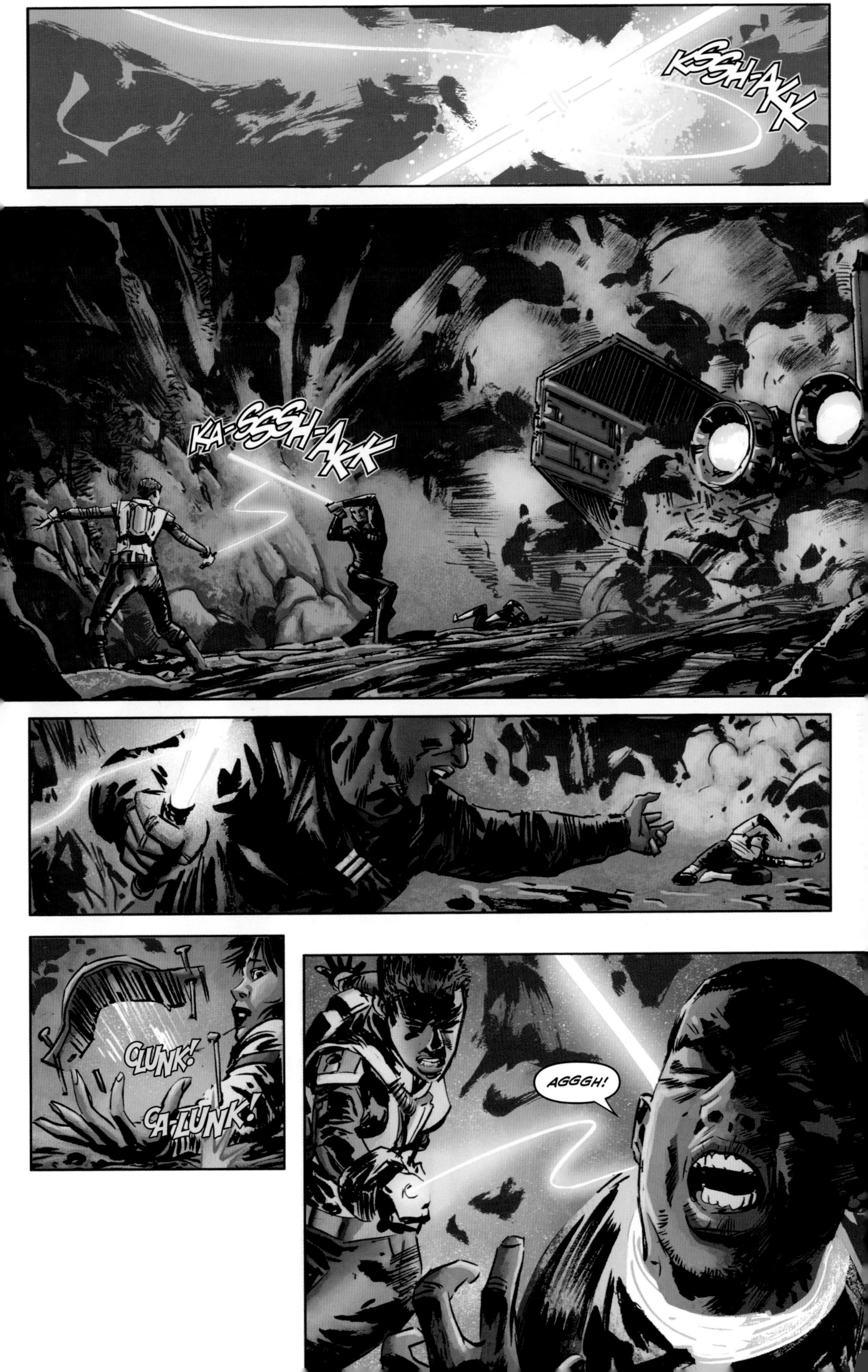
KSSH-AKK
KA-SSSH-AKK
CLUNK!
CA-LUNK!
AGGGH!

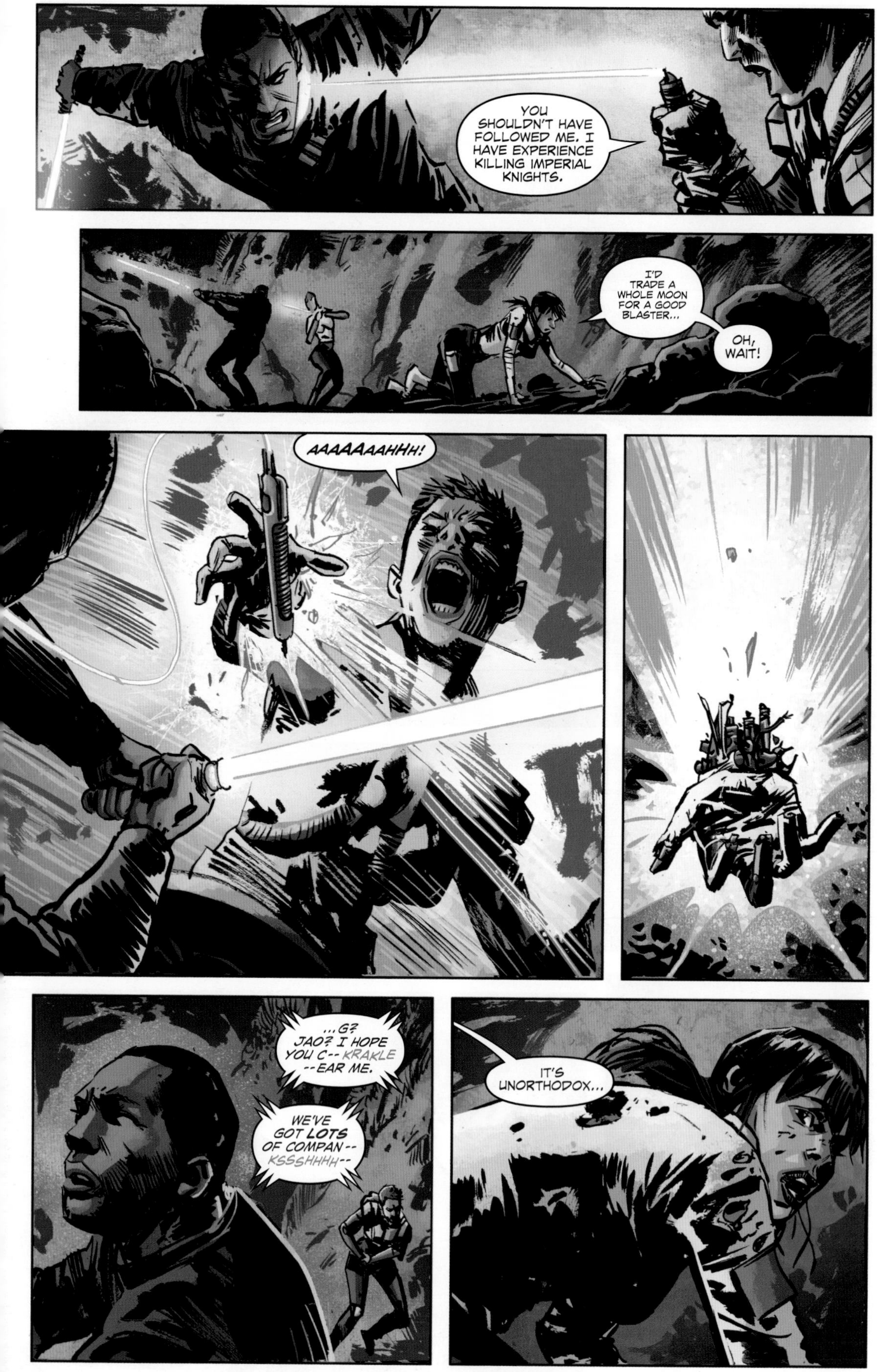
YOU SHOULDN'T HAVE FOLLOWED ME. I HAVE EXPERIENCE KILLING IMPERIAL KNIGHTS.
I'D TRADE A WHOLE MOON FOR A GOOD BLASTER...
OH, WAIT!
AAAAAAAHHH!
...G? JAO? I HOPE YOU C-- KRAKLE --EAR ME.
WE'VE GOT LOTS OF COMPAN-- KSSSHHHH--
IT'S UNORTHODOX...

BUT ATTACHMENTS *CAN* BE DONE POSTMORTEM.

OH?

I TAKE IT I DON'T NEED ANYTHING SPECIAL TO WORK *THIS?*

THE REMOTE --

*deet*

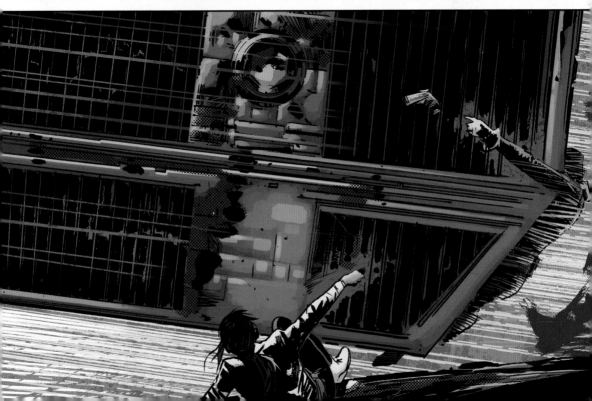

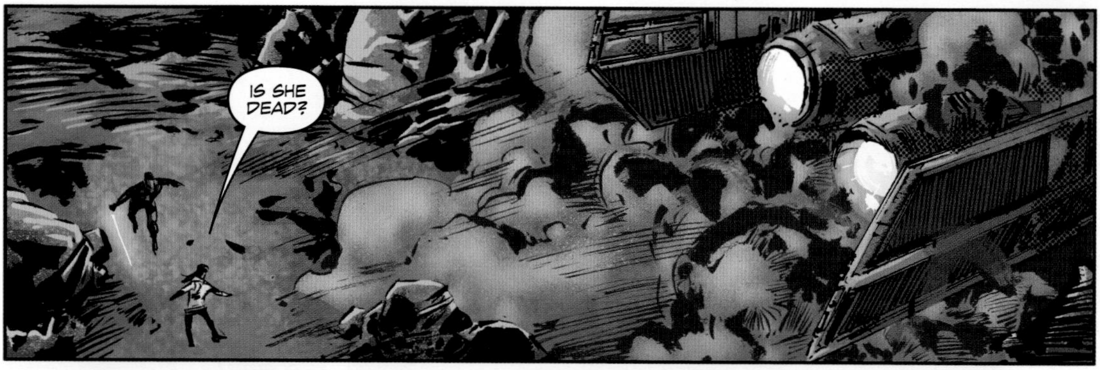
IS SHE DEAD?

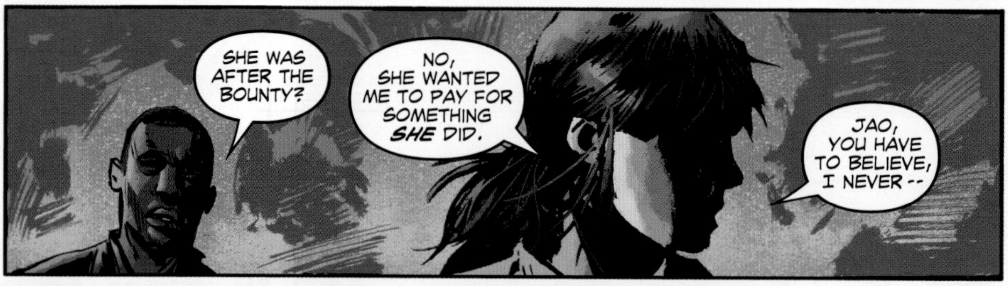
SHE WAS AFTER THE BOUNTY?
NO, SHE WANTED ME TO PAY FOR SOMETHING *SHE* DID.
JAO, YOU HAVE TO BELIEVE, I NEVER --

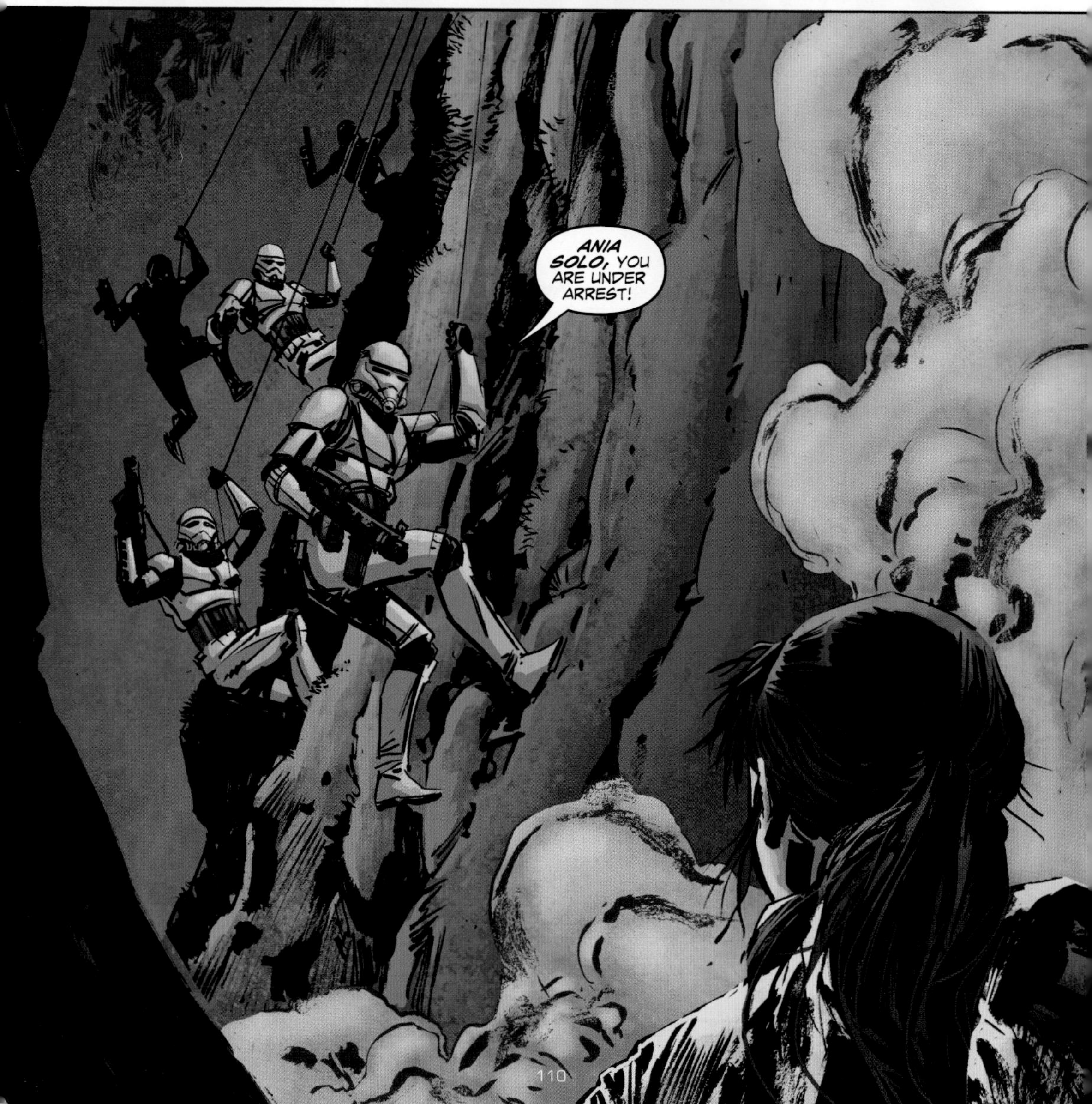
*ANIA SOLO,* YOU ARE UNDER ARREST!

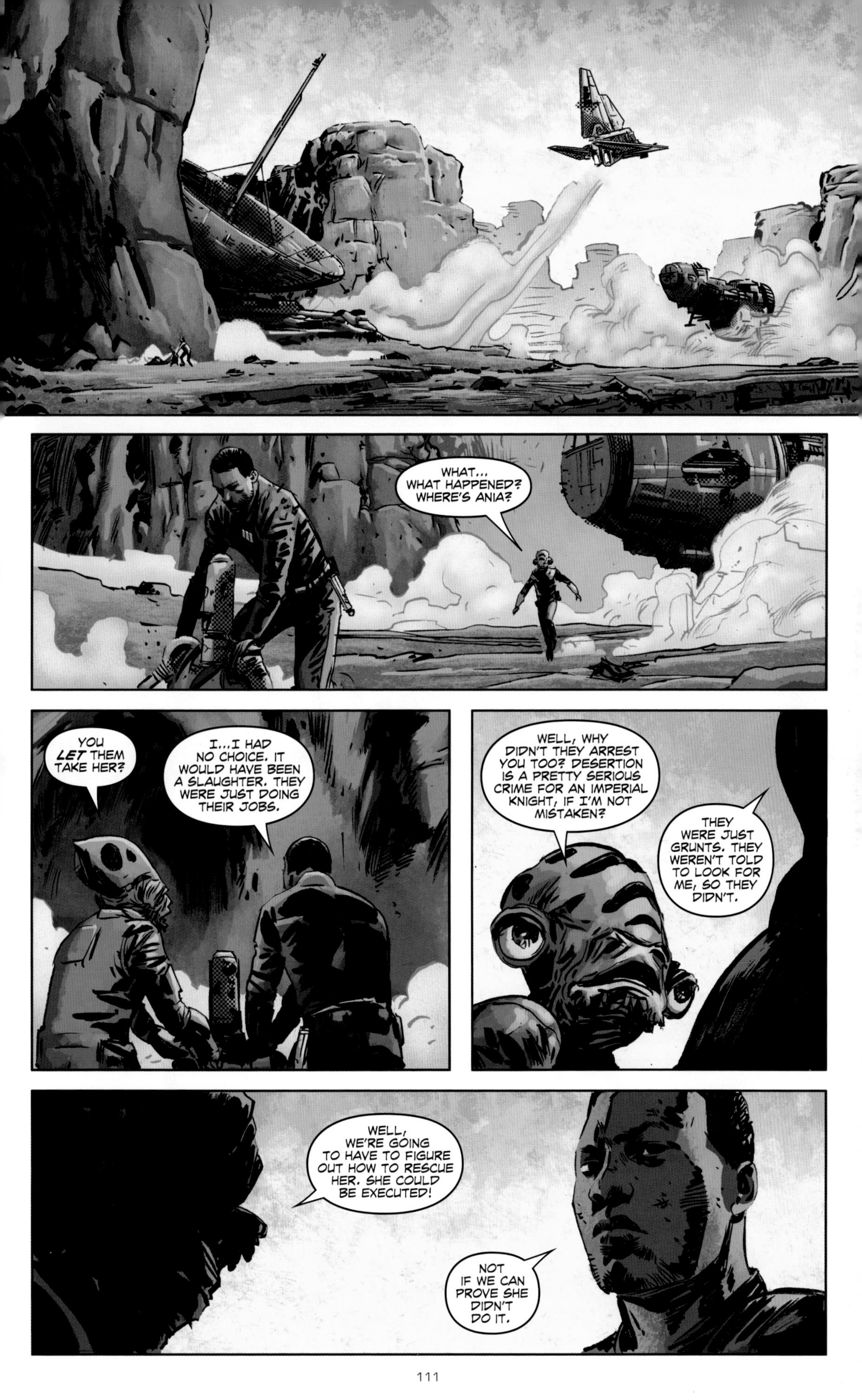
WHAT... WHAT HAPPENED? WHERE'S ANIA?
YOU *LET* THEM TAKE HER?
I...I HAD NO CHOICE. IT WOULD HAVE BEEN A SLAUGHTER. THEY WERE JUST DOING THEIR JOBS.
WELL, WHY DIDN'T THEY ARREST YOU TOO? DESERTION IS A PRETTY SERIOUS CRIME FOR AN IMPERIAL KNIGHT, IF I'M NOT MISTAKEN?
THEY WERE JUST GRUNTS. THEY WEREN'T TOLD TO LOOK FOR ME, SO THEY DIDN'T.
WELL, WE'RE GOING TO HAVE TO FIGURE OUT HOW TO RESCUE HER. SHE COULD BE EXECUTED!
NOT IF WE CAN PROVE SHE DIDN'T DO IT.

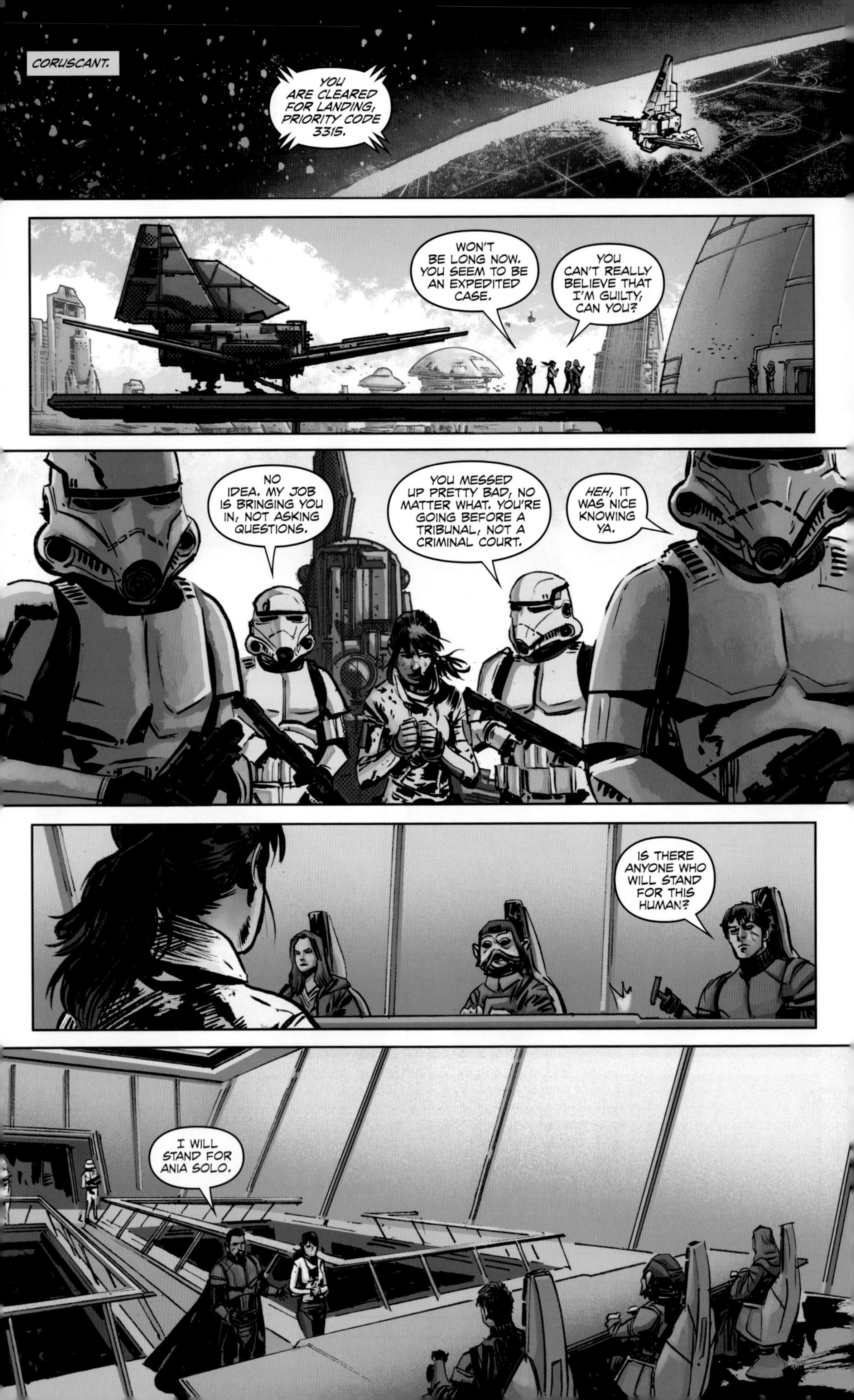
CORUSCANT.
YOU ARE CLEARED FOR LANDING, PRIORITY CODE 3315.
WON'T BE LONG NOW. YOU SEEM TO BE AN EXPEDITED CASE.
YOU CAN'T REALLY BELIEVE THAT I'M GUILTY, CAN YOU?
NO IDEA. MY JOB IS BRINGING YOU IN, NOT ASKING QUESTIONS.
YOU MESSED UP PRETTY BAD, NO MATTER WHAT. YOU'RE GOING BEFORE A TRIBUNAL, NOT A CRIMINAL COURT.
HEH, IT WAS NICE KNOWING YA.
IS THERE ANYONE WHO WILL STAND FOR THIS HUMAN?
I WILL STAND FOR ANIA SOLO.

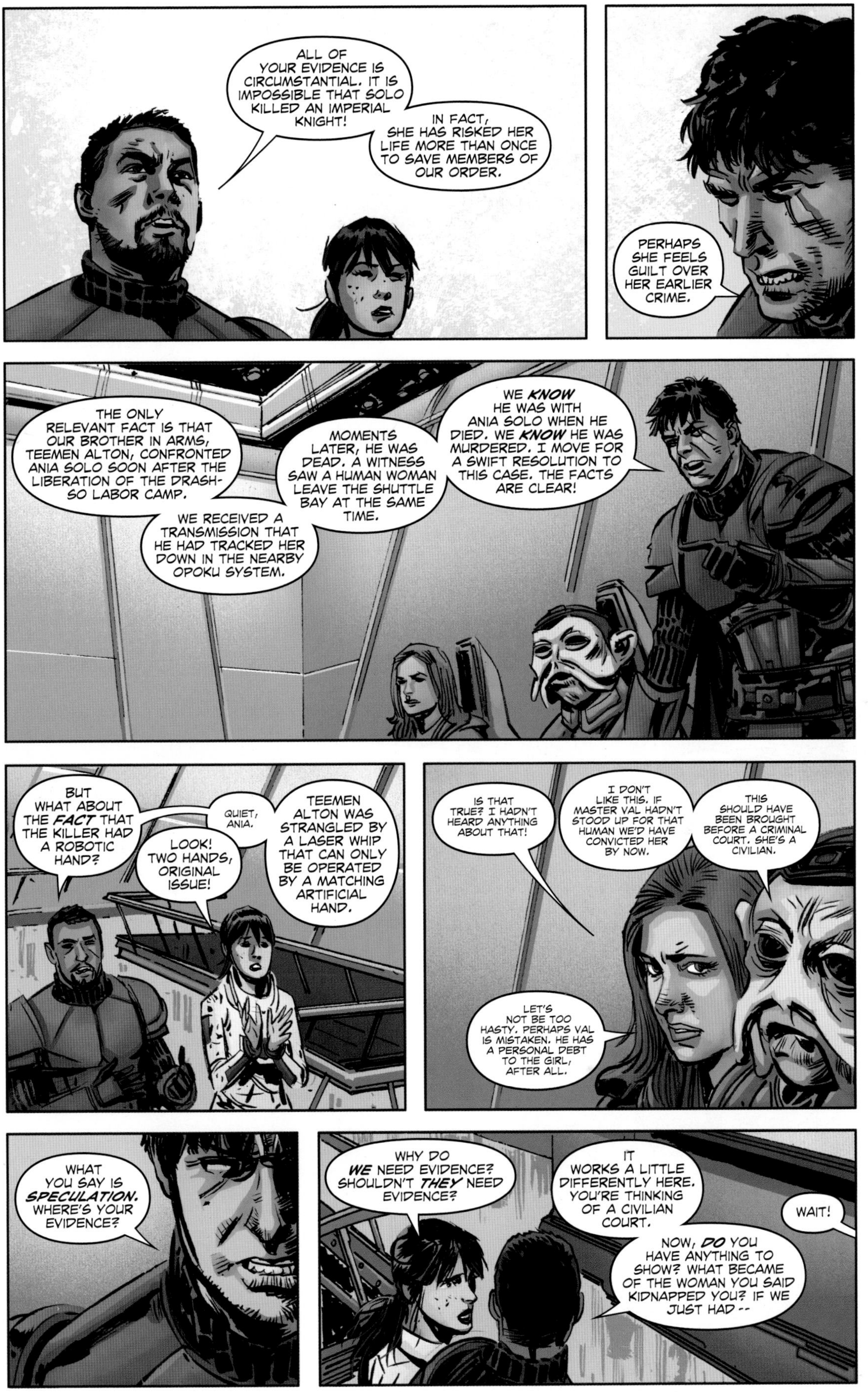
ALL OF YOUR EVIDENCE IS CIRCUMSTANTIAL. IT IS IMPOSSIBLE THAT SOLO KILLED AN IMPERIAL KNIGHT!
IN FACT, SHE HAS RISKED HER LIFE MORE THAN ONCE TO SAVE MEMBERS OF OUR ORDER.
PERHAPS SHE FEELS GUILT OVER HER EARLIER CRIME.
THE ONLY RELEVANT FACT IS THAT OUR BROTHER IN ARMS, TEEMEN ALTON, CONFRONTED ANIA SOLO SOON AFTER THE LIBERATION OF THE DRASH-SO LABOR CAMP.
WE RECEIVED A TRANSMISSION THAT HE HAD TRACKED HER DOWN IN THE NEARBY OPOKU SYSTEM.
MOMENTS LATER, HE WAS DEAD. A WITNESS SAW A HUMAN WOMAN LEAVE THE SHUTTLE BAY AT THE SAME TIME.
WE KNOW HE WAS WITH ANIA SOLO WHEN HE DIED. WE KNOW HE WAS MURDERED. I MOVE FOR A SWIFT RESOLUTION TO THIS CASE. THE FACTS ARE CLEAR!
BUT WHAT ABOUT THE FACT THAT THE KILLER HAD A ROBOTIC HAND?
QUIET, ANIA.
LOOK! TWO HANDS, ORIGINAL ISSUE!
TEEMEN ALTON WAS STRANGLED BY A LASER WHIP THAT CAN ONLY BE OPERATED BY A MATCHING ARTIFICIAL HAND.
IS THAT TRUE? I HADN'T HEARD ANYTHING ABOUT THAT!
I DON'T LIKE THIS. IF MASTER VAL HADN'T STOOD UP FOR THAT HUMAN WE'D HAVE CONVICTED HER BY NOW.
THIS SHOULD HAVE BEEN BROUGHT BEFORE A CRIMINAL COURT. SHE'S A CIVILIAN.
LET'S NOT BE TOO HASTY. PERHAPS VAL IS MISTAKEN. HE HAS A PERSONAL DEBT TO THE GIRL, AFTER ALL.
WHAT YOU SAY IS SPECULATION. WHERE'S YOUR EVIDENCE?
WHY DO WE NEED EVIDENCE? SHOULDN'T THEY NEED EVIDENCE?
IT WORKS A LITTLE DIFFERENTLY HERE. YOU'RE THINKING OF A CIVILIAN COURT.
NOW, DO YOU HAVE ANYTHING TO SHOW? WHAT BECAME OF THE WOMAN YOU SAID KIDNAPPED YOU? IF WE JUST HAD --
WAIT!

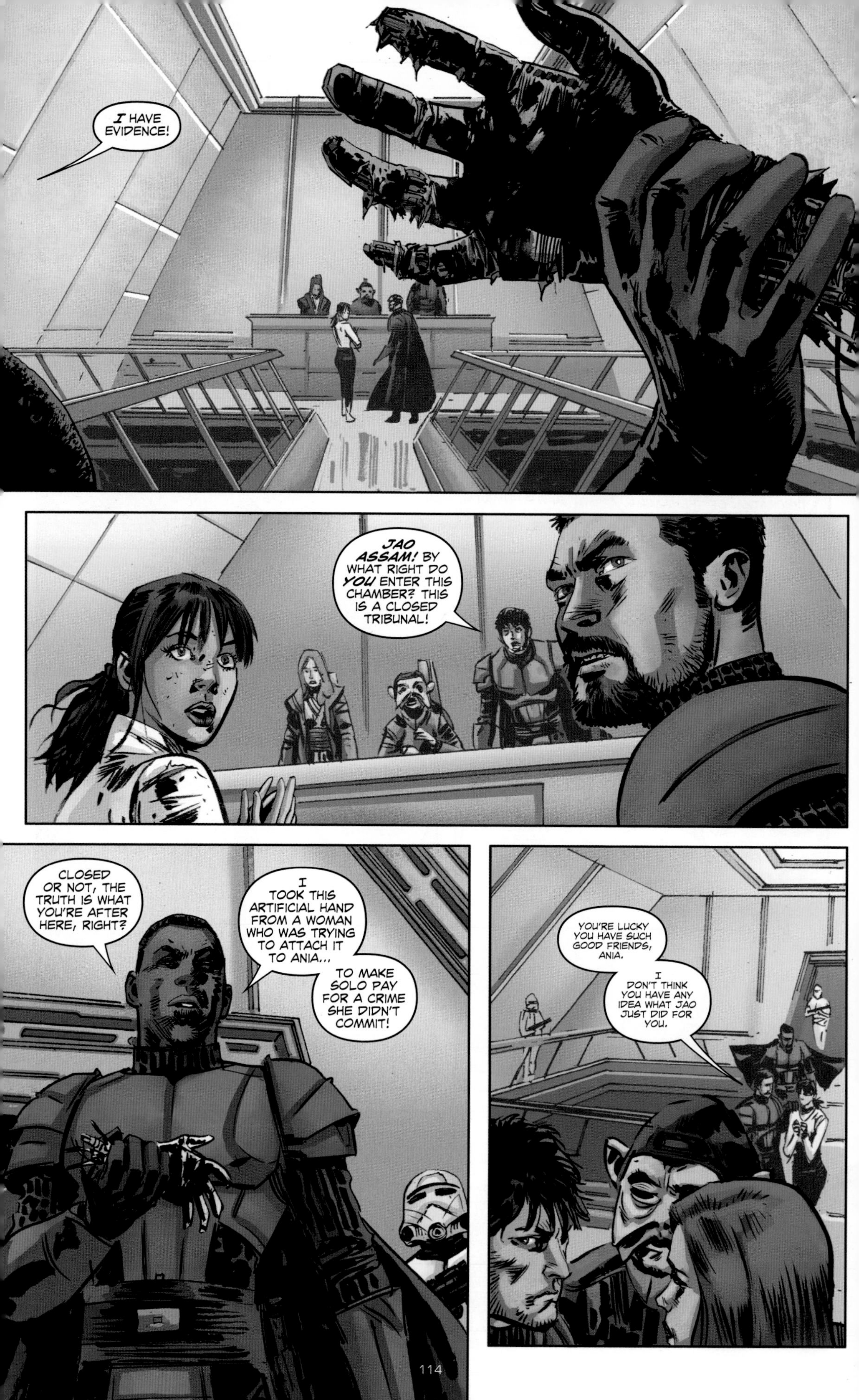
I HAVE EVIDENCE!
JAO ASSAM! BY WHAT RIGHT DO YOU ENTER THIS CHAMBER? THIS IS A CLOSED TRIBUNAL!
CLOSED OR NOT, THE TRUTH IS WHAT YOU'RE AFTER HERE, RIGHT?
I TOOK THIS ARTIFICIAL HAND FROM A WOMAN WHO WAS TRYING TO ATTACH IT TO ANIA...
TO MAKE SOLO PAY FOR A CRIME SHE DIDN'T COMMIT!
YOU'RE LUCKY YOU HAVE SUCH GOOD FRIENDS, ANIA.
I DON'T THINK YOU HAVE ANY IDEA WHAT JAO JUST DID FOR YOU.

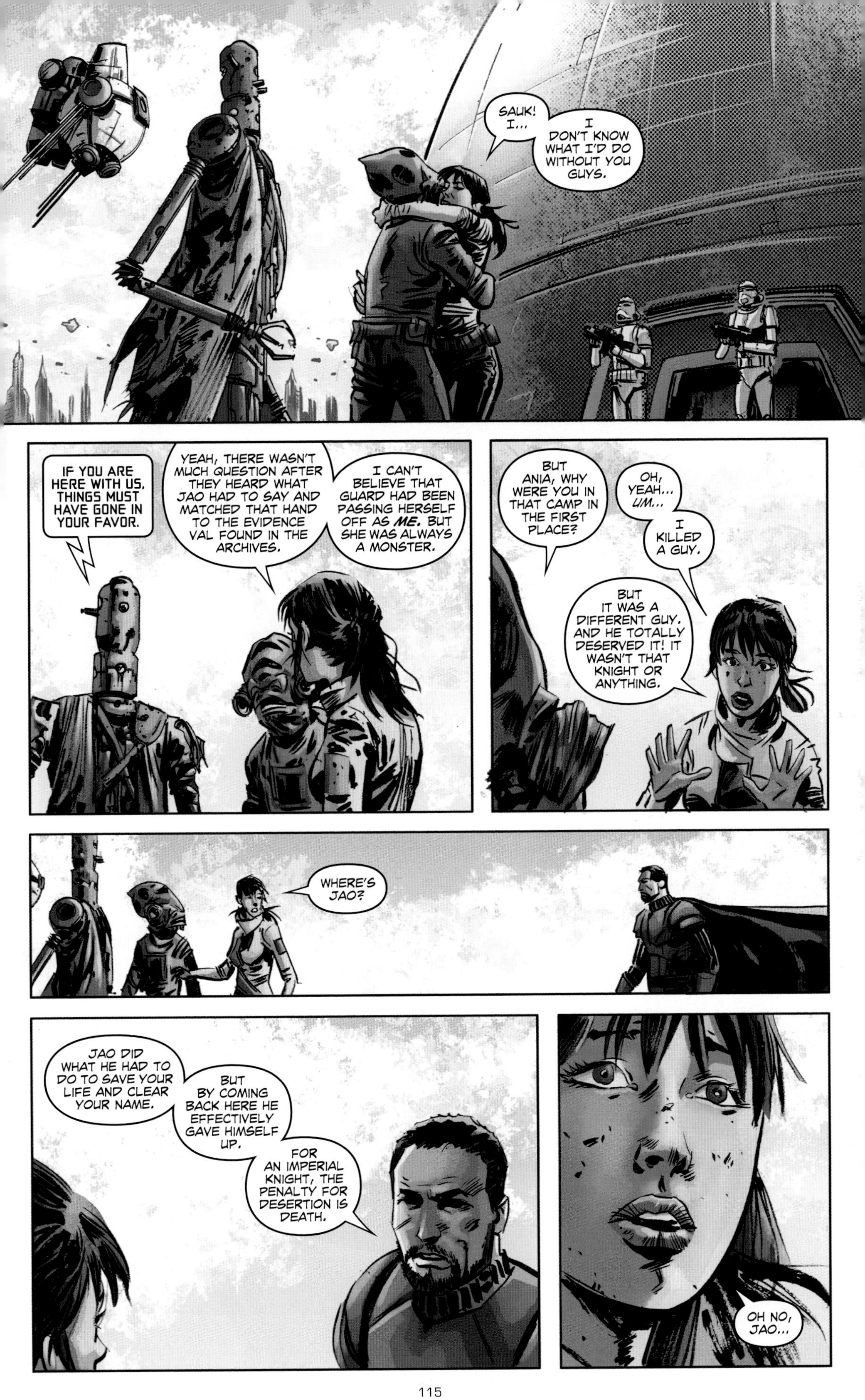
SAUK! I...
I DON'T KNOW WHAT I'D DO WITHOUT YOU GUYS.
IF YOU ARE HERE WITH US, THINGS MUST HAVE GONE IN YOUR FAVOR.
YEAH, THERE WASN'T MUCH QUESTION AFTER THEY HEARD WHAT JAO HAD TO SAY AND MATCHED THAT HAND TO THE EVIDENCE VAL FOUND IN THE ARCHIVES.
I CAN'T BELIEVE THAT GUARD HAD BEEN PASSING HERSELF OFF AS *ME.* BUT SHE WAS ALWAYS A MONSTER.
BUT ANIA, WHY WERE YOU IN THAT CAMP IN THE FIRST PLACE?
OH, YEAH... *UM...*
I KILLED A GUY.
BUT IT WAS A DIFFERENT GUY. AND HE TOTALLY DESERVED IT! IT WASN'T THAT KNIGHT OR ANYTHING.
WHERE'S JAO?
JAO DID WHAT HE HAD TO DO TO SAVE YOUR LIFE AND CLEAR YOUR NAME.
BUT BY COMING BACK HERE HE EFFECTIVELY GAVE HIMSELF UP.
FOR AN IMPERIAL KNIGHT, THE PENALTY FOR DESERTION IS DEATH.
OH NO, JAO...

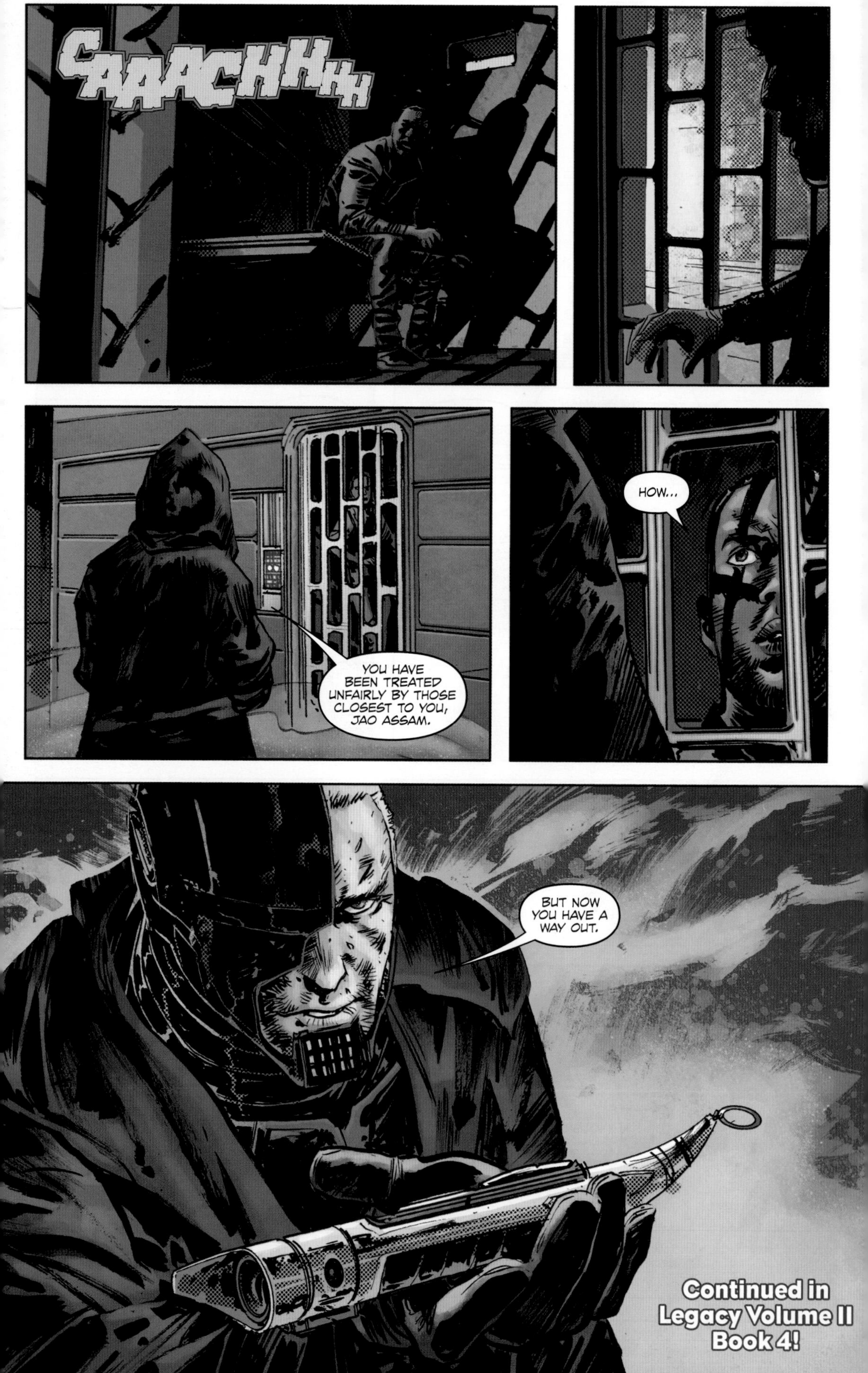
CRAAACHHHH
YOU HAVE BEEN TREATED UNFAIRLY BY THOSE CLOSEST TO YOU, JAO ASSAM.
HOW...
BUT NOW YOU HAVE A WAY OUT.
Continued in Legacy Volume II Book 4!

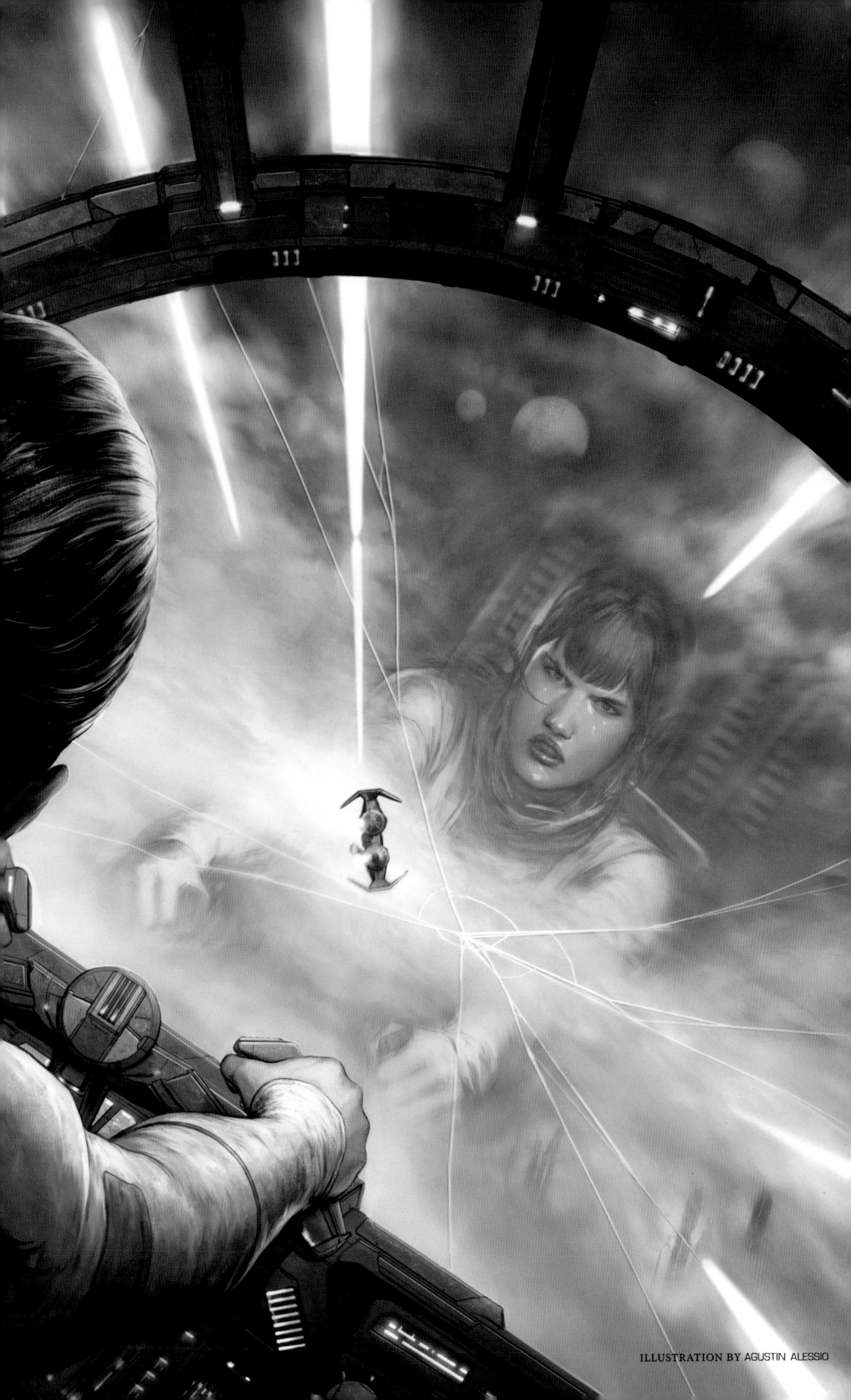

ILLUSTRATION BY AGUSTIN ALESSIO

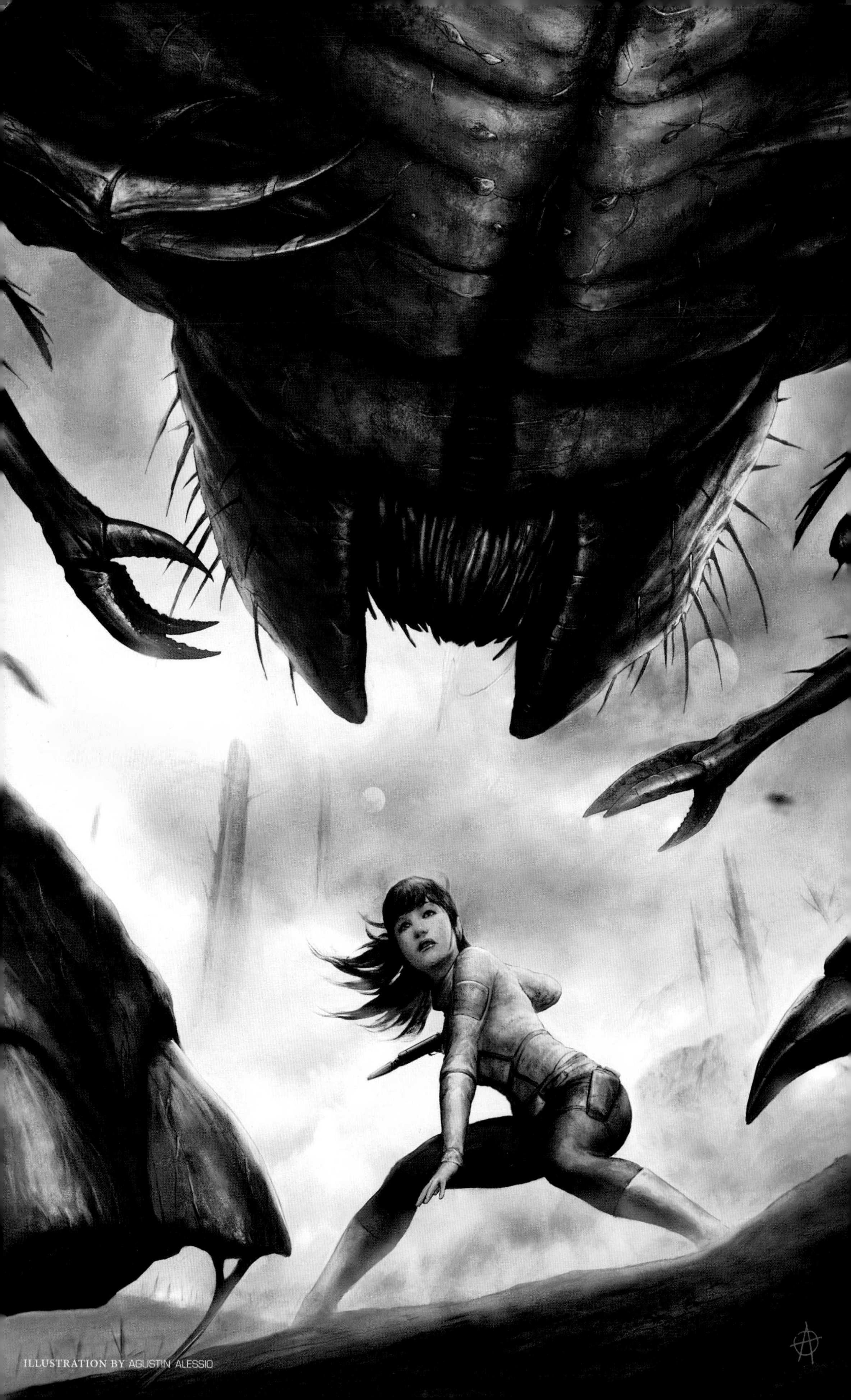

ILLUSTRATION BY AGUSTIN ALESSIO

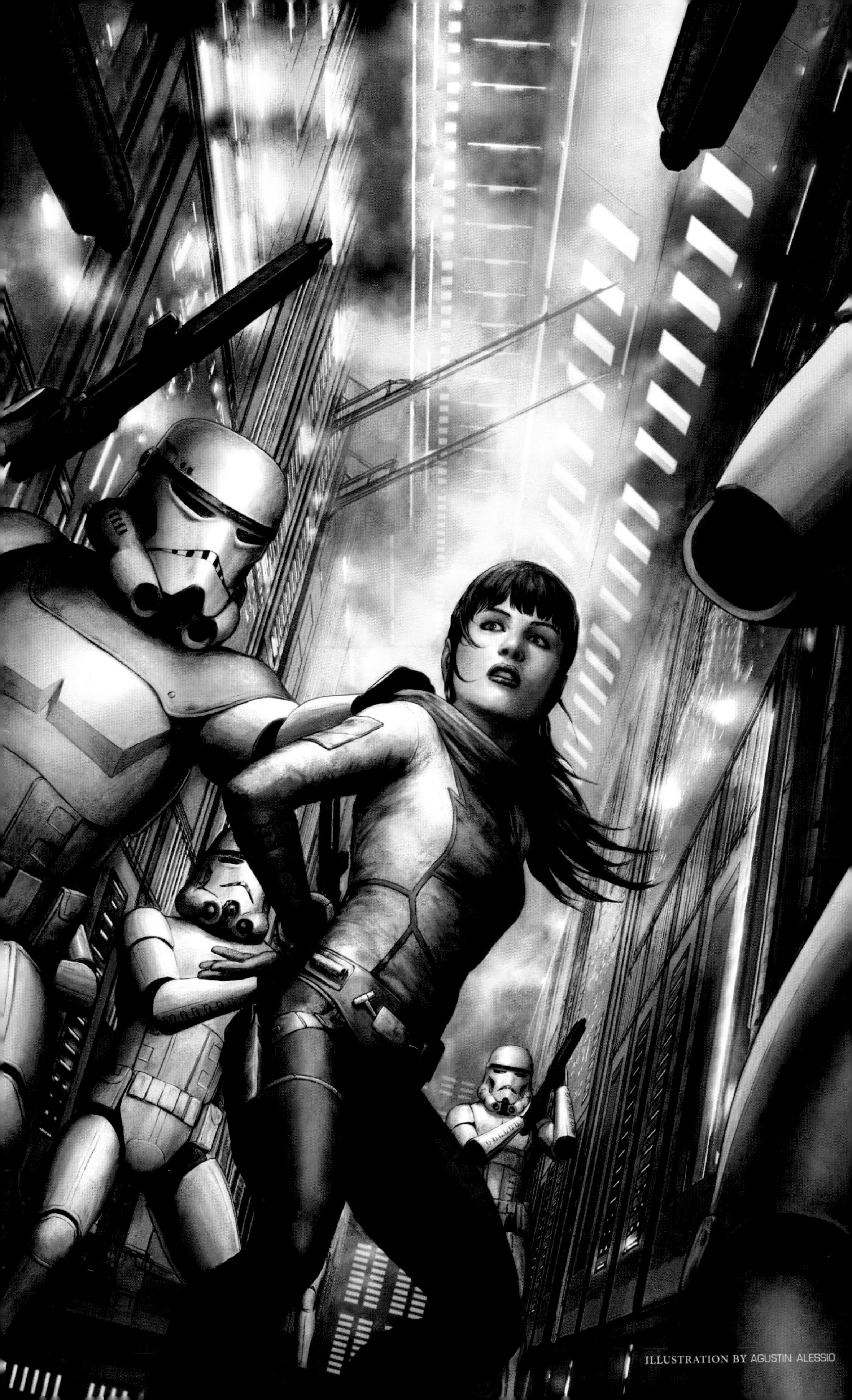

ILLUSTRATION BY AGUSTIN ALESSIO

# STAR WARS GRAPHIC NOVEL TIMELINE (IN YEARS)

Dawn of the Jedi—36,000–25,000 BSW4

Omnibus: Tales of the Jedi—5,000–3,986 BSW4

Knights of the Old Republic—3,964–3,963 BSW4

The Old Republic—3678, 3653, 3600 BSW4

Lost Tribe of the Sith—2974 BSW4

Knight Errant—1,032 BSW4

Jedi vs. Sith—1,000 BSW4

Jedi: The Dark Side—53 BSW4

Omnibus: Rise of the Sith—33 BSW4

Episode I: The Phantom Menace—32 BSW4

Omnibus: Emissaries and Assassins—32 BSW4

Omnibus: Quinlan Vos—Jedi in Darkness—31–30 BSW4

Omnibus: Menace Revealed—31–22 BSW4

Honor and Duty—22 BSW4

Blood Ties—22 BSW4

Episode II: Attack of the Clones—22 BSW4

Clone Wars—22–19 BSW4

Omnibus: Clone Wars—22–19 BSW4

Clone Wars Adventures—22–19 BSW4

Darth Maul: Death Sentence—20 BSW4

Episode III: Revenge of the Sith—19 BSW4

Purge—19 BSW4

Dark Times—19 BSW4

Darth Vader—19 BSW4

Omnibus: Droids and Ewoks—15 BSW4–3.5 ASW4

Omnibus: Droids—5.5 BSW4

Omnibus: Boba Fett—3 BSW4–10 ASW4

Agent of the Empire—3 BSW4

The Force Unleashed—2 BSW4

Omnibus: At War with the Empire—1 BSW4

Episode IV: A New Hope—SW4

Star Wars—0 ASW4

Classic Star Wars—0–3 ASW4

Omnibus: A Long Time Ago. . . .—0–4 ASW4

Omnibus: Wild Space—0–4 ASW4

Empire—0 ASW4

Omnibus: The Other Sons of Tatooine—0 ASW4

Omnibus: Early Victories—0–3 ASW4

Jabba the Hutt: The Art of the Deal—1 ASW4

Episode V: The Empire Strikes Back—3 ASW4

Ewoks: Shadows of Endor—3.5–4 ASW4

Omnibus: Shadows of the Empire—3.5–4.5 ASW4

Episode VI: Return of the Jedi—4 ASW4

Omnibus: X-Wing Rogue Squadron—4–5 ASW4

The Thrawn Trilogy—9 ASW4

Dark Empire—10 ASW4

Crimson Empire—11 ASW4

Jedi Academy: Leviathan—12 ASW4

Union—19 ASW4

Chewbacca—25 ASW4

Invasion—25 ASW4

Legacy—130–138 ASW4

**Dawn of the Jedi**
36,000 years before
Star Wars: A New Hope

**Old Republic Era**
25,000–1000 years before
Star Wars: A New Hope

**Rise of the Empire Era**
1000–0 years before Star
Wars: A New Hope

**Rebellion Era**
0–5 years after
Star Wars: A New Hope

**New Republic Era**
5–25 years after
Star Wars: A New Hope

**New Jedi Order Era**
25+ years after
Star Wars: A New Hope

**Legacy Era**
130+ years after
Star Wars: A New Hope

**Vector**
Crosses four eras in timeline

**Volume 1 contains:**
Knights of the Old Republic Volume 5
Dark Times Volume 3
**Volume 2 contains:**
Rebellion Volume 4
Legacy Volume 6

**Infinities**
Does not apply to timeline
Star Wars Tales
Omnibus: Infinities
Omnibus: Wild Space Volume 2

BSW4 = before *Episode IV: A New Hope*. ASW4 = after *Episode IV: A New Hope*.